Brilliance

101 Short Stories, Essays, And Insights To Improve Communication Skills

ARMANITALKS

TABLE OF CONTENTS

AUTHOR'S PREFACE

There are a few quotes I despise.
3 of them immediately come to mind.

The first one is:

> ## *You need to speak up for those who don't have a voice!*

I never liked this quote but couldn't articulate why.
Something just felt off.

As I got older, I realized why.
Communication skills = A skill.
Learn to speak up for yourself.

When someone is speaking up for you, it leads to bad habits.
I would know... because for a long time, my brother would speak up for me.

Whenever I would get in trouble or have difficulty sharing my perspective, he would speak up and make my position known.

I liked this because he knew me well.
He always presented my positions fairly.
But other times, I felt off because I was too dependent.

Once I began taking public speaking seriously, I realized there was *freedom* to speaking up for myself.

Capture your thoughts, hone your voice, and cultivate your philosophy.

There's a common saying that goes like:

- What gets measured, gets improved.

My remix to that is:

- What gets articulated, gets realized.

A lot of people are incapable of improving because they cannot concisely articulate what the problem is.

Another quote I hate is:

Great artists steal.

One day, I posted how much I hated this quote on Twitter.

That's when a long-time follower DM'd me and explained why I misunderstood the quote.

He proceeded to explain what the quote **really** meant.

It meant to get inspiration from the outside world.

Take bits and pieces from others.

Then eventually, you'll grow into your own artistic groove.

This was a very well-thought-out fellow.

He had great logic and crystal-clear communication.

But dear follower...

I understood the quote the first time.

I still disagree with it.

> ***I don't believe an artist should be looking out first.***
> ***I believe an artist should be looking in first.***

There are certain curiosities we were born with.

No one taught us how to be curious, it was ingrained.

Follow those curiosities.

Learn about them.

The more you learn about them, the more studying feels effortless.

The more studying feels effortless, the more production becomes a no-brainer.

By producing, you'll see what works and what doesn't.

By cultivating your own database of experiences *first,* you'll get inspired by others *second.*

The 3rd quote I hate is:

> ***How you do 1 thing is how you do everything.***

From the other quotes I mentioned, I believe this has the purest intent.

It implies:

'If you're sloppy in one task, then chances are you'll be sloppy in other tasks. So, begin to do small things in a great way.'

I really love the intent of this quote.

However, I am still not a fan of it.

Here's the reason why:
- Some people are not in the optimal environment at the moment.

A C student may be a C student because the school atmosphere is not the best learning environment for them.

The C student doesn't like to:
- Hear about someone else's theory.
- Memorize the theory without understanding how it relates to their life.
- Then be tested on a theory they never cared for.

Do you know what this student likes?

They like to build things.

They like to fail smart.

Failing dumb is born from character issues (taking shortcuts, stealing, gossiping and getting caught).

This C student wants to build something that has practical utility.

As they build, they fail and succeed in iterations.

After a series of reps, their pattern recognition muscle strengthens.

From there, they will extract their own theories from the data they have compiled.

In sitcoms, you'll see scientists creating certain formulas.

Then a group of engineers brings those formulas to life.

But in the real world, it's often the opposite.

The engineer fails their way into success.

Then a bunch of theories are built after studying the success.

Don't you see?

If you judged this C student from the measurements of success in school, then you'd always view this kid as average.

But look closer.

This C student is brilliant.

He just needs to be placed in the optimal environment for his gifts to shine.

There are 5 levels of communication:
1. Communication with thyself - Self-awareness.
2. One-on-one communication - Conversation.
3. Many-to-many communication - Group interaction.
4. One-to-many communication - Public speaking.
5. Human-to-machine communication - Media.

Many work on levels 2-5 and undermine level 1.

"Communication with myself? Ha! I need to communicate better with others," they think.

> ***In order to communicate better with others, you need to first communicate better with yourself.***

- Introspection.
- Spotting curiosities.
- Channeling desire.
- Spotting the silver lining.
- Turning destructive emotions into fuel.

These are highly practical.

A check with a bunch of 0s means nothing.

But put a 1 in front of all those 0s and now they mean something.

Likewise, communication without self-awareness leads to becoming a snake, a nice guy, or a wimp.

But put self-awareness in the front, and now you can move mountains.

We are all brilliant at something.
Something that comes easy for you is difficult for others.

Once you spot this gift, you may be the first person to undermine it.
'What's the big deal? Anyone can do this.'

I know a guy who can see a dance move once and execute it to perfection.
Whenever I see him at a wedding, he is dancing away.

I'm like:
'Bro, you're such an amazing dancer!'
He responds back with:
'Me? Nah man, everyone can dance.'

This guy must be blind.
Doesn't he see that no one dares to step on the dance floor until he starts it off?
What others do with dread, he does with joy.

This guy is gifted.

Spotting the brilliance is one thing.
But doubling down on the natural talent until it becomes a codified skill is a whole different ball game!

Steve Harvey was naturally a funny guy.

He said it was effortless for him to turn dry information and experiences into comedy gold.

But having humor alone meant nothing.

Therefore, Steve went to comedy clubs to refine his skills.

He got booed.

He got cheers.

He slept in a car.

Now he sleeps in a mansion.

Spotting a gift is something many will never do.

Limiting beliefs will get the best of them.

But from the few who spot a gift, even fewer will hone it into a skill.

A few will become a professional.

Doesn't matter how they 'feel.'

They show up for work.

That's someone who displays brilliance.

In this book, you will get 101 short stories, essays, and insights that will help you improve your self-awareness.

The more you learn how to communicate with yourself, the better you will communicate with others.

You know that person you have been judging?
"This guy is such a poor critical thinker!"

Well, that same person can make friends with just about anyone.
They know how to break the ice.
That's a skill.

A leader is capable of spotting something in others that they cannot spot in themselves.

Work on yourself first.
Place the 1 before all the 0s.
Once that 1 is sharpened, all the 0s develop mighty powers.

– ARMANITALKS

WHEN GOOD EMPLOYEES STOP CARING

I saw this article a few days ago that wrote something along the lines of:

'A record-high amount of people are quitting their jobs.'

As I read the article, I noticed something.

A lot of these people were not quitting their jobs to start a business.

They were quitting their jobs to find another job.

Which meant there was a management problem.

I do believe that a lot of people have gotten lazier as of late.

Since a lot of infrastructures are set up, the masses have no clue what consistency and grit are about.

On the other hand, too many numbers have desensitized us to other humans.

Employees included.

In this article, I am going to explain why good employees stop caring.

TOO MANY NUMBERS

Too much analytics is not a good thing.

It's easy to keep focusing on the metrics so much that we forget why those metrics exist in the first place.

'Why do they exist?'

To provide useful value.

The entity that is providing useful value is a **person**.
Not seeing that will lead to poor judgment.

We have more data tracking tools than ever.
A regular guy can have 40,000 followers on Twitter.
But do they really perceive it like that?

40,000 people are a lot of people.
However, since the followers have been digitized, we just see numbers on a screen.

If a manager sees numbers on a screen for too long, they will lose perspective.
Put the data analytics down and go back to the basics.
Learn about human nature.

THE PRIMAL NEED FOR APPRECIATION

Humans need food.
Humans need oxygen.
These are the physical sides to us.

But want to know something else?
'What?'
Humans also need appreciation.

Appreciation is a big driving factor in why we do what we do.

As a manager, if you want to get the most out of your employees, you need to evaluate the intent.
The intent comes down to viewing their work ethic.
What is it like?

Are they consistent?
Are they delivering?

If so, praise them either in front of others or on the side.
Fulfill their primal desire for appreciation.

WHY APPRECIATION HAS PLUMMETED

'Are you really saying that employees are quitting at record-high rates due to a lack of appreciation?'
That's not all I'm saying.
Clearly, this is a complex problem.
A complex problem cannot always be reduced to one answer.

However, I do believe that appreciation is something that will get the most out of the employees that you do have.
I'll share an example.

There was this time when I was the External VP of my fraternity.
I was in charge of throwing events.
Not going to lie... I hated the position.

I was doing too much small talk with others.
I'm normally a lowkey guy and I didn't want to be in all these events.

One day, I go to chapter.
I'm annoyed.
I just came from a 3-hour dinner and wanted to chill.

In this particular chapter meeting, our president introduced a new concept.

We were going to praise 1 fraternity brother for what they bought to their position.

Ironically, I was the brother chosen for this meeting.
One by one, everyone goes around the room talking me up.
They were saying stuff that embarrassed me:
'I don't know how you are put in any event and are already making friends. It terrifies me to create small talk.'

I realized that these guys appreciated the work that I did.
Once I felt appreciated, I was like:
'Let me look out for the bigger goal. I'm not just working for myself, but rather… the fraternity.'

QUIET QUITTING

There's this concept known as "quiet quitting."
I was introduced to this lately.

The concept, from my understanding, is when the employee doesn't go above and beyond in their role.
They only do what is required.

As I heard this concept, all I thought was:
'And??'

They are getting paid for what they were hired for.
Why are we putting a label on it?

You shouldn't expect everyone to be ambitious from the get-go.
Most people are just coming to their jobs for a paycheck.
This may get under a manager's skin.
But it is what it is.

When you see someone who is always doing more than expected:

LOCK IN ON THEM.

Praise them and ask them if they want more responsibilities.

INSTILLING A NEW CULTURE

When Sam Walton was scaling Walmart, he was doing what a lot of other CEOs were not doing.

'What?'

He was sharing information with his employees.

The reason he did that was because he wanted them to feel like they had ownership.

By giving them clarity, they knew WHY they were doing what they were doing.

If you pull a lot of employees to the side and ask them:

'Do you know WHY you are doing a series of tasks?'

They are going to shrug their shoulders.

That's your fault as the manager, my friend.

They should know the macro and the micro.

The micro is their role.

The macro is how their role has an impact on everyone else's roles.

By giving them clarity, you give them direction.

When you give them direction, they move with an extra pep in their step.

FOCUS MORE ON THE SOFT SKILLS

Too many tools are not a good thing.
I truly do believe this.
It makes us small-time thinkers.

Center the business on people first and technology second.
This allows you to keep the important thing the important thing.

Soft skills are more important than ever.

The basics are what I call it:
- A strong understanding of psychology.
- Proficiency in emotional intelligence.
- Team working.
- Supreme listening skills.

Focus on these and you'll see yourself attracting good employees and magnifying great employees.

WHAT I LEARNED FROM ALFRED HITCHCOCK

When I was a kid, I'd go to the local library to get books.

My mind was blown when I found out you could rent movies too.

My younger self thought:

'If I could rent movies all along, why the hell am I wasting my time renting books??'

I go to the movie section and eagerly peek through the selections.

I was very disappointed.

All the movies were whack!

Old school Planet of the Ape movies and Alfred Hitchcock movies.

Who the hell is Alfred Hitchcock??

Sound's like a bird.

Anyways, curiosity got the best of me and I decided to watch one of his films.

The movie I rented was called *Birds*.

MY EXPERIENCE WITH ALFRED HITCHCOCK

When I watched Birds, I was pleasantly surprised.

It was a thriller about when birds attack and disrupt ordinary life.

What a strange concept, I thought.

But Alfred Hitchcock was able to make it work.

Since I was pleasantly delighted by the movie, I went on to rent more of his films.

That's when I saw:

- Psycho
- Frenzy
- Rope

Each movie was amazing to me.

He was creating thrillers without many special effects.

His movies were based in the 70s, so he had little to work with.

However, despite having little to work with, he was providing a lot.

WHAT I LEARNED FROM ALFRED HITCHCOCK

'So, what did you end up learning from Alfred?'

I learned that you can produce a lot with a little.

As I got older, I once again got curious about Alfred.

More specifically in 2020.

When the lockdowns were going on, I was like:

'Let me check out some Alfred Hitchcock interviews.'

In one of the interviews, he shared a story about an actress who came to his office crying.

She was upset by something Alfred did...

Or didn't do.

Alfred asked her what was wrong.

She said:

'Alfred, most directors are giving me endless feedback on set. But you don't say anything. You don't make me change anything!'

And he was like:

'That's because you're doing a great job.'

Done.

End of the conversation.

KEEPING THE IMPORTANT THING THE IMPORTANT THING

When you have little, that's when you can do a lot.

Because with little, you have no choice but to keep the important thing the important thing.

A lot of whiners make excuses.

They are like:

'I would be able to make movies too if I had x, y, and z.'

They begin listing off all these gadgets and software that they don't have.

While completely undermining what they **do have.**

'And what do these whiners have, Armani?'

Their mind.

That's what made Alfred's work stunning.

It was the simplicity.

The simplicity allowed him to keep the story as the king.

HOW HE BECAME THE KING OF DRAMA

Alfred's fundamental philosophy can be broken down to the following line:

'Allow the audience to know more than the character.'

Wow!

It seems too simple, doesn't it?

But think about any suspense film that you watch.

All those movies have one thing in common.

The audience members know more than the idiot who is about to go into the dark forest.

'Don't go into the forest lady! The monster is in the forest!'

By knowing something that the character doesn't know, we automatically become engaged.

Think about this, my friend…

Alfred's philosophy that created endless work can be boiled down into **1 simple line.**

This further highlights how Alfred could do a lot with little.

HOW TO APPLY SIMPLICITY TO YOUR LIFE

We have so many tools nowadays.

But just collecting tools for the sake of collecting tools creates clutter.

The more clutter that you have, the more you lose sight of the bigger picture.

James Clear's blog is a good example of eliminating all clutter.

There aren't any graphics or anything like that.

Just his ideas.

A first-time reader may say that the blog is a tad bit boring.
Why not spice it up, James??

But a long-time reader loves how it isn't too flashy.
Lack of clutter allows the idea to remain king.

Therefore, when identifying how to add simplicity to your life, you need to know what you are prioritizing.
With content, it's always the idea that is king.
Without the idea, you have nothing.

Once you have centered the idea in your workflow, now tools are **only** bought in if it helps amplify the idea.
Otherwise, you can live without it.

REINFORCE THE FUNDAMENTALS

No matter which interview it was, Alfred always gave glimpses of how he viewed filmmaking as a craft.
By viewing it as a craft, it was easier to reinforce the fundamentals.

Storytelling is a subject that combines a lot of other topics.

You need to be good with words.
Need to understand human nature.
Need to understand how to activate nostalgia at will.
Be proficient with technology along with a lot of other topics.

That's why you'll see a lot of people in the later parts of their life trying to create some sort of content.

The sum of their wisdom is naturally pulling them towards telling stories.

The cool thing about our era is that we can get a head start.

Rather than mastering storytelling later in our lives, we can start early.

That's when a lot of lessons from old-school filmmakers like Alfred come to life again.

HOW TO STOP COMPARING YOURSELF TO OTHERS

Comparison leads to a lot of new information.

When comparing yourself to others, a contrast is created.

All knowledge exists in a state of contrasts.

You don't know something.

New information is presented.

Now you know something.

Therefore, comparison is not bad.

But it becomes bad when too much comparison happens.

With social media, you open your phone and are suddenly bombarded with images of people having something you don't.

Next?

> Jealousy ensues.

Next?

> Despair ensues.

Next?

> More comparison ensues.

To stop this toxic cycle, read on...

HOW COMPARISON STARTS AT A YOUNG AGE

I wrote this one newsletter where I talked about being overly competitive for a while.

I shared how I was too competitive in Toastmasters which led me to be jealous of the other speakers.

Once I stopped competing with them to compete with my prior day self, I became inspired by them.

- Creativity = Unlocked.

Once I hit sent, I received an email from a reader.

He asked:

'Why do I compare myself to others so much? I can't stop.'

I asked the guy more questions.

Eventually, I was led to his background.

He was Korean.

'Um..so?'

A lot of Koreans have strict parents.

In their household, a B is perceived as a D and a C is perceived as an F.

Whenever this guy would do good in a class, but not get an A, his parents would be like:

'What happened? Tom's kids got an A in the same class, how come you didn't?'

I interacted with that reader some more.

At a young age, he was being compared by his guardians.

The subconscious mind picked up the pattern.

And the subconscious mind held onto the pattern.

THE HOMELESS MAN

A few days ago, I was getting out of 7/11.

I bought some chocolate milk and was given some change.

As I was walking to my car, I saw this man with a dirty shirt staring at me.

He motioned his face like:

'Got any change?'

But he never said those words.

After seeing his body language, I motioned:

'Do you want this change?'

When I motioned to give him the change, his eyes lit up.

Once I gave him the change and went to my car, I felt sorry for him.

That was my default reaction.

It's because it was hot as fuck that day in Florida.

And he was waiting outside asking for money.

'Why is the homeless man's story important?'

Because I never thought for a second to compare myself to him.

It's because I saw him in a moment of struggle.

THE CONFIDENCE IRONY

In my book, Speak Easy, I break down a law known as the Confidence Irony.

This is when we undermine how confident we are.

Then we over-amplify how confident someone else is.

It's best to flip it.

View yourself as more confident than you really are.
And view others as less confident.

The only time you begin comparing yourself to others is when you find a certain part of their life where they excel.
Not only are they excelling in that field...
But that's the same part of your life where you're not doing so well.

It's like the successful single businessman who envies the family man's family.
But the broke family man also envies the successful businessman's riches.
Call that duel jealousy.

You compare yourself to others when you view them at a higher level than you.
In doses, it's fine.
But do it too much, now it becomes poison.

HOW TO STOP COMPARING YOURSELF TO OTHERS

The first thing to understand is that problems are built into nature.
Just because Johnathan seems like a golden boy in all facets of his life...
He has a great family.
A great job.
A great physique.

Doesn't mean that he's perfect.

Secretly, he does drugs and is unable to stop.
He struggles with the fear of losing everything.
And that fear only amplifies his drug usage.

By humanizing Johnathan like I was able to humanize the homeless man that day, it's easier to realize that too much comparison is a waste of time.

But gathering everyone you're jealous of and finding flaws in them to humanize them is tedious.
You don't have to do it with everyone.

Just find one person you constantly compare yourself to.
Then do your best to humanize them.

You may lack information on the setbacks they have.
But remember, problems are built into nature.
So, if you are unable to articulate what their setback is, then just **assume** they have one.
This allows you to humanize them and keep it pushing.

BE TOO BUSY TO COMPARE YOURSELF TO OTHERS

The act of finding setbacks in someone that you're jealous of is just a mental experiment to realize that no one is perfect.

But to nip this problem in the bud, the solution is to level up.
Improve a minimum of 1% daily in something.
Anything.

- Make today better than yesterday and tomorrow better than today.

Naturally, this allows you to focus more on your life and less on others.

Someone who is comparing themself too much to others most likely doesn't have much going on.

A bit of jealousy is good.

It serves as a compass.

You're jealous of Ricky's body.

Chances are you need to get in shape.

But being jealous of Ricky's body and not going to the gym is jealousy gone wrong.

Go to the gym, bud.

Focus more on that.

The tiny 1%'s adds up.

Soon, you'll realize Ricky was never your enemy.

He was simply living his life.

Hopefully, now you are living yours.

6 TIPS TO REMEMBER WHILE MASTERING YOUR CRAFT

Let's say you want to master the craft of writing.
It's not only the writing that is important.
There are behind-the-scenes forces that influence your words.

The proper reading.
The proper research.
A disciplined writing practice.
Dealing with criticism and much more.

No matter what craft it is...
Mastering it takes **work**.

In this article, you will learn 6 tips to keep in mind when you begin your journey to mastering your craft.
Which brings me to the strange tip of number 1.

1. YOU NEVER MASTER YOUR CRAFT

Think about a master in any field.
Do they ever say something like:
'I have officially mastered my craft.'
?

No.

Because if they think that, then their desire to keep practicing will plummet.
When their practicing plummets, their craft plummets.

True masters keep mastering for life.

They don't speak in finite terms.
Which has a deadline. Like:
'I have mastered my craft.'

They speak in infinite terms.
They say:
'I will keep sharpening my blade, forever.'

2. THERE IS ALWAYS SOMETHING TO IMPROVE

Stupid people think they know everything.
Smart people think they have yet to know anything.

The reason smart people behave like this is because they are aware of a lot of things.
However, one caveat of being smarter is knowing what you are ignorant on.
And the smart person knows they are ignorant on plenty...
This is a good problem to have.
Because this keeps them learning.

Similar to mastering a craft.
Maybe you have been practicing writing for some time.

Your ideas are breathtaking.
However, you have the tendency to ramble.
The sentences can be shortened.

When you have a finite mindset, you find this to be annoying.
'Damn! When am I going to figure this out already?'

But when you have the infinite mindset, you're like:
'Yes, a new challenge for me to work on!!'

3. A PRACTICE ROUTINE KEEPS YOU CONSISTENT

A lot of creators don't have an idea problem.
They have a deadline problem.

They have a deadline problem because they don't take the initiative to set deadlines.
Without deadlines, the mind will overthink.

It doesn't need to be a complex practice routine either.
The simpler, the better.

For example:
'Every Monday, Wednesday, and Friday, I will write a blog.'
'Evenings are for reading.'
'Mornings are for writing.'

To better plan your day, be sure to check out my personal organizer planner, Simplify.
Take the guesswork out so you stay disciplined.

4. KEEP LEARNING MORE THEORY

Practicing is a great way to give your nervous system more data.

You learn the theory better by doing than learning the theory strictly with the theory.

But that doesn't mean that you undermine the theory.

When you have practical experience, theory becomes a safe haven.

For a while, you were doing things a certain way.

There was a lot of guesswork involved.

But then you read a book that breaks down your moves into formulas.

When you see that your moves have already been codified by someone else, that's when you're like:

'Whoa!! There's a method to the madness!'

This is how education was meant to be in the first place.

Practical application and theory are meant to be friends, not enemies.

Therefore, lead with street smarts.

Fill in the gaps with book smarts.

5. INTERLEAVING LEARNING

While mastering your craft, you'll notice yourself becoming a polymath.

Interleaving learning is cross-combining subjects to build a holistic understanding.

But wait!

You may be tempted to study a bunch of random subjects to force yourself into a big picture view.

I recommend you don't do that.

Instead, **organically** drift off to a new subject.

When I started writing, I had to set up my site.
When I set up my site, I organically learned more about domain setup, hosting services, and WordPress.
So, I naturally hopped from writing to information technology.

Once I learned more about information technology, I realized:
'Whoa, computers are just a series of electricity turning on and off.'

What the hell is electricity...really?
So, I got curious about that subject.

Think about this:
- Writing -> electricity.

Similar hops in subjects will happen to you.
As you aim to master your craft, you will learn plenty of topics along the way.

6. CLARIFY THE VISION

The mind is prone to entropy.
It's wired to get distracted.

When Steve Jobs got fired from Apple, he went on to start a new company called Next.
His most important role was to keep reiterating the vision to his employees.

Because the employees would often drift off to majoring in the minors.

Steve would fall for that trap too.

Therefore, he had to **constantly** remind himself of the vision.

The more the vision became clarified, the more the desire built.

The more the desire built, the more the work just took care of itself!

Keep reminding yourself of why you started this craft in the first place.

Keep adding more clarity to it.

Tackle it from multiple angles.

Eventually, that vision will always remain at the forefront of your mind.

Now the work will take care of itself.

ALWAYS STAY SHARPENING THE BLADE

A strong purpose is not built from hoping to retire on a beach and drinking sour amaretto's all day.

True purpose is becoming awesome at something.

Anything.

If you follow the ArmaniTalks brand, then you are aiming to get better with words.

Stick with the skills.

By mastering 1, you begin to master plenty.

And if you ask me...

That beats being a beach bum any day.

How to Deal with Changes in Life Like a Winner

Change is a part of reality.
Those who try to suppress change often end up dealing the worst with it.

It's much better to deal with change.
Expect it.
Conquer it.

One of my first times realizing the importance of dealing with change was when I was forced to read this book called Things Fall Apart in high school.

For most books, I SparkNotes'd it.
But something in my gut told me to read this book.
So, I read it.

It was a book about a powerful warrior in Africa.
The book highlighted his gradual journey to gaining physical strength, growing a family, and winning respect in his tribe.

It seemed like he was going to be a winner.
But things began to change.

A new religion set up shop in his village.
Soon, he was finding it difficult to adjust to the new religion.
The culture was shifting.
His son abandoned his roots and converted to the new religion.

The powerful warrior saw his life falling apart.

I won't spoil the book for you.

So, allow me to share how to deal with changes in life.

THE 2 PARTS OF REALITY

The 2 forces of reality are:

- Constant.
- Change.

In terms of human experience:

Awareness is constant.

But what changes is your life (mind & body).

- Your body has changed from a baby to now.
- Your mind has changed from a baby to now.

Another example is the screen that you are reading this blog from.

The screen remains the same.

But during your web surfing session, I'm sure you saw a lot of different content.

YouTube posts.

Other blog articles.

And tweets.

- Screen = Constant
- Content on the screen = Change.

These 2 parts of reality are baked into the human experience.

WHY PEOPLE HATE CHANGE

'If change is one of the forces of reality, why do so many people hate it?'

They hate it because of the emotional strings.

The subconscious mind loves familiarity.

It's the conscious mind that wants to evolve.

Have you ever had that moment when you saw your friend making moves?

Let's say one of them started a business and has been crushing it.

Now you want to start a business.

Your imagination is engaged and you can hear the coins pouring in.

One problem...

You keep self-sabotaging yourself.

The motivation is plagued with self-doubt, analysis paralysis, and inconsistency.

Why?

It's because the subconscious mind wants things to remain the way it always has.

You have a nice cozy job.

Everything is predictable.

Why switch it up?

The subconscious mind doesn't like change too much.

It **loves** predictability though.

HOW TO DEAL WITH CHANGES IN LIFE

I believe it's smart to willingly introduce changes to your life.
If things have been working for too long, then it's wise to switch it up.

One of the simplest examples is the gym.
If you go to the gym and lift the same weight all the time, then there is no growth.
The general rule of thumb is to change it up.
Make it difficult for your muscles to adapt.

It's the same with reality.
Occasionally introduce changes to your life...
It doesn't have to be volatile changes either.

Let's say you are someone who is always going for a walk on a treadmill.
Well, switch it up and go walk in the park.

'Okay... what's the point of that? I'm still walking.'
Doesn't matter.
It's the act of **willingly** introducing change that is key.
By introducing gradual changes every now and then, the subconscious mind no longer detests change.

DEAL WITH IT

Here's some uncomfortable advice.
It may piss you off.
The advice is:

- Deal with it.

'Deal with it? This is your bright advice?!'
Okay, I'll switch up the words to make it more powerful:

- Thrive under it.

I recall in my first internship… one day, I got to work late.
Once I got to work, there was this guy named Hoa who came to me and was like:
'Whoa, you're here?? I was worried.'

For a bit of context, this was my first engineering-related job.
I was very nervous about being exposed as a fraudulent engineer.
Hoa took me under his wing and taught me the ropes.
We built a close bond.

I thought he was being sarcastic with his comment, so I was like:
'Very funny, Hoa. I know I'm 20 minutes late, but there was a lot of traffic!'

He still had a serious face.
Then he said:
'You didn't hear? The new management that bought our company just fired half of the staff. Amy and Braulio are gone.'

Just like that, half of the company was slashed.

This was a tiny company where everyone knew each other.
I soon heard people crying in the walkways.

But what's done was done.

We couldn't do anything about it.
So, we needed to find a way to thrive.

THE ADAPTABLE NERVOUS SYSTEM

'You never know how strong you are until you have no choice.'

Over time, the few remaining members of the company
adjusted to our coworkers' departure.
We learned their:

- Systems.
- Workflow.
- Processes.

We became smarter through the tragedy.
They eventually found new jobs as well.
We were all better off in the long run.

All change has a silver lining buried within it.
Over time, the silver lining will present itself.

DEAL WITH CHANGE AND GROW WITH CHANGE

No matter which field you are in..
Which state you are in..
Or which stage you are in...

Change is inevitable.

There are 2 forces of reality:
- The constant and the change.

Awareness always remains the same.
It is nature that goes up and down.

Accept the reality of nature.
And it will no longer be intimidating.

How to Stop Making Everything About Yourself

To stop making everything about yourself, listen to listen, rather than listening to respond.

- Listening to listen is when you listen in streams.
- Listening to respond is when you listen in fragments.

'Can you give me an example of listening to respond?'

Sure.

Imagine Sam has been learning about commercial real estate as of late.

One day, his cousin Rohit is in town.

Sam takes Rohit out to eat.

Sam asks Rohit what he has been up to.

Rohit says he has started studying commercial real estate as of late.

If Sam was listening to respond, then simply hearing *commercial real estate* was all that was needed for him to stop listening.

Commercial real estate resonates with Sam's experiences.

So, now he stopped listening and is looking to respond.

Sam desperately wants to say:

'I too have been learning about commercial real estate!'

But if Sam was listening to listen, then 'commercial real estate' wouldn't be such a **sticky** phrase.

He's not stuck on that fragment of the conversation.

Instead, he is still listening to the stream of Rohit's response.

Which ends with Rohit saying:
'That's when I realized commercial real estate wasn't for me. My real love was always engineering.'

DANGERS OF ASSUMING

'Why do so many well-intentioned people make everything about themselves?'
There are a lot of reasons for this.

Sometimes, it's a poor focus.
Other times, they are relating to your story to build more rapport with you.

And other times, it's because they are assuming.
Assuming is dangerous to your charisma.
That's why there is the quote:
When you assume, you make an ass out of u and me.

This is also why it's difficult to listen to people you are close with.
There's a high degree of familiarity.
You think you know everything about them.
When you think you already know most things... the likelihood of assuming **skyrockets**.

Sometimes, the assumptions hold to be true.
Other times, the assumptions are dead wrong.

It's important to melt away assumptions and remain curious.
The more curious you are, the easier it will be to stop making everything about yourself.

DEALING WITH AN EGOTISTICAL PERSONALITY

Talking to an egotistical personality is draining.

This is when you are being socially intelligent.

- Listening.

- Responding.

- Asking questions.

But they still have this draining energy that sucks the life out of you.

Maybe this is a person you can't get away from.

What then?

If it's a person you can't get away from, then use them as an emotional workout.

Just like going to the gym requires pain to grow...

Dealing with difficult personalities builds social skills.

Other than that, the main thing we can do is control our behavior.

Avoid being an egotistical person.

There will be times when we accidentally get caught in the act.

Our attempt at showing that we related to their story caused us to take the spotlight away from them.

Their body language shows they are not pleased.

Own up to it and say:

'My bad... You were saying?'

Occasionally taking away the spotlight isn't bad.

But not giving the spotlight back is a felony in all 50 states!!

WHAT DOES AN EMCEE DO? | TIPS FOR EMCEEING AN EVENT

There's a difference between a speaker and an emcee for an event.

Both are important.

Just know that the 2 are different.

By knowing the difference, you'll be able to perceive public speaking from multiple angles.

Most events that are scaled often have both a speaker and an emcee.

By learning the intricacies of both positions, you'll feel confident no matter which position you are called to take.

At the end of the day, both positions require words.

But how the words are delivered is different.

DIFFERENCE BETWEEN A SPEAKER AND EMCEE

The speaker has an in-depth talk.
While the emcee is the glue guy.

'Hmm, the in-depth talk seems much more important.'
Not quite.
Both serve a unique function.

As the glue guy, the emcee is the **bridge** between the speakers and the audience.
They will be the person:

- Entertaining the audience.
- Introducing the speakers.
- Transitioning from 1 speaker to the next.

The better of a job that an emcee does, the more at ease a speaker is.

If the emcee sucks, then the speaker and the audience will feel uncomfortable.

'How do you determine if the emcee sucks?'
If they don't know a lot.

One of the main traits of an emcee is to **know a lot.**

They should know the setup of the event location beforehand.

They should know interesting facts about the speaker.

And they should have a rough idea of what the speaker will be talking about!

HOW TO PREPARE AS AN EMCEE

Normally, there is an event coordinator that will ask a person to be an emcee.

It's best to buddy up with this event coordinator from the beginning.

They will be able to give a rough idea of what the event is about.

From there, it's best to get an introduction card from the speakers.

This is basically a short summary of the speaker.

These cards will have the credentials of the speaker, why they should be taken seriously, and an idea of what the talk is about.

An emcee can read off the cards.

But in my opinion, it's better to memorize the cards.

By memorizing the cards, the emcee seems more professional.

Also, by memorizing the cards, it's easier to transition from speaker to speaker.

While others are walking around in the forest.

The emcee has a bird's eye view.

OPENING MONOLOGUE

Have you ever seen an award show before?

Normally, the emcee or the host of the event has an opening monologue.

This opening monologue is a short funny talk to keep the mood light.

A lot of the audience members came as guests with someone who was invited.

So, as guests...they have no clue what to expect.

In the opening monologue, it's smart to give a rough idea of what the event is about.

Let's say the event coordinator wants to throw a seminar on leadership.

Then in the opening monologue, you can:

- Tell a funny story of when you were under the supervision of a poor leader.

- Explain why this seminar is needed.

- Explain how the audience will learn leadership in this seminar from quality speakers.

The opening monologue is the first thing before introducing the speakers.

From there, it's a game of transition.

BEING THE HYPE MAN

Where the speakers talk about their topics in depth...
The emcee is the glue guy.
You just keep the event going from point A -> point B.

This is easier when you have the hype man mentality.
Introduce the speakers with some enthusiasm.
And once they are done with their talk, be like:
'Oh my diddly daze...That was fire!'

Well, not in those exact words but you get my point!

By being the hype man, you'll notice you allow the speaker to get in their groove much faster.
This builds a great atmosphere in the event.

'Do you recommend I get to know the speakers even before the event?'
That would be the ideal scenario.
But it's not always doable.
For a lot of large scaled events, speakers are traveling from out of state or from overseas.

But you can do some research on them prior to the event.
Maybe they have a YouTube channel or a blog.
Then it will be much easier to be a hypeman.
The atmosphere is now lit.

HAVE FUN

To be the glue guy, you mainly need to be having fun.

You can do a lot of things wrong...

But if you overall radiate a fun, energetic presence, then your role as the emcee will be judged in a positive light.

Just remember this:

- You control the tempo.

In many ways, you are the most important position while also not the most important position.

Some would say the audience members are the most important.

Some would say the speakers are the most important.

But without you, the audience members and the speakers are twiddling their thumbs!

The oxymoron of being the most important and not the most important allows pressure to fall away.

Just keep that perspective.

Now you will have the ability to have a lot more fun!

EMCEEING AND BEING THE GLUE GUY

You never know when you will be asked to be an emcee.

If you want to prepare, then join a Toastmasters club and volunteer to be the head Toastmaster.

You'll get a feel for what it's like to keep a cadence going for an event.

Create memories for yourself.

And help create memories for others.

That's the essence of being an emcee!

How to Speak Up for Yourself Without Overthinking

Chaos and social skills go together.

At one moment, people are talking about one topic.

The next moment, they are on a new topic.

By the time they are on a new topic, you're annoyed.

'What the hell! I just formulated my points for the last topic.'

This only gets tougher if you found yourself getting embarrassed on the last point.

Where someone put you down and swiftly transitioned.

I'm going to share some truths on learning how to speak up for yourself.

But first, it begins with a few faulty quotes.

3 Quotes That I Hate

One quote that I hate is:

Great artists steal.

This gets the artist too focused on copying rather than leveraging inspiration.

Great artists don't steal.

Great artists learn from the world.

But before they can learn from the world, they must first learn from themselves.

Another quote I hate is:

There is no such thing as a new idea.

Sure, this quote is true if you focus on the end result.

But nowadays, more people are curious of HOW the idea was reached.

And the HOW is always different from person to person.

Therefore, when focusing on the HOW, ideas have no choice but to be unique.

The final quote I hate is:

You need to speak up for those who don't have a voice.

The reason I hate this quote is because it makes a person feel like a victim.

Yes, there are groups who need others to speak up for them.

They are in such devastating circumstances that they need representation.

But if you're reading this article, then chances are you're not one of those people!

With your fancy internet...

Learn to speak up for yourself.

WHEN TO SPEAK UP FOR YOURSELF

I know a guy named Anand.

He is a very opinionated guy.

He has opinions about:

- What type of ice cream is the best.
- How eating boneless wings is for pussies.
- And how football is the best sport out there.

It's one thing to have an opinion.

It's another thing to drop everything and debate about those opinions.

And it's one thing to debate.

It's a whole different ball game to debate in order to FORCE someone to behave another way.

As you can tell...

Anand is a tityboy.

He's a guy who is not building anything.

He spends most of his time speaking up for himself because he has nothing better to do.

Too much time on his hands.

Therefore, speaking up for yourself is not always a good thing.

Sometimes, it can be a detrimental thing.

'How do I know when to speak up for myself and when to let things slide?'

That's a subjective question that cannot be given an objective response.

However, there are some clues to look out for.

SPOTTING FUNDAMENTAL PRINCIPLES

Fundamental principles are non-negotiable.

Spotting these non-negotiables take time.

'Why does it take long?'

Because you need to be CERTAIN they work.

Once spotting the principles, it's easier to spot the signal from the noise.

Now it becomes easier to know **when** to speak up for yourself.

That's because someone is doing something that defies your non-negotiables.

One of the fundamental principles I have with the ArmaniTalks brand is:

- Don't compete against others.
- Compete against your prior day self.

I break down this rule in the Level Up Mentality book.

If I'm dealing with someone who wants me to create content talking shit about someone, then my red flags go off.

I'll say:

'Nah, that breaks a fundamental law.'

Decision-making is crystal clear.

Let's try another example.

Imagine Peter and Susie get into a relationship.

Peter's one rule is that infidelity will not be accepted.

One night, Susie gets drunk and kisses a guy in the club.

The next day, Susie breaks the news to Peter.

She says she was drunk and doesn't remember.

Now what?

Well, a person without any principles regarding infidelity will be in a pickle.

They will be like:

'Well, she was drunk. Hmm... I need to think this through.'

But Peter's decision is already made.

He ends the relationship.

Speaking up for yourself is not only done with words.
It's done and solidified through actions.

SPRINGING INTO ACTION

A lot of real-world scenarios are blurry.
What is obvious for 1 person is ambiguous for another person.
That's because different humans have different orders of value.

It all stems from the fundamental principles.
The more the principles are followed, the more the body alerts you when something is off.
The body will start firing of sensations like:
'Yo, this doesn't seem right.'

When the body is firing off like that, it's best to speak up **immediately**.
Rather than thinking:
'Hm... let me think of the exact way to string this sentence together.'

When people talk about listening to the gut, what does that really mean?
Look closer...
The gut instinct doesn't just happen in the gut.
Instead, it's a series of sensations that fire off in the body.

Speak up immediately when the body tingles.
You'll sound more convincing with less preparation rather than preparing too much.
The raw emotion and authenticity will spill out.

That's how you speak up for yourself.
Ready, fire, and aim.

SPEAKING UP & SPEAKING ASSERTIVELY

The word, *assertive*, gets a bad rep.
But that's because assertive is confused with aggressive.

Aggressive is when you are being unnecessarily hostile.
Assertive is when you are standing for the truth.

Aggressive is having poor manners.
While assertive is confidently telling someone that 2+2=4.

It doesn't matter if a group of people tell you that 2+2=5.
You KNOW it equals 4.
Since you KNOW it equals 4, it's easier to deliver the message without creating too many enemies in the process.

A Dummies Guide on How to Spot Fake News

If you have no clue how the media business model works, then chances are you will get brainwashed.

It's not a matter of *if*, it's a matter of *when*.

The sad reality is that many of us are prone to get brainwashed.

It's because we don't know everything.

When we don't know everything, that's when we need to understand.

To understand means to stand under.

And when we stand under an authority, we give them power over our minds.

For example...

I am not going to cut myself open to see what's going on in there.

I will give control of my mind to a medical professional or a medical textbook to tell me what's going on inside my body.

It becomes more complex when we are giving power over our minds for other topics.

Like social issues, opinions, and 'facts' that are meant to help us make practical decisions.

In this article, I'm going to give some frameworks on how to spot fake news.

So you are not becoming a zombie from the Walking Dead.

THE PURPOSE OF JOURNALISM

The purpose of journalism is to spread information so the consumer is self-sufficient.

A lot of the current mainstream news organizations are the polar opposite of that.

They aren't trying to make the masses feel independent.

They are trying to make others feel more dependent.

Maybe dependent on the government, a political party, or a news organization.

Why?

This is when having some basic understanding of the business model of mainstream news organizations helps.

THE BUSINESS MODEL OF MAINSTREAM NEWS ORGANIZATIONS

Companies make money by selling things. You sell a:

- Product.
- Service.
- Ad space on your platform.

Traditional news organizations often do the last one.

They have shows that are meant to give value through delivering news.

From there, advertisers would like to promote products and services during available time slots.

Therefore, for the corporation to make more money, they need more views.

This is when these organizations aim to create content that will get clicks.

Clicks often spike through negativity.

Once the emotions are there, that's when more people tune in.

This is when the initial purpose of journalism gets lost.

Rather than creating content that makes others feel independent.

They create content to make others feel dependent.

So the viewers will tune in again and again.

Not all organizations do this.

But in this era, many have fallen victim to the trend.

And there is a reason why.

THE ROLE OF TECHNOLOGY IN MEDIA

The beauty of this era is that it's easier than ever to become a media company.

With the rise of information technology, all you need is a microphone and ideas.

This makes it harder for traditional media.

Because now old school letterheads have more voices to compete against.

The competition mindset towards media is sad!

Because media is a positive-sum game.

Ironically, the tiny organizations have more leverage because they don't have too many overhead costs.

They don't have to get a massive amount of views to break a profit.

Which allows them to dive into long-tail keywords and nuanced topics.

Technology has changed the game.
And this causes old-school businesses to get desperate.

SPOTTING FAKE NEWS

Thus far, I have shared why fake news exists.
And by the way, this is not new by any means.
This has been happening for ages.

The first step to spotting fake news is to know a lot.
This allows you to separate what is legit vs what is bs.

For example:
If someone starts lying to me about dolphins...
I won't be able to distinguish fact from fiction because I don't know much about dolphins.
I'll just nod my head and will believe what they say.

I need to know about something to spot biases.
Often, you'll spot biases by the language someone uses.
A whole bunch of emotion and sweeping generalizations.

BUILDING MEDIA LITERACY

Just because it's on tv doesn't mean it's true.
Just because it's on the internet doesn't mean it's true.

Someone with elevated levels of media literacy knows how to:
1.   Spot the intent of the media.
2.   And create media.

I believe #2 leads to more development of #1.

When you create some form of media, that's when you are capable of developing awareness and a gut feeling.

It's easier to spot biases.

By the way, biases aren't bad if you own them.

This brand's name is called ArmaniTalks.
Not SaulTalks.
Therefore, my readers want to hear my perspectives.
ArmaniTalks does not claim to be a news organization.

Most of the media you consume may be like that too.
Where you follow a particular author to hear their biases.

See how someone frames themselves.
If they are saying that they are a news organization that lives on facts...then it's vital that they live up to that proclamation.

As Warren Buffet once said:
"You can hold a rock concert and that's OK. You can hold a ballet and that's OK. But don't hold a rock concert and advertise it as a ballet."

SPOTTING FAKE NEWS

A lot of people are talking about how coding should be taught in early education.
That coding is just as important as learning English.

I agree with this.
Coding is important.

But more people need to learn media literacy.

What coding is to computers, storytelling is to humans.

A story commands someone's nervous system and dictates their future.

A person with a bright future who gets caught up in fake news no longer has a bright future.

Therefore, learn to spot fake news by knowing a lot.

And once you know a lot, create some content.

That's when you'll develop a new sunglass to perceive reality.

Storytelling is influential and that's how the powerful get more powerful.

How to Connect People Like a Winner

'Is networking and connecting the same?'

No.

Networking is when you are trying to make yourself known.

Connecting is when you are trying to make others known.

When someone pictures a charismatic person, they immediately think:

- Someone who knows how to tell jokes, break the ice, and be the center of attention.

On the flip side, a lot of charismatic people are lowkey.

They don't need all the attention on them.

This is a great trait of someone who can connect.

In this article, you will get an introduction on how to make an introduction.

Power connectors are powerful forces in the social skills world.

Allow us to learn how to become one.

Connecting Mindset

Connecting people is a lot like recommending a book to someone.

Me going to a friend and saying:

'Hey, you should read this book because I liked it.'

Is **not** a compelling reason for them to read the book.

On the other hand, let's say I am well read.

I see that this person is struggling with connecting other people.

In this case, I'd say:

'You should read this book called the Power Connector by Judy Robinet. She breaks down how to connect people.'

Point being, we need a few variables to connect properly:

1. Know people.
2. Know what people need.

EXAMPLE OF CONNECTING

Let's say I've written plenty of books and know the entire writing process.

From creating the manuscript, to editing, to proofreading, to cover design, etc.

I meet Sally.

She is an upcoming author.

She is a great writer, but an awful designer.

I know that my graphic designer, Zeg, is looking for more clients.

And he is gifted with creating compelling book covers.

I introduce Sally and Zeg.

From this connection, all parties win.

Sally gets a book cover made.

Zeg gets money in his bank account.

And I get the pleasure of adding value.

In the social world, the law of energy exists.

The energy you put out there is the same energy that comes back.

Even if you don't collect a referral fee or anything like that...

That energy will be returned to you in another form.

WHICH MEDIUM SHOULD YOU CHOOSE?

There are multiple ways of connecting others.

It can be done in person.

It can be done digitally.

Or it can be done with a blend of both methods.

Where you digitally introduce each other to see if they will vibe.

If they vibe, then they meet offline.

I'm here to tell you that the medium does not matter too much.

Focusing too much on the medium will make you lose focus of the bigger picture.

'What was the bigger picture again?'

Create a connection that leads to a win-win.

- *Emails.*
- *Group messages.*
- *Live meetups.*

They are all pointed towards the same goal.

And that's creating connections.

WHAT TO DO IF SOMEONE INTRODUCES YOU

When someone introduces you to someone else, it's smart to keep the initial connector in the loop.

By doing this, the connector can connect you to more people in the future.

A past client of mine once introduced me to a guy he met at a networking event.

Let's call the past client of mine, Tom.

And the guy he met at the networking event, Joseph.

Tom told me that Joseph wanted to make videos on LinkedIn.

But he was camera shy.

Luckily for me, Tom and I worked together on that **exact** service.

So, Tom recommends that Joseph check out my services.

In my initial call with Joseph, nothing solidifies.

He was curious about the service, but not committed at the moment.

We talked for a few, then wrapped up with some final words.

2021 begins and Joseph hits me up again.

He emails me:

'Armani, I'm ready.'

Once his payment came into my PayPal, I message Tom and was like:

'Thanks a lot for the referral, Tom. Joseph and I decided to work together.'

After getting the update from me, Tom sent over 3 more referrals!

Therefore, it's smart to hit up the initial power connector and give a confirmation that the interaction went smoothly (or not so smoothly).

WHAT TO DO NEXT

'Okay, now I see what connecting is about. What do I do next?'
Just keep your ears open.

I wouldn't set goals like:
'I am going to create 40 new connections this year!'
That gets you too outcome-focused.
You will be tempted to create a connection more for ego's sake than for relationship's sake.

All you need to do is sit back and keep your ears open.
Normally, behind other people's whining, you will see an opportunity to make connections.

I had a friend who was whining about how he didn't know much about websites.
He wasn't too sure of how hosting, web design, and domain registration worked.
 Good.
I have a WordPress guy for that.
Behind the whining, I got the idea to introduce him to my website guy.

You don't want to connect in a way where it will make your life harder.
I know my WordPress guy has a team, he's not a solopreneur.
But if he was a solopreneur, then me giving him additional work will take away his attention from my site.
There are complexities that form every now and then with connecting.
But the main thing to look out for is creating a relationship where **all** parties win.
Yourself included.

CRITICAL THINKING VS LOGICAL THINKING: WHAT'S THE DIFFERENCE?

There's some confusion between critical thinking vs logical thinking.

People think they are the same.

But that's not the case.

Thinking they are the same is an honest mistake.

They seem similar at first glance.

However, in this article, we are going to share the clear **distinction** between the 2.

Not only are you going to learn the distinction, but I'm also going to give you a funny real-world example highlighting the difference.

By understanding the basics, you will improve logical thinking and critical thinking.

Without further ado, let us begin.

THE DIFFERENCE BETWEEN LOGICAL THINKING AND CRITICAL THINKING

Logical thinking is potential energy.
Critical thinking is kinetic energy.

Logical thinking is a series of:
- *'Because of this, this happened'* connections.

Critical thinking is a series of:

- *'If I do this, this will happen'* connections.

For logical thinking, you don't always need to get your hands dirty.

But with critical thinking, you always need to get your hands dirty.

You'll see a lot of people who make logical sense when they talk.

But when it comes to taking action, they act like a dufus.

Any idea why?

'No... why?'

It's because they haven't gotten their hands dirty (take action).

They use someone else's logic to fuel their thinking.

Although this strategy is not harmful...

It does not lead to supreme intelligence.

SECRET INGREDIENT OF CRITICAL THINKING

'I sort of see what you are saying Armani, but the difference is not solidified yet.'

All good. We will solidify the difference shortly with an example.

But before I give the example, I want to talk a bit more about critical thinking.

There is a special ingredient in all critical thinkers.

Can you guess what it is?

'Uh... a high IQ score?'

No. The special ingredient is **desire**.

'Desire?? That sounds like an emotional intelligence word. Why are you using it in this article for?'

It's because desire is the precursor to experimentation.

And experimentation is the precursor to critical thinking.

Have you ever seen one of those pictures of an iceberg before?

The one where you see the tip, and the rest of the berg is submerged under water?

Like this....

Normally this image is used to talk about the myth of an overnight success.

Today, I would like to help you perceive this iceberg in another light.

Critical thinking is the tip of the iceberg.

But what is submerged underwater is **desire.**

Allow us to transition to the example right now.

EXAMPLE OF THE SMELLY BREATH

You ever had that moment when you needed toothpaste, but ran out?

'Yea, plenty of times.'

Go back to that moment.

It's 5 am in the morning.

You're waking up so early because there is going to be a cute mail woman delivering the mail.

Your breath smells awful.

You're running low on toothpaste.

And all the convenient shops around you are closed.

So, you go to the toothpaste tube and try to squeeze it.

At this moment, the desire is pretty low to get the toothpaste.

At the back of your mind, you're thinking:

'I doubt I'm going to get any paste. I should probably wait until the stores open.'

You squeeze the tube like a wimp.

You're about to quit with your experimentation.

Then suddenly, the image of the cute mail woman pops up.

You think:

'I can't possibly greet her with this stinky breath! I must get the toothpaste out.'

Desire is rising.

Now you begin getting crafty.

The experimentation is becoming more dynamic.

You're no longer squeezing the tube like a wimp.

There is intention.

You move your hands to the middle of the tube, not just the top.

When you squeeze the middle, you see a bit of paste show its face, but it goes into hiding once you try to put it on your brush.

At least you're on the right track!

You begin moving your hands down the tube.

From your experimentation, you see that pressure is king.

When you squeeze from the bottom, you get more pressure.

Not only that, you begin twisting the bottom of the tube in a circular motion.

Now the pressure is at an all-time high.

TOOTHPASTE BEGINS FLOWING OUT!!

You needed 1 squirt.

You now have enough for 5 squirts.

The trip to the convenience store has been saved for another day.

Now you get to greet the cute mail woman as the best version of you.

BREAKDOWN OF THE EXPERIMENT

What did I say critical thinking was?

'You said it was a series of, *if I do this, this will happen,* connections.'

Correct. And that's exactly what you did in the example above.

You had desire, otherwise, the experimentation would not have happened.

From the experimentation, you collected a bunch of data.

Learning from the data led to the insight of the importance of pressure.

Applying the pressure gave you the toothpaste.

The final rundown of the experiment was:

- If I run low on toothpaste, I can use pressure to my advantage.

- If I use the pressure, then I will get more paste.

- And if I need more pressure, then I will go straight to the bottom of the tube.

What are the 3 bullets above showing?

'It's a series of, *because of this, this happened,* connections.'

What are those connections called?

'Logic.'

Correct, you were paying attention!

BE A DOER AND A THINKER

The problem with today's society is that very few people experiment.

They lack guts.

Due to their lack of guts, they parrot other people's experimentations, logic, and ideas.

But a rare few are rolling up their sleeves and getting their hands dirty.

They do this because they have the desire.

Desire is built from a compelling vision.

From that desire, they experiment.

They analyze the data.

They build critical thinking skills.

Then they cultivate sharp logic born from first-hand experiences.

I call that having skin in the game.

7 PRODUCTIVITY HACKS TO MAXIMIZE EACH DAY

I think everyone out there wants to be more productive.

This allows them to end the night with a good feeling.

The feeling of accomplishment.

Productivity is difficult to understand through theory alone.

It must be experienced.

The main thing to have is direction.

Without direction, none of the productivity hacks out there will help you.

That's like the guy who eats a bunch of junk thinking that supplements will save them.

'Does the direction need to be grand?'

No, it can be something small.

The direction can be:

- I'm going to build a daily writing practice.

- I plan to fit into my suit before my sister's wedding.

- I want to start that comic book company.

Once you're in motion, it helps to look for little refinements that will take you to the next level.

Let's see if any of these productivity hacks will help you out!

1. DON'T CHECK YOUR PHONE TILL 1-3 DIFFICULT TASKS ARE COMPLETE

The first thing the average person does when they wake up is check their phone.

Facebook, Instagram, Tik Tok, etc.

Maybe they see some negative content in the morning.
Do you know what happens next?
'What?'
The rest of their day feels **choppy**.

How you start the morning will set the tone for the rest of your day.
Don't check your phone at all until you get 1-3 of your hardest tasks done for the day!
That will set the right tone.

2. LEVERAGE INCENTIVES

I used to hate rest.
Thought it meant I was doing something wrong.
Later on, I learned that rest would lead to more productivity.

The are multiple ways to do this.
For me, I work very intensely from the morning until evening.

But roughly around that 7:30 pm to 8:30 pm range, I want my mind to be off.
Knowing that I have relaxation waiting at the end of the day makes me work harder when I am working.

3. AUTOMATE UNNECESSARY DECISIONS

You ever seen those famous people who wore the same thing every day?
'Yea, why do they do that?'

Because they don't want to keep deciding what they are going to wear every day.

- Decision = Automated.

And there are certain stuff anyone can automate.

For me, it's food.

I eat the same thing every day.

I don't want to keep thinking about what I am going to be eating, therefore, I automated this step.

Yes, I love the meal.

On a side note: I do intermittent fasting. So I don't eat till the end of the day. I mentioned in the last point how incentives are key. Knowing that I have relaxation AND food waiting for me after my productivity period drives me to work with even more intensity.

Point being, you can stack incentives to create a new beast to work towards!

4. LEVERAGE TO-DO LISTS

A to-do list is a great way to keep the important thing the important thing.

It's even better if your to-do list is simple.

If you see big paragraphs staring at you, then chances are you will not do them.

Boil those big paragraphs down to simple worlds.

Rather than say:

- I will go to the gym and workout X, Y, and Z followed by this stretch, followed by this meal...blah blah blah...

Just write:

- Gym

Here is a simple to-do list to help you get started:

5. CUT OFF TOXIC PEOPLE AND/OR HANG WITH PRODUCTIVE PEOPLE

It doesn't matter how productive you are.

If you have a roommate who is always trying to get high and eat wings, that environment will be toxic.

Best to create your own productivity zone (which we will be breaking down shortly).

Maybe you're at the stage of your life right now where you cannot just cut this roommate off.

So, go to a library.

Or any place where people are working.

Simply seeing others working will inspire you to not be a lazy sack of shit.

That's the power of mirror neurons.

6. DRESS UP AT HOME

Let's say you work from home.

Do you think someone will be more productive:

- Wearing pajamas and working

or

- Dressing up in formal clothes and working

???

'Formal clothes.'

Why?

'Idk.'

Because clothes influence psychology.

Wear shoes too and spray the cologne you normally put on before working.

- Wearing shoes just makes you present. Idk why, it just happens...
- And the scent of the cologne triggers the past memories of productivity.

Game time!

7. CREATING A PRODUCTIVE ZONE

This zone is strictly meant for working.

You have your laptop there.

Answer emails there.

Write your content there.

Keep that zone just for working, not for goofing around.

'Uh....duh Armani.'

Not duh.

Some people combine their work area with their play area.

Which I don't recommend, especially if you are struggling with productivity.

Block out this zone just for work.

Once you leave this zone, it'll be easy to enter into relaxation mode.

BONUS TIP: TRACKING TRANSFORMATION

I did p90x a while back (a 90-day workout program).

At first, I didn't like it.

Didn't see many changes.

Looked like I was getting chubbier.

But as some time went by, I noticed that I was getting leaner.

Once I noticed I was getting leaner, I began appreciating the chubby pics.

It showed how far I had come.

Seeing how far I had come made me associate a positive feeling with productivity.

If you can find some sort of way to document your transformation, that'll be a gamechanger.

I don't know exactly how you will do it in your life.

That's something you have to get creative with.

Just look to set up something that shows:

- Where you were -> Where you are

USE THE PRODUCTIVITY HACKS THAT WORK FOR YOU!

The productive mind turns a:

- 30-minute task into a 28-minute one.

While the unproductive mind turns a:

- 30-minute task into a 3-hour one.

Create a direction for your life.

That's the theme of the story.

And occasionally try a productivity hack to add more life to each chapter!

HOW TO DEAL WITH ADVERSITY LIKE A WINNER

It may be hard to imagine, but adversity is a good thing.

Some can deal with it.

And others fold under the pressure.

I never had a big problem with failures.

It stung at first, but I always thought it was a part of the game.

'Why did you think like this?'

Because I was a loser growing up and things rarely came easy for me.

It was very difficult for me to figure something out.

I looked to my left.

I looked to my right.

And what was difficult for me was easy for others.

I hated that.

But little did I know, those stages of setbacks were building character.

The ability to deal with adversity happens when we reframe failures as data.

In this article, we are going to talk about how to welcome in all kinds of data so we can learn from it and power up to new heights.

WHAT IS SOFTWARE?

Think about how powerful software is in our generation.

It's changing industries overnight.

Uber is a software.

Amazon has software.

And your phone is filled with software!

Can you define software?

'Uh…'

Software is a process that manipulates data.

That's the crystal-clear definition that should make you more introspective.

'What the hell? Why would I be more introspective about that? I don't have software.'

You absolutely do.

It's called the mind.

And you have data as well.

It's called your experiences.

Without data, software is good as useless.

Without experiences, your mind is good as useless.

WHY PEOPLE ARE AFRAID OF FAILURES

In the school system, the most important things were quantified down to grades.

You were evaluated in terms of:

- A, B, C, D or F

Never understood why they skipped E!

I got love for you E.

The grades are a frozen interpretation of our efforts.

The grades didn't factor in work ethic, consistency, networking skills, or any other soft skills.

It just came down to whether you passed or failed.

This binary measurement from school transferred into the real world.

And this form of thinking often turns someone into a coward.

They turn into a coward because they optimize their life to avoid failures.

However, anytime innovation, risk-taking, and greatness are involved....

Failures are a must.

Show me a great person...

And I'll show you someone who welcomed uncertainty and tackled it brick by brick.

How to Be Okay with Failures

To be okay with failures, it's important to categorize.

There are good failures and bad failures.

Which one do you want to hear about first?

'Bad.'

Bad failures are character issues and repeated mistakes.

If you made a mistake once, that's something to learn from.

But the more the mistake is repeated, the more that it can be labeled as a 'bad failure.'

A bad failure can be boiled down to something that does not lead to much wisdom or behavioral changes.

Good failures are setbacks and losses that lead to wisdom and refinements.

An example is when an entrepreneur releases a product that did not do well.

There are wins in this activity.

One win is that the entrepreneur released a product.

The entrepreneur gained experience in market research, how to organize people to create a deliverable, how to launch, and much more

The loss will hopefully spark the entrepreneur to tighten up their game some more.

Make micro-adjustments.

Soon, the multiple losses will blossom into an upcoming W.

VIEW FAILURES AS DATA

Big data.

Artificial intelligence.

When they are separate, their powers are reduced.

Big data cannot be processed by regular computers.

You need the powerful computers with advanced infrastructure to process big data.

Artificial intelligence without much data leads to sloppy outputs.

Optimization has been reduced.

But combine the 2 forces??

You have magic.

Big data can seamlessly be processed by artificial intelligence.

And artificial intelligence creates beautiful refined outputs once big data has been fed into it.

I saw this one toy self-driving helicopter that was supposed to fly around a track.

It kept bumping into things!

So sloppy…

But the more laps it took, the more data it accumulated.

The artificial intelligence of the helicopter took in the data of the surroundings.

It observed what the helicopter was doing right AND wrong.

After a whole bunch of bumping and bruising, the sloppy helicopter soon became more refined!

It began seamlessly flying around the track.

The process was so refined that it looked like a cartoon.

View failures as data.

View introspection as the software.

Then the artificial intelligence of your nervous system will make refinements over time.

Just keep pushing forward.

BUILDING CHARACTER & DEALING WITH ADVERSITY LIKE A WINNER

One common attribute of all winners is that they faced adversity and rose back up.

These are people with street smarts.

Coming back from adversity is not a physical act alone.

It's not as simple as a person physically standing up.

Instead, the process of coming back from adversity is a game of attitude.

Anyone can physically show up.

That requires little talent.

Few people can physically show up with peak enthusiasm.

They are enthusiastic despite getting punched in the face 15 times.

'Why are they so enthusiastic for?'

It's because they have their mind on the big picture.

They are collecting data from the wins AND losses.

Their movements are slowly becoming more refined.

And they are showing others how to deal with adversity like a winner.

This is the type of emotional intelligence that all humans possess.

But only a few will ever tap into it.

6 TRAITS OF SOMEONE WITH HIGH SELF ESTEEM

Self-esteem is self-image.
It is the perception of thyself.

There are some obvious traits of those with low self-esteem.
They gossip a lot, go out of their way to take others down, and are pretty harsh on themselves during their private time.

It would be simple to just reverse those traits and come up with the traits of someone with high self-esteem.
But it's not that simple.

The progression towards high self-esteem is a journey.
And it's **lifelong**.

This group of people is constantly getting better and gradually bringing up others with them.
In this article, we will learn a few traits that make these people so profound.

1. THEY ARE WORKING ON A PROJECT

It's difficult to build confidence without work.
Work purifies the body, mind, and intellect.
From that state of purification, clarity is produced.

Google *Confidence*.
Often, you'll see some remix of the word 'clarity' comes up.

To build that level of perception, they had to put in the work to build a complex system.

A complex system is a bunch of interconnected parts that lead to the creation of something new.

It can be building a dream body.

Creating a money-generating business.

Cultivating a relationship...

And much more.

Just know that confident people are building **something**.

2. THEY HELP OTHERS UP

In Wallace Wattle's book, The Science of Getting Rich, he talks about the advancing personality.

The advancing personality is someone who is TOO BIG for their place.

There's no denying they are going to the top one day.

We all met someone like that before.

What allows the advancing personality to advance is the *impression of increase.*

'What's that?'

It's when they leave others better off than they found them.

Wallace is very specific about this, so read closely:

It doesn't matter who they are interacting with...the advancing personality does their best to leave an impression of increase in those they interact with.

Whether it's a business client or a kid who is buying a soda from them.

Giving the impression of increase translates to high self-esteem over time.

3. THEY AVOID GOSSIPING TOO MUCH

I said *too much* rather than *at all.*

I think in an ideal world, a person doesn't gossip at all.

But I don't think that's realistic.

I think it's much wiser to weigh the holistic content material.

Are they predominantly talking about people?

Or do they sometimes talk about people, blended with topics on ideas, projects, and self-improvement?

Those with high self-esteem often talk others up (more on that shortly).

They will promote other people's business, their family, and their actions.

That's spreading good energy.

4. AVOIDS FOLLOWING A HERD

Nowadays, I see some of the most ridiculous trends:

- People hitting other people on the face with a purse.
- Licking the top of an ice cream and sticking it back in the fridge.
- Eating Tide pods.

This happens with low self-esteem people.

They are seeking guidance on how to tame their mind.

Rather than looking at the mirror for answers...

They look to social media trends for answers.

Someone with high self-esteem is like a tree.

Their roots are planted into the ground.

They water those roots by hanging with quality people, consuming quality information, and relaxing.

The tree strengthens.

When the tree strengthens, they do not act like an aimless bag floating in the wind.

5. THEY ARE TEACHERS

One thing that I've seen with all high self-esteem people is that they are teachers.

Not the type of teacher who turns every conversation into a lecture.

Instead, they know when someone needs help.

Then they explain the topic in such a clear and concise way that the other person feels like an idiot for not understanding.

You'll be surprised how this is **not** a common practice.

Low self-esteem people teach to show off how smart they are.

Using big words, incessantly sprinkling in their credentials, and not placing much emphasis on the student.

A person with high self-esteem is balanced in their approach.

They are well versed in a multitude of fields because they are building something.

Then they are well-spoken to explain that information.

6. HYPE MAN (OBSERVANT)

Have you ever seen a person who could fight, but rarely made others aware of how well they could fight?

This was not the type of person who was getting into random bar fights.

On the other hand, the tubby man who could barely walk without running out of breath is the one barking the most!

Why the unusual behavior?

Because competent people are at ease with themselves.

That doesn't mean they are being so humble that they aren't promoting themselves.

Instead, they aren't going out of their way to brag and hog the spotlight to show off.

High self-esteem people are more than happy to be a hype man.

A hype man is not some sort of cheerleader who jumps up and down acting like a dummy.

Instead, a hype man is:

Someone who notices relevant information often overlooked by others. Once the relevant information is spotted, they magnify it to bring awareness to it.

I have a short story in my book, **Word Play**, where I break down how the beloved hype man operates.

Get Here:

ARE YOU ON THE PATH TO BUILDING HIGH SELF ESTEEM?

This list is just scratching the surface.
I may have another blog post down the line.
Who knows...

What did you think?

Did you resonate with some of the traits?
If so, great!

If you felt like the traits were the exact opposite of you, that's still good to a certain degree.

Self-awareness sparks massive self-improvement over time.

The desire to improve just needs to match the awareness levels.

4 WAYS ON HOW TO BE MORE APPROACHABLE AT WORK & EVENTS

There was a time I was at gym class in the 6th grade.
Just minding my own business.

Suddenly, a kid named Cartier blurts out:
'Armani, why do you always look so mean?'

When he said that, a bunch of the other kids in the gym class agreed.
They were like:
'Yea, Armani looks so mean that I'm afraid to approach him!

I was shocked.
This was one of the first times I was made aware that I looked mean.
As a little kid, I was able to wave this off.
However, as an adult, not being approachable is a fast way to lose out on opportunities.

It sucks to be judged for something that you're not.
You are not standoffish, even if you look standoffish.
In this article, we are going to discuss 4 ways on how to be more approachable at work, social events, and in life.

CORRECT WAY TO VIEW APPROACHABILITY

First of all, there are some levels of approachability beyond our control.

A person can only make so many adjustments to their mean face.

If they are trying too hard to be approachable, that'll lead to:

- A nice guy.
- Clinginess.
- Being fake.

Therefore, the best way to build approachability is by asking:
How do I allow others to know my character?

When this is set as the intent, we keep ourselves as the focal point.
This allows us to stay rooted in our personality, so we don't become a people pleaser.
This question also allows us to make the initiative to make improvements along the way.

Approachability is a blend of physical and mental adjustments.
Allow us to go through some ideas.

1. RESTING BITCH FACE IS A PROBLEM

Humans process tons of information with their eyes.

So, if they are met with a scowled face, then chances are they will run the other way.
'What do I do about the resting bitch face?'
Think about thorns…

Have you ever gotten a thorn stuck in your foot?
'Yea.'
What did you do?

'I got another thorn and used it to poke out the thorn from my foot.'

Why didn't you use your fingers?

'Because my fingers were too big while the other thorn was tiny and efficient.'

Just like we used a thorn to remove a thorn.

Use a resting bitch face to remove a resting bitch face.

1. Make your face look 10x meaner.
2. Hold it for 6 minutes.

Once done, let go.

How do you feel?

'Wow, my face feels loose and relaxed!'

That's a peek into slowly melting away the resting bitch face.

2. TONE DOWN THE SASS AND SARCASM

Sarcasm is a very polarizing personality trait.

Some people **love** it.

When they see someone with sarcasm, they are in awe.

This type of person loves deadpan comedy.

On the other hand, there are a number of people who find sarcasm rude and condescending.

Sarcasm in itself is not bad.

But if you find yourself struggling to look more approachable, then it may be wise to tone down the sarcasm just a bit.

Build more rapport, then assess if the person is the type to be open to sarcasm.

3. DO THE APPROACHING FIRST

One of the most approachable people from my last job was the one who always did the approaching.

She was this girl named Melanie.

Melanie was in her mid-30s, had risen dramatically in her career, and was quite attractive.

This made it difficult for her to be approachable. Others were intimidated by her.

Especially because she managed so many people on the floor.

I'm sure she was aware of this issue.

Do you know what she did??

'What?'

She did the approaching first!

When she would introduce herself, ask questions, and crack jokes.... others would be like:

'Melanie, you're way nicer than I thought!'

From there, her reputation as an approachable person built.

4. CREATE MICRO BODY LANGUAGE ADJUSTMENTS

Doesn't it feel strange to go to a networking event when you're new in town?

You're hopping from person to person struggling to think of conversation material.

There was this winery I went to in Virginia for a social.

I just moved to Virginia and didn't know anyone.

So, I went by myself.

I began having a conversation with a guy named Sam.

He was talking about his career and was getting into it.

From the corner of my eye, I could see a guy who was hovering aimlessly looking for someone to talk to.

I looked at the guy, made subtle eye contact, smiled...

Then I SLIGHTLY shifted my body outwards as if I was making room for this stranger to come to the interaction with me and Sam.

After the SLIGHT shifted body language, he came my way.

We introduced ourselves.

With body language, micro has the potential to translate into macro.

- A smirk makes an impact.

- A gentle touch on the shoulder makes an impact.

- And slightly opening your body to invite someone in makes an impact.

LEARNING TO BE MORE APPROACHABLE

These are 4 ways on how to be more approachable at work, in business, and in life.

Apply what works and gently build more social opportunities.

Some people can just show up to an event and have a herd of people come their way.

They may be a celebrity, has a harmless face, or possesses an elevated level of magnetism.

View that as a rare occurrence.

For the most part, people have to work on improving themselves from a physical/mental level to be more approachable.

Social skills are the holistic education for life.

And you only stop learning once you die.

CHEATCODE TO A BETTER LIFE

The following post is from the ArmaniTalks Twitter Account.

Sleep well

Meditate

Journal

Visualize

Do yoga

Know financial literacy

Have hobbies

Get sun

Workout

Eat healthy

Drink water

Have a social support system

Know when to rest

SLEEP WELL

I used to sleep on my sleep.
Scraped a few hours a day.
Bad move.
Aim to get 7-8 hours.
I get it, not easy in today's busy world.
But make it an effort, and your production & happiness will

MEDITATE

Meditation has changed my life forever.
I used to be this overthinking squirmy fuck.

But once you begin meditating routinely, life slows down.

Concentration improves.

Happiness improves.

Clarity improves.

I do 10 min when I wake up & 10 min before sleep.

JOURNAL

Journaling is a game-changer.

I treat Twitter like a journal because I typically have my phone on me.

But you can do a Word Document or physical journal.

Just get your thoughts & feelings written.

Bonus: Do so every day and your writing skills will improve.

VISUALIZE

Tbh, I don't visualize like most people in silence.

If I'm visualizing, I better have some lit music.

Otherwise, it feels like work.

My visualization routine has me envisioning positives AND negatives.

If it's a negative scenario I plan out my rise as well.

DO YOGA

Seriously, do yoga.

And no, it's not easy as many of you may think.

Yoga allows you to synchronize your mind, breath & body.

Very powerful.

I use the yoga routine from p90x3.

But try a few routines out yourself and see which one works best for you.

FINANCIAL LITERACY

'I'm financially literate. My mommy said I was.

Ha.

Your mommy lied to you.

You are not just born financially literate.

Tame your ego.

Learn from books, ask questions to the right people, and become more curious.

Learn this language inside & out fam.

HAVE HOBBIES

Major key.

Life is going to kick your ass many times.

Make no mistake about that.

Your hobbies will always keep you grounded even in your dark times.

Have a hobby to keep you creative, one that makes you money & one that keeps you in shape.

GET SUN

I'm not going to start giving you all these concepts on why the sun is good for you.

I just know ever since I have been going for a walk every day outdoors, my life has improved.

Go ahead and give it a try.

Leave your darkroom & Netflix binge session and get some sun.

WORKOUT

Working out is not only good for you physically, but mentally as well.

'Mentally??'

Yep.

Tbh, consistently showing dedication to your body is more mental than physical in my opinion.

Have a workout routine and stick to it.

Don't be a bum.

EAT HEALTHY

Put your twinkies & cup noodles away and take your fatass to the kitchen, homie.

Learn how to cook.

Do not be dependent on fast food.

Many view cooking as 'work' but not really.

Learn a few dishes and you will realize it is fun.

Recipes are everywhere online.

DRINK WATER

Staying hydrated is very important.

Proper hydration will have you thinking clearly & efficiently.

However, do not overhydrate.

Drinking too much water is just as bad as not drinking enough water.

Use a water calculator online to find out your optimal level.

HAVE A SOCIAL SUPPORT SYSTEM

Have friends & family you can count on.

We are social creatures by blood.

If you do not have a squad, go on and build one.

People are not going to just break into your house asking to be your friend.

Know when to work, know when to unwind.

KNOW WHEN TO REST

People think always working is a badge of honor.
Nah.
You need to rest.
Otherwise, you risk burning out.
You cannot run a smooth engine if it's always running.
Learn to maintain it by resting intelligently.

This is my Cheatcode to a better life.

FEAR OF CONFRONTATION??

No matter how tough someone looks, for the most part, they don't like confrontation.

The type of confrontation where demands are laid out, tonality is raised and ultimatums are given.

The reason why the general public doesn't like confrontation is because they have a thing called a brain.

And the brain operates on the path of least resistance:

- It wants the easiest way to do something.

And confrontation is far from easy.

You may be the kindest person out there.

But unfortunately, that doesn't mean that someone won't confront you.

Sometimes, the confrontation was your fault.

Other times, it wasn't your fault.

In these scenarios, what's the best game plan?

Spoiler Alert

There is no perfect game plan.

Instead, it starts off by clarifying the right definitions.

Evolve definitions, evolve thinking.

And hopefully, evolved thinking leads to evolved behavior.

ASSERTIVE VS AGGRESSIVE

In my book, Speak Easy, I talk about the clear distinction between aggressive and assertive.

The 2 are often confused for one another.

- Aggressive is when a person is unnecessarily hostile.
- Assertive is when a person is articulating the truth.

Aggressiveness shows low social intelligence.
Assertiveness shows high social intelligence.

An example of assertive is articulating why someone broke a contract.
Running them through the details of the contract.
Providing evidence.
While talking to them with respect.
The tonality is smooth & gentle.

Aggression on the other hand is yelling at the person and putting them down.
But hey…I'm not judging.
There are times when the quality of work is so poor that a little bit of aggressiveness gets the job done faster than assertion alone.
May not be the politically correct thing to say…but it is what is.

For the most part though, it's wiser to be assertive over aggressive.
This leads to fewer burned bridges and more relationships intact.

EXPECT CONFRONTATION IN YOUR LIFE

Expecting a surprise is a great way to control the narrative.
It prevents things from rattling you so quickly.

Expecting confrontations is a marvelous way of bringing an accepting attitude towards occasional hostility.

'But me? I'm a kind dude. I don't see anyone confronting me!'

Just because you don't see it happening doesn't mean it won't happen.

I had a buddy a few years back who was playing basketball with a group of kids.

He was torching them in a game of 21.

Out of nowhere, one of the players sucker-punched him and knocked him out cold.

He fell to the ground on his face.

Which required him to get surgery and wear braces for the next few years.

Obviously, this may not be a regular scenario.

But expecting unexpected moments brings a sense of composure.

Emotional intelligence is not about running away from feelings.

It's about learning to coexist with all feelings.

IT'S RARELY PERSONAL

'Okay, I expect confrontations to happen every now and then. Now what?'

Now, it's a game of not taking it personally.

By not taking it personally, it's easier to articulate ideas rather than articulating impulsiveness.

You ever got angry and accidentally took it out on someone else?

'Yea.'

Did you despise the person you were yelling at or were you angrier about the act that set off your fuse in the first place?

'The act from before.'

Exactly. It's often the same case for others.

Most people are not acting out because of you directly.

It may be from a behind-the-scenes event that caused them to lose it.

An example is when Will Smith slapped Chris Rock at the Oscars.

At first glance, it seemed like Will Smith was agitated by the G.I. Jane joke.

But if you read Will Smith's recent memoir, it's easy to tell that other variables were involved.

He always felt like a coward for not defending his mom growing up from his dad, so I believe the joke set off a subconscious narrative to not let the same mistake happen with his wife.

I break down the slap heard around the world in this video.

Point being, the slap was not personal towards Chris Rock.

ARTICULATE THE IDEAS AND MOVE ALONG

Clarity is the ability to perceive things with an equal eye.

Once it's no longer personal, it becomes easier to **see** things.

When personalization has melted away, the bowl of water is no longer shaking.

The bowl of water is still.

Making it easy to see through the water.

With an unruffled mind, it becomes easier to articulate your points without fear.

Just because you have an unruffled mind doesn't mean the other party does.

View them as not knowing any better.

The ability to view someone as not knowing any better is a ninja-like way to build emotional intelligence.

When both parties are ruffled, words often turn into fists.

But when ATLEAST 1 party is unruffled:

1. They create a higher social value for themselves.
2. Reach resolutions quicker.

These 2 traits are unlocked whether you are doing the confronting or getting confronted.

Articulating ideas with an unruffled mind turns the ruffled person into unruffled too.

Humans have a thing called mirror neurons.

We subconsciously mimic.

Good or bad.

CONFRONTATIONS, COMPOSURE, AND COOLNESS

The best social strategy is to mitigate confrontations.

However, during the process of leveling up, life happens.

Confrontations sneak up out of the blue moon.

It may be from an aggressive landlord.

A bitter ex.

A great business partner turned rogue.

Etc.

Finally...

'Yea?'

If you were in the wrong, instantaneously melt the
confrontation with an apology.

Not a regular apology.

But an apology with a few reasons as to why you were wrong.

Sometimes, confrontations serve as great feedback.

We were in the wrong.

Now we know better.

6 SOCIAL SINS THAT PISS OTHERS OFF

A social sin is a move that leaves the other person drained.
With perception, humans focus on the big picture.

The big picture often comes down to feelings.

- Did you make the other person feel empowered or drained?

With perception, generalities beat details.
And pleasure beats pain.

Let's say you have given your friend, Bucky, 50 rides to the airport.
Never even asked him for gas money!
But one day, you slapped him in front of a group of people for insulting your sister.

There is a HIGH chance that the 1 painful moment beat the 50 positive moments of giving him free car rides.
This leaves Bucky with a distasteful attitude towards you.

Obviously, there are other variables involved like the depth of your relationship with Bucky, his maturity levels & his ability to forgive.
But for the most part, socially intelligent people aim to reduce social sins.

Some social sins are obvious.
While other social sins are not that obvious.
In this article, we will explore the not-so-obvious social sins.

1. Always Getting Offended by Something

In this era, people are soft.

It's because they don't build anything.

They have a buffer from the real world which affords them the luxury of being offended by everything.

A sensitive person has the capability of ruining the vibe of the entire interaction.

Creativity happens when people are having fun.

From fun, riveting ideas emerge.

And riveting ideas allow the social interaction to feel light & for time to fly by.

But when someone easily gets offended by jokes...
The dynamic changes.

Creativity walks out the door.

Time slows down.

And it becomes a pain in the ass to go through the interaction.

2. Unwanted Advice

Normally, it seems like a positive trait to give others advice.

If one person knows something, they should inform the other person, no?

Not always.

Sometimes, giving advice is smart.

Other times, giving advice is stepping over boundaries.

Give advice when they directly ask you for advice.

Or if they are about to make a **dire** mistake.

Other than that, if they are talking about their day or an upcoming project & you begin lecturing them with advice...

It'll often leave a poor taste in their mouth.

There is an art to letting others make their own mistakes so they can learn from it (hopefully).

Rather than always butting in.

3. TALKING ABOUT NICHED TOPICS

This is the era to have all sorts of fascinating interests.

But being too niched in conversation material is a fast way to bore people.

Especially if you can tell the other person doesn't care.

I know someone who is overly detailed with NFTs, Bitcoin, nodes, and all that.

He is so compelled by the information that he is certain that others **must** hear about the information.

The thing with our interests is that it seems REALLY important to our nervous system.

Those strong feelings create the narrative of:

'Others MUST know this information. I'm looking out for them.'

While in reality, it's the ego that's creating the 'altruistic' narrative.

Others probably don't **have to** know about this niched topic.

Be socially dynamic and adjust conversation material when needed.

4. NOT INTRODUCING PEOPLE PROPERLY

You ever had that moment when you were interacting with a friend.

Then this friend runs into someone you don't know.

They begin chatting with this stranger for a LONG time but never introduces you.

What next?

Well, you go on your phone.

Shuffle your body.

And look around aimlessly with a goofy smile on your face.

Still, your friend and this stranger are carrying on a conversation without acknowledging your presence.

Social sin!!

Winners introduce like winners.

Introduction for dummies:

1. Introduce both parties.
2. Create conversation material to get the parties integrated.
3. Fall back and conduct the flow of the conversation to make sure everyone is participating.

5. LACK OF ENTHUSIASM WHEN HEARING OTHERS TALK

Enthusiasm is not just about being physically present.

It's about being mentally present too.

You ever had that moment when you thought you did a good job listening to someone else?

But when it was their turn to listen to you, they seemed uninterested?

That's a social sin.

The best conversations happen when all parties are interested.

This is a tough problem to have.

Because the more interested you are, the more you notice how few people are interested in others.

It's easy to want to be offended and show little interest back.

But this is a great time to work out your social muscle and keep interest.

Cultivating curiosity towards a boring or uninterested person is a way to build further enthusiasm for the future.

6. PEER PRESSURE & ADDICTIONS

A part of growing up is seeing the different habits others adopt at different parts of their life.

Not only do they pick up good habits...but also drop the destructive habits.

I had this fraternity brother who was struggling with alcoholism.

His life was spiraling out of control.

Getting into fights, breaking things, and getting bloated like the blueberry girl from the Willy Wonka movie.

Eventually, he decided to seek help and get sober.

One day, we all attended a wedding together.

There were 2 guys at the wedding convincing him to drink.

They were good guys who didn't mean any harm.

From their paradigm, it was 'only one night' of drinking.

But that was the mistake.

They were evaluating the scenario from THEIR paradigm.

With addictions, it's best not to peer pressure someone to go back to their old ways, no matter how small the activity may seem to you at the time.

With addictions, things work in chains.

All it takes is 1 tiny activity to get them back to their old ways.

Plus, let's say they listen to you.

The next day, when the flurry of emotions subside, they'll associate the pain of breaking their sober streak with you.

Best to support someone who is making significant changes in their life.

BUILDING SOCIAL KNOWLEDGE & MELTING SOCIAL SINS

Knowledge, self-improvement, and social skills all go together.

The more you self-improve, the more you know.

The more you know, the easier it becomes to avoid making social sins.

A sad thing about those who make social sins is that they have no clue they are doing it.

After reading this blog, no need to judge others who make social sins.

Assume they don't know any better.

This will lead to more charm from your end.

HOW TO RESPOND TO MEAN COMMENTS & CYBERBULLYING

Mean comments are not a new phenomenon.

Nowadays, it just happens to be *visible*.

Back in the day, if someone was gossiping about you, you may have never heard it.

Other times, when you did hear about it, their voice was temporary.

Eventually, their voice disappeared, and the memory faded.

But nowadays, it's easier to FREEZE hate.

Where you make eye contact with the mean comment over and over again.

It's easy to ask:

'How can I make others stop being so mean to me?'

It's tougher to ask:

'How can I remain composed no matter what the world throws at me?'

This blog will take the path of toughness.

Mean comments will eventually just be comments.

WHAT EXACTLY IS A MEAN COMMENT?

To learn how to respond to mean comments, we need to define it.

A mean comment is:

A comment that has been written with negative intent.

Even this definition is blurry.

Because a lot of social media users write mean comments because they are bored.

They have no ill intent towards the person they are making fun of.

But they just write the comment to temporarily be a part of a community.

Social media has made it easier to insulate a hater from the world.

It's hard to insult someone when you are making eye contact with them.

But behind a screen, it's easier to type and hit enter.

Understanding why people leave mean comments will free up a lot of turmoil within.

They predominantly leave mean comments because:

- They hate you.

- Are bored.

- Want to see you do better.

How to Respond to Mean Comments & Cyberbullying

If I called you an alien, would you be sad?

'Of course not.'

Why not?

'Because I am not an alien.'

Then why do you get sad when someone calls you a loser?

'Uh...'

It's because you may feel like a loser at times.

The fix for remaining unbothered with mean comments is to level up.

You are too busy improving to sit idle and read (or think) about mean comments all day.

In the level-up process, it's not like we ignore mean comments.

We read it just like anything else out there.

However, we are not dwelling on it.

That's the biggest difference.

A person who is not doing any form of leveling up will take the insult of being called an alien seriously.

They will be like:

'Why'd the person write that I was an alien? Is it because I have a big head? I knew I had a big head! I'm so sad.'

A person who levels up views means comments as motivation to level up further.

'Wait, I can use mean comments to level up?'

Yeah, you can.

ALL MEAN COMMENTS ARE NOT CREATED EQUAL

Some mean comments are mean.

While other mean comments are *insightful*.

Want to know a stellar way to not be bothered by mean comments and cyberbullying?

'How?'

Learn from them.

There was a guy who told me that the beginning of my YouTube videos was stiff & lame.

He hated it.

I took in the words and realized his mean words had some truth to them.

I noticed while starting a video, my face was stiff, and it would gradually loosen up over time.

My goal was to have it loose from the get-go.

That mean comment was insightful & I never took it personally.

Not taking things personally makes your life much easier and allows for more areas of improvement.

THE DANGER OF WRITING BACK MEAN COMMENTS

I know some people who clap back at haters.

But I think that's a waste of time.

Mainly because words have a powerful effect on your subconscious mind.

Reading another person's words is one thing...

But writing your own words is a whole different ball game.

If you're spending minutes, hours, and days writing mean comments back, that's not good for the subconscious mind.

Too much negative energy.

It's hard to be great when you are willingly participating with that energy.

'Is it wrong to get revenge bro???'

Sometimes, I see the logic behind revenge.

But writing back to mean comments is a first-world problem.

You'll see people treat this as a big problem when they don't have much else going on for them.

Remember this bud:

The mind is BUILT to solve problems.

When you don't have enough problems to solve, it will create its own.

That's why leveling up is such a great fix.

It's because as you level up, you invite empowering problems into your life that will lead to dividends once you solve them.

While writing back to mean comments will just lead to more mean comments.

Haters are not people you try to logic with.

Instead, turn them into a joke.

VIEW MEAN COMMENTS AS JOKES

Jimmy Kimmel has this section of his show where celebrities read out mean comments they received on Twitter.

This bit on Jimmy Kimmel's show has become legendary.

The celebrity reads off the mean tweet, the audience laughs, and the celeb often laughs too.

The mean comment has officially become a joke.

When you turn darkness into humor, thick skin builds like non-other.

Also, you build creativity.

Another thing I noticed from Jimmy Kimmel's show is that a WIDE range of people get mean comments.

It's not just 1 person getting attacked.

Seeing others experiencing mean comments allows you to not personalize attacks or cyberbullying.

Look out for the mean comments which will help you level up & ignore or find humor in the mean comments which don't allow you to level up.

This is a simple solution to cyberbullying so we can learn how to respond (not react) to mean comments.

3 BODY LANGUAGE MOVES TO SKYROCKET CONFIDENCE

The body can be your best friend or worst enemy.

The body often becomes an enemy when you have no clue it is capable of being a friend.

That's when it starts slouching, feeling heavy & walking without purpose.

However, if you realize that your body is a tool...

Then you'll realize all tools are meant to be used with intention.

In this article, I'm going to give you 3 body language moves to build confidence.

This is a primal way to build confidence.

No narcotics or supplements needed.

POOR BODY LANGUAGE MOVES

Before talking about the good parts, let's talk about the bad parts.

What is poor body language?

Poor body language moves make you look smaller.

There are some 5 foot 2 people who walk BIGGER than someone who is 6 foot 2.

It's because the 6 foot 2 person is slouching.

Chin is heavy & drooping.

Shoulders are scrunched.

They are looking at the floor while walking.

All poor body language moves.

When you look at this 6 foot 2 person, does it look like they have somewhere to go?

Or does it look like they are dreading to go wherever they are headed?

Often, it will be the latter when we look at poor body language moves.

Walk like you're about to pick up a billionaire dollar check.

Automaticity, there is a purpose in your strides & fire behind your eyes.

HOW TO LEVERAGE YOUR BODY

To leverage your body, there are some hot spots we can use for instant confidence.

These 3 moves are sensitive to changing our mindset.

Allow us to go through each of them and I will explain my logic for each body language move.

SMIRK

The smirk often gets a bad rep.

It's seen as an arrogant move.

However, I disagree.

Crossing your arms across your chest is seen as a 'defensive' move.

For some people, it may be.

However, you'll also notice a lot of powerful people crossing their arms.

Therefore, this move is open to interpretation.

Likewise, the smirk is not only for arrogance.
Instead, a lot of times, it implies cool, calm, and composed.

The smirk is a subtle version of the smile.
You may not always have the need for a blatant move like the smile.
However, a light smirk is often appropriate because it looks like your default facial gesture.

Also, a smirk releases endorphins in your brain.
Endorphins are 'feel-good' chemicals that allow you to feel empowered.

Try it out:
Smirk.

Feel that?
Much better, right?

RAISED CHIN

A raised chin automatically brings you back to the present moment.
Let's go through an experiment.

First, have a droopy chin.
How do you feel?
'I feel mopey and unconfident.'
Now *gradually* raise your chin.
How do you feel?
'I feel calm & more present.'

Present.

That word is key.

A raised chin brings you back to the present moment which leads to calmness.

Heck, you can combine a raised chin with a smirk for even more confidence.

Try both moves out for yourself.

You'll feel a tingling sensation in your heart.

SQUINTED EYES

'Armani, why does eye contact feel so difficult?'

It's because with eye contact, you feel like your WHOLE body is being watched.

Eye contact makes you feel like you are under a microscope.

And if you are already feeling unconfident, then the spotlight will make matters worse.

Gently squinting the eyes fool you into thinking that your whole body is not being watched.

It feels like you have a shield when you squint the eyes.

Try it out real quick.

You'll notice you feel sensations around the rest of the body as if a force field is being activated.

Not only do you feel better, but the person you're speaking to enjoys it as well.

Some people have creepy eye contact.

Wide-eyed & stalker vibes.

A gentle eye squint creates a chill vibe which builds rapport.

 Bonus Move: Stand Up Straight

The good ole posture never fails.
Posture is a superpower.
Stand up straight.

'I find it difficult to stand up straight, any tips?'
Yes.
Get a textbook, put it on your head & try to walk with it.

In the beginning, the book may slide off your head.
Over time, you'll build **micro muscles** to help balance the book.
Walking with a solid posture will eventually be autopilot.
Confidence will eventually be autopilot as well.

PRACTICING BODY LANGUAGE MOVES

'These moves are great, but how do I practice them?'
I recommend gradually incorporating one of these moves into your life.
No need to overwhelm yourself and do them all at once.

Let's say you're having a conversation and feel nervous.
Well, **gradually** squint your eyes more.

Let's say there is a group of people telling you a story and you feel anxious.
Well, **gradually** fix your posture.

Feeling nervous before a speech?
Gradually raise your chin and bring yourself back to the present.
 Notice what all these sentences have in common.

GRADUALLY.

Avoid jerky movements.

Jerkiness shocks the subconscious mind & creates weird vibes for the person you are interacting with.

While gradual movements ease you into a new mode of thinking over time.

Others will appreciate you for it.

LEVERAGING BODY LANGUAGE MOVES TO BUILD CONFIDENCE

Confidence is earned through pain, vision & building something valuable.

But there are small cheat codes that will make your journey much easier.

Body language is one of those cheat codes.

The body is a tool that will aid you or destruct you.

Use the smirk, squinted eyes & raised chin to feel more confident than ever.

Practice building a great posture too.

Driving was once difficult.

It felt like there were too many moves to do at once.

Nowadays, you do all the moves at once without a second thought.

Your body is a vehicle with the same capabilities.

Incorporate a few of these powerful body language moves & you'll eventually feel confident on autopilot!

Mind Mapping 101: What's a Mind Map & Ideas on How to Do It

It's that time of the month again.

You are feeling creative but not really.

Uh oh…

Time is being wasted.

How is it that others are creating so many ideas…. but you are stuck?

It's because they have systems in place to generate ideas at will.

Maybe they have a creative writing journal.

Maybe they have backup content in place for a day like this.

Or maybe…

They are leveraging mind maps.

'Mind maps?'

On Google, mind maps are defined as:

- A diagram that is used to visually organize information.

'Hm… I don't know how that will help me.'

It will help you.

Mind maps are useful for any field out there.

Why Use Mind Maps?

The thing with creative fields is that it's hard to measure with the senses.

A lot of things are happening in the mind, out of sight.

With minds maps, we use the process of externalization.
'What's that?'
Externalization is when you take the content from your mind
to the outside world.

This blog is a form of externalization.

The more you externalize, the more that your senses get
engaged with creativity.
Creativity is no longer a random blob of chaos to the senses.
Instead, creativity becomes visible.
Now it's easier to train as an artist & athlete.

HOW TO MIND MAP FOR DUMMIES

There are different techniques and softwares for mind
mapping nowadays.
But I'm going to keep it simple.
I like the good ole' paper and pencil.

1. **I create boxes of knowledge & see how they
   connect.**
That is my one and only step.

If you are solving a problem, then it will be easier to know
which boxes of knowledge to put on your paper to spot the
connections.
Let's say I have a speech coming up.
I know my audience is going to be filled with young
entrepreneurs.

What do I talk about?

That's when I create boxes of knowledge on my paper:

- Entrepreneurship
- Emotional intelligence
- Critical thinking
- Weightlifting practice
- Time management skills
- Solving problems

As I'm creating the boxes, I notice a few possible connections.

For example, *entrepreneurship* is a real-world class on *solving problems*.

My problem-solving process is:

1. Prioritize problem
2. Troubleshoot
3. Articulate the problem
4. Create direction
5. Research & experiment
6. Assess results
7. Contract relevant teams

It would be more efficient for my paper if I don't write all 7 steps on the mind map.

Instead, I create another knowledge box titled:

- Problem-solving process

As I link the different knowledge boxes together, I get a bird's eye view of the subject.

I mind map at least once a month (preferably the first day of the month).

Or often, I do it as a task to unwind at the end of the day.

For me, creating mind maps is therapeutic & fun.

WHO SHOULD MIND MAP?

Have you ever seen one of those people that could see around the corner?

It seems like they were working so hard to come up with these insights.

But if you asked them, they would say that they were just showing some common sense.

Big picture thinkers *see* the big picture.

What small picture thinkers need critical thinking for comes intuitively to the big picture thinker.

There is this false understanding that big picture thinkers were born that way.

Some may have had a natural inclination towards systems thinking growing up.

But for others, this form of thinking was trained into their being.

That's where mind maps come in.

Any field where you benefit from:

- Recalling information
- Connecting information
- And creating useful insights

Will benefit from a mind maps practice.

Tons of people learn, but they never actively recall the information.

So, they forget.

Tons of people recall information, but they have no clue how the information ties to anything else.

And tons of people understand how concepts tie together, but they are unable to provide any useful insights.

A mind map practice allows you to recall, connect & create information.

What an integrated approach!

MIND MAP EXERCISE

Find a recurring problem in your life right now.

Got it?

'Yessir.'

Now aim to solve the problem **today**.

'Geez Armani, the problem of mine is severe. I can't possibly solve it today.'

All good. Set the high stakes anyways. Often, you'll get your best creative insights when your back is against the wall.

Get a pencil & paper.

Then:

- Creating knowledge boxes
- Connect knowledge boxes

Let's say you are getting sued for using a picture on your site that you were not supposed to use.

How do you resolve it?

Knowledge boxes:

- Negotiate with the person suing you
- Sue them back
- Research the law to see if you did anything wrong
- Create a payment plan

Etc.

How you connect the knowledge boxes is up to you.

USING MIND MAPS FOR ENDLESS CREATIVE IDEAS

You'll be surprised by how many different fields connect with each other.

Through my mind maps, I was able to see a stellar connection between content marketing and farming.

I noticed there wasn't much content on content marketing (no content on content? Make it make sense!).

Didn't know where to look.

One day, I discovered farming.

Content resembles farming in many ways.

Content is like a digital seed.

SEO optimizing is like watering the seed.

Over time, the seed turns into a plant, aka the traffic.

And then the plant creates fruits, aka money.

I saw the STUNNING parallel between content & farming by using mind maps and getting a view of the big picture.

Which useful insights are waiting for you?

5 TIPS ON HOW TO RELAX & FEEL CALMER

For some people, it's easy to relax.
Their life is just one big relaxation.

- Chilling.
- Dragging their feet.
- Not moving with any urgency.

For others, learning to relax is going to require work.
Their mind is always running.
And they need to learn how to slow down.

Complex systems need time to relax.
'Huh?'
A computer for example isn't always able to run.
It needs some downtime after a while.

Likewise, it's the same with a human.
They need some downtime as well.
I have a few tips on how to relax.
Take whichever tips work and discard which don't.
Before I give you the tips, I need to explain why relaxation is tough for some.

WHY SOME PEOPLE FIND IT DIFFICULT TO RELAX

'Why is it easy for some to relax while others find it difficult?'

It's because of different fundamental beliefs.

The group who finds it difficult to relax often works a lot.
Their work is either productive or destructive.

Destructive work is when you're moving a lot, but not empowering anyone for the best.
Not even yourself.
- Overthinking, worrying, complaining to others.
This is technically work, just not the good kind.

The other kind of workers are doing work that benefits others.
- They have a business.
- An important role at their job.
- Serve as a leader in their family etc.

For this latter group, the reason they find it difficult to relax is because of **guilt**.
They associate some form of guilt with relaxing.
They feel like they are wasting time.

TIP 1: ARTICULATE THE IMPORTANCE OF RELAXATION

It's one thing when some random guy on the internet tells you to relax.
It's a whole different ball game when you are capable of articulating the importance of relaxation for yourself!

Why do **you** think you should relax?
'Uh...because it's good for me?'
That's vague. See if you can get more specific.

Leverage logic.

Assume that your future self has understood the value of relaxing.

But your present self is still not sold.

Somehow, your future self was able to teleport to the present to **logically** explain why you should begin relaxing.

What would your future self say?

Even though this seems silly, when we intellectually grasp a concept, we are much more likely to implement it.

TIP 2: FIND RELAXATION ACTIVITIES THAT DON'T MAKE YOU FEEL GUILTY

One reason that a lot of people find it difficult to relax is because their activity of choice makes them feel guilty the next morning.

They feel disgusted.

Then they associate the disgusted feeling with the entire act of relaxing.

Are there any activities that allow you to feel good and relax?

So, you don't feel guilty the next morning?

This isn't to say that you only implement productivity into your life.

Only being productive is a fast way to ensure you're not productive.

Trying to be too perfect causes self-implosion.

Just brainstorm to see if there are any acts that you can do which are not only good for you but allow you to unwind as well.

- Journaling, reading a fiction book, playing basketball, etc.

These tasks work out our creativity or physique.

Let's say you don't have something like that.

See if you can *tone down* the activity that has you feeling guilty in the morning.

Rather than cutting it off cold turkey, moderation is the way.

TIP 3: SETTING TIME TO RELAX

If you don't say:

'At this time, I'm relaxing.'

Then chances are you'll feel guilty when you do relax.

The narrative will be:

'Man, I should be doing something! Why am I just sitting on my ass for?'

This is why setting a relaxation interval is the way to go.

It doesn't have to be super precise or anything.

It can be something like:

'After the sun goes down, I'm going to be chilling.'

If you want specificity, you can go for that too.

The main point is setting a time interval for relaxation.

This allows for unwinding to be much easier.

TIP 4: EARN YOUR RELAXATION

One of the best ways to disconnect the feeling of 'guilt' with 'relaxation' is to earn your relaxation.

'What do you mean?'

I mean exactly what I said.

Earn your relaxation!

When you are in the productive periods, go hard.
Do what you gotta' do

Then when the productivity zone is winding down, that's when you can be like:
'Damn, I really earned that chill session.'

This does 2 things:

1. You go hard during the productive zone.
2. You cultivate an empowering attitude towards relaxation.

To make sure you go extra hard during your working zone, a to-do list is a gamechanger.
It's so simple & gives you direction for the day.

You can check out *Check List*, which is a to-do journal to keep your day productive.

TIP 5: SWITCH IT UP

The final tip is to switch it up.
If you have a routine that works for you, then stick with it.

But if for some reason, what was once relaxing is now a chore, that means the body is craving some variety.

Experiment with other activities.
You can even ask others to see how they relax.
People love talking about themselves.
When you ask, they'll be quick to give some suggestions.

A little bit of variety goes a long way!

IMPLEMENTING THE TIPS ON HOW TO RELAX

These are my tips on how to relax.
Did any of them resonate with you?

If so, great.
If not, then find your own tips.

You ever had that moment where you were productive for a long time.
Then suddenly, you became lazy...
Not just for a few days.
But for a few months??

'Whoa, I actually did have plenty of moments like that. Why did that happen?'
That was your body treating itself to some relaxation.
So, if you can consciously sprinkle relaxation into your lifestyle then the guilt will fade away.

How to Stop Obsessive Thoughts

Have you ever met someone who was obsessed with talking about other people?

Normally, the person was normal.

But when a particular individual was bought up, this normal person would turn abnormal.

I knew a guy like that.

He was normally soft-spoken & stood behind the scenes.

But if the name *Trump* came up, his personality would change.

Suddenly, this quiet doctor would become the center of attention & get into heated debates.

This wasn't a one-time occurrence.

I saw his behavior change multiple times.

If he spent so much time talking about Trump, how much time did he spend thinking about him??

That's "Trump Derangement Syndrome."

Just imagine....using your #1 tool to think about another man.

Obsession is not bad.

What's bad is the **target** of obsession.

Obsession used correctly is a mental technology.

In this article, you'll learn how to stop obsessive thoughts about other people.

We aren't going to leave it there though.

We will use obsession towards our favor!

OBSESSION = MIND SEEKING A THEME

Imagine if I gave you a book with a bunch of random chapters.
Would you like that?
'No.'
Why not?
'Because I can't extract the meaning...'

So, I give you the digital version of the book and say you can do whatever.
I guarantee if the desire is strong enough, then you will begin rearranging the book to put the chapters in order.
This is a primal desire of the mind seeking a theme.
The theme is invisible while the content is visible.

It's the nature of the human to focus on the visible.
Everything they can see.
But as a human matures, their mind seeks a theme.

When you don't give it a theme, it looks for a theme.
An unguided mind does not always look out for your best interests.
Instead, it acts weird & defaults into thinking about other people.
To learn how to stop obsessive thoughts, you want to ask:
'Do I have any theme for my mind at the moment?'
Sit on this question.

THE MIND WITH A THEME

One of my favorite books on entrepreneurship is Made in America by Sam Walton.

Sam is the founder of Walmart.

At the end of the book, Sam said he made a lot of mistakes.
Would he undo any of those mistakes?
No... because he gave his life to Walmart.

He said he spent his life thinking about Walmart.
That's what allowed him to excel in his field.

Sam wasn't busy thinking about other people too much.
Even if you are well-wishing...thinking about other people too much is not good.

Let's say Johnathan is obsessive over his little brother because he loves him.
The intent is pure.
However, the subject matter is wrong.

If Johnathan continues to obsess over his brother, then Johnathan will become overbearing.
Plus, he will drain his own mind.

The mind is meant to dwell on concepts, not people.

That's why Sam Walton became a giant.
What is a business?
Business is a series of concepts and connections.

By giving the mind the theme of his business, Sam didn't become weird like the quiet doctor.
This allowed Sam to give back to his community.

Although a lot of people want to talk shit about capitalism nowadays...

Sam's work led to the employment of many people, tons of money raised for charities & education for the kids in his community.

Obsession done the right way.

USING OBSESSION TOWARDS YOUR FAVOR

To learn how to stop obsessive thoughts, it's all about changing the theme from:

- People -> concepts

The question is:

What is a concept??

A concept is a system.

A system is composed of:

-Creator

-Parts

-Processes

The parts and processes mean nothing without a **purpose**.

Therefore, the concept comes to life when there is a purpose.

That's when the *creator* has a direction on how to connect (*process*) the *parts*.

'How long do I work on a concept?'

A concept is worked on for life!

We never fully figure it out.

Sam Walton died knowing he could have made way more changes to his precious Walmart.

That's a **good** problem to have.

By working on 1 concept, you learn the science of nature.

'Why is that?'

It's because we live in a world of systems.

All systems have the same creator, process, and parts formula.

If you can understand 1 system in-depth, then you can understand all systems with ease.

Focus on concepts.

WRAP YOUR MIND ON 1 IDEA

Obsession used correctly is the same thing as creativity.

I often hear, 'focus leads to creativity.'

Guess what??

Obsession is focus's older brother!

It's easy to tell who is working on that 1 big idea, and who isn't.

A mind without the 1 big idea is much more likely to:

-Get offended quickly.

-Get brainwashed.

-Hop from thought to thought.

-Feel depressed much more.

Instead, gear the faculties of the mind to have a theme.

Just like you had that DESIRE to put the random chapters of the book in order.

There is a DESIRE within you that wants to put the thoughts of the mind in order.

That will happen when we learn how to stop bad obsessive thoughts (thoughts about people).

And when we learn how to start good obsessive thoughts of concepts.

This is the cheat code for creativity.

OBSESSION IS FOCUS'S OLDER BROTHER

Obsession done correctly leads to:

-Tuning out distractions.

-Skyrocketing intelligence.

-Taking fewer things personally.

-No longer whining about celebrities and politicians.

I feel bad for the mind that thinks about other people all day.

Thinking about people is normal.

But all day??

Fam, find something better to dwell on!

SYSTEMS THINKING: HOW TO BE MORE CREATIVE IN THINKING

There's a big misconception in thinking that you're not creative.

With that mindset, it's like pushing a boulder up the mountain.

Instead, when you have the default perception that you ARE creative, things are much easier.

'If I'm so creative, then how come I don't feel like it?'

It's because you were rarely rewarded for it.

Take my word that you're creative.

Throughout this article, you'll get a systematic breakdown of discovering this truth for yourself.

A creative mind sees the entire picture rather than the individual dots.

Another word for creative thinking is systems thinking.

Our goal is to stop viewing ourselves as a node thinker and be a systems thinker.

It's a process well worth the effort!

Let's learn how to be more creative in thinking

Only then can we build the confidence that we desire.

WHAT IS CREATIVE THINKING?

At the fundamental level, systems are made up of 2 components:

- Nodes
- Links

Nodes are the parts.

Links are the connection of the parts.

All systems have a purpose.

Without a purpose, a system does not exist.

It's just a random collection of things near each other.

'What does systems thinking have to do with learning how to be more creative in thinking?'

As I said earlier bud, creative thinking and systems thinking are the SAME exact thing.

The sooner you realize this, the better.

To help you realize this, let's do a tangible example and an intangible one.

What are you reading this blog from?

'My cellphone.'

What are the nodes (parts) that make up your cellphone?

'Hardware, some software, antenna, etc.'

Will those parts be worth much by themselves?

'Not really.'

So what do we do?

'We LINK them together to create the phone.'

Correct!

I'm sure your phone provides tons of useful value.

In this context, the useful value is to read this blog.

Now off to an intangible example of a system:

This blog!!

I have a bunch of thoughts (nodes).

Then I interconnect those thoughts (links) into a blog article.
Then this article provides useful value on how to be more creative in thinking.

'I'm sort of getting it, but what does that mean for me?'
Excellent question.

SYSTEMS UNIVERSE

There is a big mistake that we live in a physical universe.
That's like watching the movie and thinking the movie is real.
No, the movie is simply a plot behind a screen.
All you're doing is looking at the pixels.

We live in a SYSTEMS universe.
To learn how to be more creative in thinking, learn to spot the systems in your life.

Do it right now.
Look around you and spot 5 systems.
I'll start off.

1. I see the laptop that I am typing on.
2. There is a podcast microphone stand.
3. There is the mouse.
4. My watch.
5. And my YouTube camera.

The goal isn't to just see the final product.
The goal is to see the nodes & links within the final product.
Prime your mind to think like this through practice.

I'll zone in on 1 of my 5 systems.

My podcast microphone stand.

The microphone is being held by a stand, and the stand is hooked onto a table.

When I look at the final product, I see a bunch of parts that were strategically linked together to provide me an enjoyable podcasting experience.

Pick something simple.

'Does a book count as a system?'

Let's answer the question with some questions.

Does a book have nodes?

'Yes. The cover, pages, words, etc.'

Are the covers, pages, and words linked in a certain fashion to provide useful value?

'Uh... yea.'

Then your book is a system.

The more you keep spotting systems in your daily life...

The more you learn how to be more creative in thinking.

GRADUATING TO A CREATOR

It's one thing to just notice creations.

It's another thing to create.

The beauty is that you don't need to be a creator in all fields to learn how to be more creative in thinking.

But you do NEED to create in at least 1 field.

I don't mean copying other people and just parroting them.

I'm talking about creating some original content.

There is a false platitude that 'no ideas are new.'
Those who peddle this platitude often just regurgitate what others say without any cognitive effort.
Big mistake.
These people do not view the world in systems.

I want you to try this exercise.
Create 5 nodes with 5 words.
- Example: Mouse, Watch, Clorox, Demon, Risk.

Now I want you to link those nodes together to create a sentence.
"The mouse and the demon looked at the watch counting down and realized it was a risk to use dirty Clorox wipes."

'Um....that sentence was useless!
That's not the point of the exercise.

The point was that you can create unique content by using nodes and links in a personalized fashion.
I guarantee you, before reading my sentence, you would have used the 5 words in a completely different fashion.

The goal of a creator is to spot nodes & link them in new combinations.
This is how you learn to be more creative in thinking.

GOLDEN ERA OF CREATIVITY

I believe one of the greatest ways to learn how to be more creative in thinking is through storytelling.

Create some form of content.

It requires the lowest start-up cost from what I've seen.

That's not to say that you can't start gardening.

Or buy a toolbox and build some birdhouses...

But with content creation, all you need are words and an intent to connect those words in new ways!

Did you know that you have 30,000+ thoughts a day?

I'm sure you can gather a few of those thoughts & connect them into a system.

Aka: A story.

The more you practice, the more you rewire your mind to think in a brand new way.

It's the way of a system...

STEPS TO PROBLEM SOLVING LIKE A CHARISMATIC ENGINEER

A great communicator is a great problem solver.

'Really?'

Yes, what do you think the communicator is talking about?

The phrase 'influencer' gets thrown around a lot nowadays.

That phrase is immediately associated with communication skills.

'Do you like that?'

Nah, I don't.

I think it's much better to view a great communicator as a:

- Charismatic Engineer.

This is a person who explores problems in the real world.

Runs experiments.

Analyzes the results.

Then communicates the results in a charming way.

View communication skills as a masterclass on learning steps to problem-solving.

However, problem-solving may be a foreign concept to you.

It may seem too scary.

So, let's dumb it down.

IDENTIFYING THE PROBLEM

There is a phrase in engineering called 'troubleshooting.'

This is when the engineer is trying to find out what the issue is.

'Is this step really that important?'
Yes. Those who skip it will waste a lot of time.

Ironically, a lot of people do skip it!
They just being problem-solving on something that may or may not be a problem.

Troubleshooting comes down to asking questions.

I'm sure you've had a moment when your internet went down & you had to call the call center.

They'll ask questions like:

- *When did your internet go down?*

- *Does your internet routinely act up?*

- *Can you try resetting the router & tell me what happens?*

This is a real-world look into them troubleshooting so they can identify the problem.

ARTICULATING THE PROBLEM

'Okay, I identified the problem, now what?'
Articulate it.

'Huh? I already found out what it is. Why articulate it?'
Because this adds clarity.

Another reason an engineer often fucks up is because they can't control their emotions.

If you have ever seen what happens when your favorite sites like Instagram, Twitter, and Facebook are down...you'll be shocked.

So many people panicking.

A bad problem becomes worse.

Engineers need emotional control.

Especially when they have stakeholders asking them, 'WHAT THE HELL HAPPENED???'

Pause.
Breathe.
Articulate the problem.

'Okay, I articulated the problem in a sentence. Now what?'
Say another sentence to clarify it even more.
'Why?'
So, you can go from a general understanding to a clarified one.

Back to the call center rep who has troubleshooted the internet issue.
They will say:
'This is the only user from the neighborhood who is experiencing internet issues.

Then they will say:
'The internet issue has been happening as of late.'
This is where some people will stop.

But then, the smart rep will further articulate by saying:
'They did mention they got a pet recently. I wonder if the pet has been chomping on the wires & causing damage?'

This insight is profound.

By gradually articulating the problem more, this call center rep has learned that the issue is hardware-related.
So, he will send a hardware engineer to the customer.

I obviously dumbed down this issue a lot.

But hopefully, you can see that it's all about making connections.

Learn more about articulation skills in the Speak Easy book:

UNDERSTANDING BASIC LOGIC

What intimidates people about problem-solving is that they immediately think of something scary.

That's false. Problem-solving is fun!

It's like a story unfolding in real-time.

All we need is **basic** logic.

Logic comes down to, *"because of this, this happened"* connections.

Aka: Cause & effect.

"I saw that I was missing my keys.

I had my keys when I came home from work.

Therefore, I know my keys are at my place.

I know I put my keys on top of my wallet.

This time, I put the wallet at a new location because I got distracted.

Let me find the wallet & I'll find my keys."

This is a simple chain of going backward.

A lot of innovative problem solving is from looking forward.

Let's say you are normally great with eye contact.

However, with some people, you struggle.

Articulate the problem & try to solve it.

Ask why?

Then keep collecting data, refining & experimenting until you reach a conclusion.

Avoid Hand Holding When Learning Steps to Problem Solving

Great problem solvers are killed because they lack courage.

It's impossible to learn problem-solving without effort.

It's a game of experimenting, failing, and continuing.

As cliche as it may seem, you don't fail until you quit.

A lot of the 'failing' is you collecting data for the next rep.

This builds a holistic understanding of the field.

Before, you were looking at the dots. Now you see the picture.

1. Identify the problem.
2. Articulate the problem. Keep refining the articulation to get specific on the problem.
   1. Often, at this step, the problem solves itself.
3. Use basic logic of cause and effect to gather a solution.
4. Experiment, gather data, refine, and continue.
5. Once you have a solution, articulate it.

Problem-solving is a cumulative process that adds up over time.

A lot of those engineers who managed Instagram when it went down have an RCA call the next week.

RCA stands for Root Cause Analysis.

This is when the engineer breaks down why the problem occurred, what the fix was & how they can ensure this issue will not happen again.

'Whoa, there is a lot of communication skills that go into problem-solving.'

Problem-solving IS communication skills.

Anyone who separates the 2 is a fool.

PRACTICE THE STEPS TO PROBLEM SOLVING ON YOUR OWN

There are so many problems around you.

'How do you know?'

Because we live in a complex system.

A system is an interconnection of parts that leads to creation.

Whenever a system is involved, problems are a feature, not a bug.

Within systems, there are subsystems.

Example:

Your apartment is a system. It's a collection of furniture, rooms, closets, etc.

Within your apartment, there is a restroom which is also a system.

Within the restroom, the place where you brush your teeth is a system.

The parts include a sink, toothbrush, floss, toothpaste, mirror, etc.

On this day, you notice you barely have enough toothpaste to get a squirt out.

Problem?

 If it is a problem, how are you going to brush your teeth?
A hurricane just hit & all the places around you are closed.
Therefore, you NEED to gather toothpaste from this tube.

You have a problem, my friend.
Articulate it.
Use logic, experimentation & refining to reach a conclusion.
Report your findings.
That's the charismatic engineer.

HOW TO GET OUT OF A RUT WITH THE CURIOSITY QUOTIENT

Are you currently stuck in a rut?

There are different phrases for this:

-Stuck in a funk.

-Out of the groove.

-Losing love for life.

This often happens to someone when they have the 'what's even the point?' mentality.

This narrative can last in spurts or much longer.

Even the biggest winners occasionally have a rut.

Picture how you wake up feeling in the morning.

Some people just wake up sad without having any reason to be sad.

Then throughout their day, they feel enthusiastic again.

How long your rut lasts will depend on **you**.

Is there a way to use a rut to level up?

I believe so.

WHAT A RUT SAYS ABOUT YOU

'So, a rut can be temporary or last for a long period of time?'

Correct.

Some people's ruts become their personalities.

Rock bottom without a deadline turns into an altered personality for the worst.
Depressed, dark, and overly whiney.

A rut is faced when a person feels like they aren't growing.

This may happen in a relationship with someone else.
Relationship with yourself.
Or a relationship with the world.

Often, when there is a rut, there is also a sign of blurriness.
Clarity has been lost.

When clarity has been lost, emotions become foggy.
Now the driver needs to turn the windshield wipers ON.

SECRET TO GETTING OUT OF A RUT

There are certain states that cannot coexist with each other.
'Can you give me an example?
Sure.

I used to love *matches*.
It's cool to brush the stick alongside the matchbox to get fire.

Occasionally, in Bangladesh, the lights would go out.
When the lights went out, the room was PITCH BLACK.

That's when the person who was the closest to the matchbox would take action.

SPARK.

Fire is lit.

Although the fire didn't light up the entire room.

It was not enough to light up some of the room.

The visibility of fire drowned out the pitch-black darkness.

The darkness represents the rut.

Fire represents curiosity.

Even a little curiosity will allow you to pull yourself out of the depths of darkness.

CURIOSITY QUOTIENT

I rarely see a winner talk about their IQ score.

I rarely see a winner even know what their IQ score is!

Just another man-made exam that has people focusing on the wrong things.

Normally, it's someone without street smarts who talks about their IQ a lot.

In the real world, what matters more is the Curiosity Quotient.

This is a rather new field... but that's not even fully true.

Humans are naturally curious, modern research is just catching up and creating the label 'Curiosity Quotient.'

There is no exam for this primal trait.

Your internal world is the compass.

'Is curiosity something we are born with or something that is cultivated?'

Both.

Learning how to be curious despite pain is a sign of a high Curiosity Quotient.

This is when a person runs towards the pain rather than away from it.

When a person is in a rut, the last thing they probably want to do is be curious.

Not smart, buddy.

During this moment, you can build your curiosity even more.

HOW TO GET OUT OF A RUT WITH CURIOSITY

To become curious, learn the art of letting labels fall away.

At this point, let the body lead.

That is what curiosity is about.

When you let the body lead, it builds street smarts.

There are sensations that the body feels indicating that you are moving closer towards a curiosity.

Like those dudes on a beach who hold a metal detector.

They are trying to find the treasure chest...

So, they keep scoping around the beach trying to find where the gold lies.

Likewise, learn the art of not being too intellectual.

This is why the IQ exam is something that can make you a coward.

You think too much.

Great communicators view thinking as a tool, they don't make thinking the master.

That's foolish.

List out 3 things that you're curious about.

'Um...sharks, basketball, and podcasting.'

Name 3 more.

'3 more?? Nah, that's all I have.'

Name 3 more.

'Um...remote controllers, finance books, and remote controllers.'

Despite you naming 2 more, not 3, that was a level beyond what you **thought** was capable.

'Yea, you're right. Now what do I do?'

You learn about the curiosities.

GETTING OUT OF A RUT AND LEVELING UP

When you are in a rut, you may think:

'Geez, let me free up the calendar. I need to relax!'

Personally, that makes my rut worse.

Resting for some time is fine.

However, too much free time leads to acting like a sloth.

It's much better to have a *filled* calendar.

That's a form of therapy right there!

Not a filled calendar where you are overworking.

But a calendar filled with curiosities.

No clue where to get started?

Get curious about fitness.

I've been really curious about pull-ups recently.
Bought a pullup bar and began doing pullups.

Then I began doing this pyramid challenge where you do 1,2,3 pullups then count down to 3,2,1.
Since then, I've been curious about how high I can push the reps too.

After the pullups habit, I have had more energy.
Since having more energy, I wrote a novel that will be released later this year.
And since writing the novel, I've been working with my narrator to get him in the zone as he brings the characters to life.

A little curiosity got the ball rolling!

EMBRACE DARKNESS TO EMBRACE LIGHT

Even winners slip and fall.
What makes a winner, a winner, is that they stand back up.
Over and over again.

That process of standing back up is how a winning attitude is cultivated.
The standing up process instills a spirit that radiates FIRE.

When the winner falls and is in a rut, they allow themselves time to be sad.

But eventually, they look for methods on how to get out of a rut.

If you made it this far, then you are the mythical winner.

You're displaying your Curiosity Quotient and showing that you want more.

BREAKING THE BAD HABITS: DUMMIES EDITION

You ever seen someone push a domino before?
One domino is pushed, and a bunch comes toppling down.

'Are you saying that's what it's like with habits??'
Slow down, bud.
Just picture that domino scenario with me real quick.
'Okay, I'm picturing it....'
That's the kind of world we live in.
Interconnected.

Not only is the world we live in interconnected, but so is our body and mind.
The macro and micro are identical.
Interconnectedness runs deep.

'I thought you were going to talk about breaking the bad habits I've piled on?'
Yes, that's precisely what we are going to do.

And for us to do that, first acknowledge the interconnected...
It will make your journey easier.

DEFINING A BAD HABIT

One person's bad habit is another person's relaxation.
Let's give an example.

A highly productive person who is a great businessman, fit, and takes care of his family.

He ends the day with video games.

At this point, he *has* to end the day with video games to unwind.

Is it bad?

That's up for debate.

This is also a lesson.

Trying to eliminate every single bad habit may seem noble, but it'll often cause you to implode.

A human is not meant to be 'perfect.'

Even machines have bugs and need downtime.

If this human is productive in so many other facets of his life, then video games may go from a:

- Bad habit -> rest.

Before classifying something as a bad habit, acknowledge interconnectedness.

If this person is playing video games so much that it is destroying his business, fitness, and relationships...

Then it's a bad habit.

Otherwise, it's smart to consider it as rest.

HOW TO STOP A BAD HABIT

The trick to stopping a bad habit comes down to:

1. Associating the feeling you feel **after** doing the bad habit with the habit.

2.   Replacing the bad habit.

Let's break down this formula.

Typically, for number 1, the person attaches the feeling they get DURING the habit with the habit.

Let's use Adam the Alcoholic as an example.

Adam drinks a lot because he enjoys how he feels **while** drinking.

However, he hates the way he feels the morning **after** drinking.

Adam gets hangovers easily.

The reason that Adam is in the loop of drinking a lot is because once his hangover is gone, he *forgets the hangover*.

Then the next time the thought of alcohol comes in his mind, he envisions how he felt WHILE drinking.

This is a smart time for Adam to remember how he felt the next morning during the hangover rather than while drinking.

The headache, stinky breath, chapped lips, etc.

Get detailed.

This will associate a feeling of **disgust** with the act.

Now off to the 2nd part of the formula... replacing the bad habit.

Some people quit cold turkey and never look back.

I knew this one kid who was obsessed with weed.

Once he got high, he'd would eat tons of fast food.

After some time, he met this girl on a dating app.

The picture he posted was of when he was skinny.

2 months go by, and she wants to meet him in person.
He's alarmed!! He is fat as fuck and needs to lose 30 pounds.

For the next couple of weeks, he quits weed and starts exercising.

After the weeks were up, he never touched weed again.
He stopped exercising too.

I initially thought he replaced the weed with the gym, but that wasn't the case.
He just quit cold turkey.
Therefore, it's possible to quit turkey if the desire is strong enough.

However, that's **not** the optimal path.
Much better to replace the bad habit.

This is when someone may immediately say, 'replace it with something productive.'
Which works, sure.

But I recommend replacing it with something 'fun first and hopefully productive.'
Fun has the feeling of lightness, while productive has the feeling of seriousness.
The brain will often choose the path of least resistance.

I like writing and writing is productive.
So, I got lucky.

I know a guy who quit smoking by eating Reese's peanut butter cups.

Although the candy isn't productive, it outweighs the negative effects of smoking.

After he stopped smoking, he found a way to replace Reese's with healthy brownies.

It's a process.

THE MINDSET TO BREAKING THE BAD HABIT

Thus far, you're probably going through this article and are like:

'This idiot is not being forceful like I expected. I thought he was going to vehemently tell me to just stop the bad habit!'

I view humans as neurolinguistic programmed machines.

These machines have a thing called the subconscious mind.

The subconscious mind is beyond logic.

I know this because there were many times I tried to logically stop a bad habit.

And each time, I took an L.

It's smarter to view yourself as an emotional creature with a high likelihood of fucking up.

If you're really smart, you should think the likelihood of you fucking up is 95%.

Ironically, you become way more creative and prepared that way.

Sort of like how you become more patient when you assume a rude person doesn't know any better.

That's when you empathize with the rude person rather than clap back.

Likewise, assume that you are an emotional creature before a logical one.

This mindset will lead to more significant improvements.

BREAKING THE BAD HABITS & CREATING A NEW YOU

View habits as software that run without you thinking.

You're capable of installing new software at will.

However, gotta get rid of the viruses as well!

When dropping bad habits, avoid viewing yourself as 'too perfect.'

Fighting the subconscious mind is like swimming against a tsunami.

Rather than swim against the tsunami, surf ALONG with it.

Identify if the habit is really bad or if you're just chilling.

You can view it as bad if it's spilling over to other parts of your life.

cough interconnectedness *cough*

Then associate the feeling of how you feel AFTER doing the habit with the habit.

And finally, find a respectable habit to replace it with and ease yourself out..

BUILDING SELF-AWARENESS AS A LEADER

Everyone wants to be a leader.
Few want to act like a leader.

'Are bosses and leaders the same?'
Not quite.

A boss is a title.
It's a job position.

A leader is an attitude.
Others will be able to tell if you have leadership qualities to you.

Being a leader is not glamorous.
Instead, it's a class on building self-awareness.
It's the ability to view yourself from a 3rd party perspective.

Why is self-awareness as a leader so important?
And more importantly, how can we develop it?

WHAT IS SELF-AWARENESS?

Normally, we are viewing life from a 1st person perspective.
We see life from our own eyes.

Self-awareness is that moment when we shift from:
- 1st person perspective -> 3rd person perspective.

Rather than viewing ourselves as the subject.

We temporarily view our mind, body & intellect as objects.

This is a **profound** shift in thinking.

Self-awareness is often built during times of introspection.

When we see why we act the way that we did.

'Is self-awareness only built when dealing with ourselves?'

No.

Some of the most crucial data comes from how you deal with other people.

OTHERS ARE A MIRROR TO OURSELVES

I knew this one kid who would always talk shit about others when it came to Fantasy Football.

Let's call this kid Timmy.

Timmy would read blogs, listen to podcasts & educate himself in the field of football.

So, by the time the tournament came, he thought it'd be easy for him.

But that wasn't the case.

Routinely, Timothy would get obliterated by people who didn't take Fantasy Football that seriously.

Those kids just played for fun.

This enraged Timothy.

He began gossiping about them & creating the narrative that they got lucky.

Timothy's behavior towards others is a direct reflection of himself.

He felt inadequate.

And the inadequacy was highlighted from the lens of Fantasy Football.

If Timothy had awareness, then he'd objectify himself.

He'd ask more questions rather than act out behaviors.

- *Why do I downplay the other players?*
- *Why is Fantasy Football so important to me?*
- *And why don't I assess how I can get better?*

SELF-AWARENESS & LEADERSHIP

Leadership is a training ground on self-awareness.

And at one point or another, we are going to be called into a leadership position.

I have good news and bad news.

Which one do you want to hear first?

'Bad news.'

The bad news is that you'll see most people's behaviors do not live up to their words.

They'll tell you one thing & do something else.

'Okay, and the good news?'

The good news is that other people's mishaps are GREAT opportunities to build self-awareness.

To objectify yourself, it's best to understand the **full** spectrum of emotions.

Not only the emotions that you enjoy.

Picture a person who picks up a rope & toggles the end.
It will create a sinusoidal motion.

The top represents pleasant emotions.
The bottom represents the unpleasant emotions.
Our goal is to learn all parts of the rope.

HOW TO BUILD SELF AWARENESS AS A LEADER

In my book, Level Up Mentality, I break down how the mind works from an engineer's perspective.
The book's goal is to harness **all** emotions & direct it towards **one** grand goal.
The final chapter talks about the importance of RECORDING your Level Up Journey.

'Why is recording yourself important?'
Because you view yourself as an object.

A fat kid who is losing weight without taking progress pictures is making improvements, sure.
As 3 months pass by, his friend is amazed!
'John, how did you lose that much weight?? This is a miracle!'

When John sees how his friend reacted, he feels a ton of enthusiasm.
Now he works out even more determined.

That enthusiasm?

He could've felt it earlier if he kept recording his process &
progress.

Recording does not mean just taking videos.
It can be writing down your thoughts.
That's what journaling is.

A leader who does not record any form of content is like that
fat kid who may or may not be making progress.
Awareness is limited.

RAGE IS A COMPASS TO BUILD SELF AWARENESS

Find what enrages you.
I can't stand it when someone messes with my deadlines.
I like being on time.
That's me.

If you are going to miss a deadline, tell me.
Keep giving me updates...

What I can't stand is when someone promised me a certain
date.
Disappears for weeks.
And comes back to say:
'Hey, looks like I'll need another 2 months.'

This made me so furious because I dealt with multiple people
from around the world like that.
Rather than snap at them.
I decided to see why **I** hated to miss deadlines.

'Why?'

Well, it wasn't ever about the deadlines.

It was about the disrespect.

I thought those people were taking advantage of me because they didn't respect me as a businessman.

That's where the rage came from.

Over time, when I saw different people from around the planet behaving like this.

I realized it wasn't personal.

It was a human nature thing.

Also, dwelling on those who missed the deadlines caused me to underappreciate those who delivered way ahead of time.

Anyways, what this taught me was to consistently ask for updates.

Not in a micro-managing sort of way.

But in a way where both parties were on the same page.

Ironically, this deepened our bond.

The talent & I were building rapport.

What enrages you?

Rather than acting out that rage...

1. Figure out why you think it pissed you off so much.

2. See how you can adapt.

3. Reprimand the worker if needed.

You'll see step #3 is rarely needed when you build self-awareness in step #2.

BECOME A SELF-AWARE LEADER

A leader who stops being a follower is a leader who stopped being a leader.
Rather than talking down on people, learn from them.

They are your portals towards building more self-awareness.
Expect people are not going to make sense.
But expect yourself to adjust anyways.

When you can keep adjusting...
Not only do you build self-awareness as a leader.
You start to win the respect of the people you command.

That's a win-win.
Now keep winning more.

THE 9 SIGNS OF SUPREME SOCIAL IQ

'Social IQ, is that even a thing? Show me the test for it!'
Okay, relax there, buddy.

In the world of social skills, street smarts are engaged.
A person with elevated street smarts doesn't go asking for tests all the time.
They understand the value of intuition and gut.

In today's post, I'm going to break down one of my popular tweets which is:
The Signs of Social Intelligence.
Be sure to follow me on Twitter if you don't follow me already.

Each of these signs are valuable when you are trying to make an impression.
Get these right & you'll find others being magnetized to you.
Let's go through each one with a detailed explanation!

SIGN 1: TRUSTWORTHY

I don't know your belief systems.
Nor do I care.

But I will tell you this.
Life is better when you factor Karma into the mix.

Karma is measured by:
- Did you make a decision with the grand system in mind or yourself?

Every now and then, we move selfishly.
That's the nature of the mind.

However, if we can keep training the mind to not be a scumbag, it will be a long-term win.
I know someone who is smooth.
Can create a conversation with anyone.
Funny as hell.
And rising daily in his field.

Only problem?
He is a well-known scumbag.

His short-term wins are now leading to long-term failures.
His lack of trustworthiness is making him a liability to work with.

Be trustworthy.
Live up to your word.
When you don't live up to your word, be the first to acknowledge it.
That's how karma works in your favor.

SIGN 2: ABLE TO CREATE SMALL TALK

You may not like small talk.
I know a lot of people don't.

However, small talk is necessary.
'Why is small talk necessary?'
Because it creates the foundations for the interaction.

It's difficult to jump into a conversation with a stranger and start talking about the meaning of life.

Some may be down for that.

However, others are going to be like:

'What the hell?'

View small talk as stretching before lifting heavy at the gym.

Lifting heavy from the get-go will lead you to pull a muscle.

Speaking about deep topics from the get-go will lead you to come off as awkward.

Instead, start off light.

Create foundations.

The goal of small talk is to find the similarities between you and the other person.

Gear your questions like that.

Even if you find no similarities at the end of your interaction.

I guarantee you'll know the person much better.

SIGN 3: ABLE TO CREATE NUANCED CONVERSATION

This is the graduation from small talk.

If you're making small talk the entire time, then you missed the point.

Become a charismatic person with depth.

That's what social IQ is all about.

In my book Charisma King, I talk about how social intelligence & self-development go together.

Anyone who separates the 2 is a fool.

Because without self-development, you become too focused on the tactics, rather than the purpose.

Social intelligence falls out of living a life filled with purpose.

This allows you to seamlessly create nuanced conversations about a variety of topics.

And the topics you don't know about?

It's easier to fall back and ask questions.

JOIN CONVERSATION SKILLS CLASS FOR DUMMIES

SIGN 4: REMEMBER NAMES

'Why do I keep forgetting people's names?'

How often do you use the name once you get it?

'Uh...'

That's why.

Not using someone's name after you got it is like buying seasoning, but never using it on your food.

Yuck!

On the contrary, using the names too much may be weird.

Therefore, view names like a seasoning.

Let your body be the guide.

When the body is the guide, you'll develop an intuition for what feels right & when you're overdoing it.

But the key to understand is:

Remember names by using names!

SIGN 5: CAN HAVE A BIG CIRCLE, BUT CHOOSES FOR A SMALL ONE

From the entire list, this may be the most confusing.
Why a small circle?

Contrary to mainstream sayings, popularity is not measured by how big the circle is.
A big circle often leads to surface-level relationships & more betrayal.

From my experience, the better strategy is to have:
-A lot of acquaintances
-Few friends.

Friends are the nucleus.
Acquaintances are the valence electrons.

Acquaintances are people you know on a surface level.
The surface level is not bad by any means!
The human brain is not meant to know everyone inside and out.

Friends are the handful of people that we have connections with & go through the ups & downs of life with.
The nucleus leads to emotional stability.

Not being able to distinguish friends from acquaintances is the reason for loneliness.

SIGN 6: OBSERVATION TO THE SMALL DETAILS

Know this.

Remembering the small details will allow you to remember the big details.

Remembering the big details does not guarantee that you'll remember the small details.

People with high social IQ remember the small things.

It's the information that others don't notice.

If someone mentioned that they were going in for a job interview 2 weeks ago…. then immediately transitioned to another topic.

Then in 2 weeks, the socially intelligent person will ask:

'How'd the interview go?'

The small details also train the mind to be more creative.

The more it is looking out for the small stuff, the less time it has to worry about social anxiety.

Social anxiety often happens when the mind is focusing too much on itself.

Instead of focusing on the other person.

SIGN 7: GIVES THOUGHTFUL COMPLIMENTS

A compliment is invisible.

However, it holds power.

It's capable of charging up someone else's nervous system.

But there is a catch!
Give laser-like thoughtful compliments.

A compliment is good when it's personal to them.
And it's personal when it's specific.

If you just say:
'Hey, good job.'
That's way too general.

But if you say:
'Your ability to stay focused for so long while maintaining enthusiasm makes you irreplaceable. Good job.'
Now the person will feel the compliment in their nervous system.

Also, if you lead people, know how to give compliments.
People like it when you praise their skill.
People love it when you upraise their work ethic.

SIGN 8: LASER-LIKE LISTENING SKILLS

Many people can't listen properly because they don't know the difference between hearing and listening.
'I thought they were the same?'
Nope!

Hearing is physical. Only the senses are engaged.
Listening is physical and mental. The mind and the senses are engaged.

Listen better by getting curious about the other person.

Get more curious about the other person by thinking that they know something that you don't.

This knowledge they have can shift your perspective **forever**.

Therefore....listen astutely.

Simply by creating this narrative, you don't try to listen.

Listening just happens.

Try it out for yourself.

JOIN CLASS TO BUILD LISTENING SKILLS.

SIGN 9: HIGH-LEVEL EMPATHY

Empathy is a word that has been highjacked in the mainstream.

It gives the vibe of coddling & crying with someone.

Not quite.

Empathy is to see yourself in someone else.

This allows you to perceive unity before diversity.

What do you and the other person have in common?

'Uh...'

The bodies are different.

The content in the minds is different.

However, you guys are both **aware**.

The awareness unites the 2 of you.

By perceiving the unity first, it's easier to empathize.

Also, empathy leads to less anxiety & fear.

Anxiety and fear are often caused by a feeling of separateness.

But when unity is perceived first, it leads to a more enjoyable experience for both parties.

LEVEL UP YOUR SOCIAL IQ

Social IQ can be trained.

It's just a game of finding what you need to improve.

After going through these 9 signs, hopefully, you're capable of seeing what you are strong on.

And what you can improve.

Solid social skills allow you to build a social asset out of thin air.

At the core of every subject, you'll run into people talking to each other.

4 EFFECTIVE TREATMENTS FOR SOCIAL MEDIA ADDICTION

Social media is a powerful tool.

With great power comes great responsibility.

With great responsibility comes great pressure.

In this digital landscape, social media addiction leads to a mental disease.

'What is that mental disease?'

Mind-wandering.

The inability to control your mind at will is a sad fate.

Anxiety is on the horizon.

However, I do not believe in cutting off social media cold turkey.

My 4 treatments for social media addiction are much different than the traditional advice.

I believe we must stop viewing the tool as the master.

DOES SOCIAL MEDIA ADDICTION EXIST?

No one can ever tell if someone is paying attention.

Only the other person knows whether they are paying attention or not.

Social media addiction is difficult to spot because it is not only happening physically.

It is something that is happening mentally.

Externally, we can see them constantly checking their phone when it beeps.

That's visible to the eyes.

But what's not visible is the chain of thoughts that get activated after the physical motion of checking the phone.

Once they are done looking at their phone & look back at you...

Is their mind present or are they putting on an act?

SYMPTOMS OF SOCIAL MEDIA ADDICTION

There are data engineers, algorithms, & software engineers looking to keep you **hooked**.

The longer you are on their platform, the longer your attention can lead to some sort of monetization for them.

Your concentration levels are not their concern.

Your lack of concentration levels are their concern.

SYMPTOMS OF SOCIAL MEDIA ADDICTION INCLUDE:

1. Mood is heavily influenced by what is happening in the digital landscape.

A lot of views? You're happy.

Little views? You're sad.

A lot of likes? You're happy.

Little likes? You're sad.

2. Thinking about social media when you are not on social media.

This is when the monkey mind is activated.

You're at the concert you have been waiting 5 months for.

However, for the entire concert, you're on Snapchat rather than with the singer.

3. Loss of Focus.

This is when the mind is constantly hopping around.

Social media addiction is not the only reason for a distracted mind.

But it has played a large part in the matter.

4. Social media negativity influences real-world behavior.

There are new 'movements' going on in social media all the time.

And I wouldn't even call them a *movement*.

I call it propaganda disguised as a movement to spark outrage.

Are you participating in a lot of that nonsense?

Is it affecting your real life?

Then chances are you are suffering from social media addiction.

ACKNOWLEDGE THE BENEFITS OF SOCIAL MEDIA FIRST

My philosophy is to acknowledge the BENEFITS of social media first.

Rather than quitting cold turkey, acknowledge how social media is a tool.

Quitting something cold turkey rarely works.

Often, it works temporarily and then the victim comes back worse than before.

Acknowledge the benefits of social media.

'Like?'

Like how you can network with so many people on the planet.

How you can stay in touch with people that you used to use phone cards for.

90s babies understand what phone cards are.

What about all those accounts that post empowering content online?

That empowering content provides tips, tricks & strategies to skyrocket your learning.

You can learn about anything!

Communication skills, finance, fitness, etc.

Also, social media makes it easier to build a business.

Back in the day, there were all these unnecessary middlemen taking away profits.

Nowadays, you can build your tribe & directly communicate with them.

This brings me to YOU.

You can create content to teach yourself & others along the way.

This is when you chronicle your journey to the top.

4 SIMPLE TREATMENTS FOR SOCIAL MEDIA ADDICTION

The reason I talked about the good parts of social media first is to help you view it as a tool.

Sort of like a digital car.

When we view the car as a tool, it becomes easier to spot when we are using it **incorrectly**.

Is driving a car in the water smart?

'Of course not!'

Why?

'Because it is not being used like it was designed!'

Correct.

So now that we found the proper usage of social media, let's talk about some treatments for social media addiction.

1. OPERATE WITH INTENT

Relaxing isn't a bad thing.

It's actually a good thing.

But relaxing when you were thinking about working is a bad thing.

That's how a lot of social media addiction happens.

Someone was supposed to be working.

Then they take a "10-minute bathroom break" to scroll on social media.

10 minutes turns into 1.2 hours.

Distraction muscle has been exercised.

When you are working, work.

When you are relaxing, let yourself know that you are relaxing.

This exercises intent.

2. HAVE PERIODS OF NO SOCIAL MEDIA THROUGHOUT THE DAY

There should be a certain part of the day when social media is not touched.

For me, that's in the morning & night.

In the morning & night, I do my analog activities.

And in the middle of the day, I'll check social media when needed.

Seeing that you can survive without social media is awesome!

It shows that just because others are scrolling all the time, doesn't mean you have to.

3. AUTOMATE WHAT YOU CAN

Twitter can get addicting very fast.

Especially with the fast-paced nature of the algorithm.

Automation is outsourcing the task to the best of your abilities.

In the Twitter example, you can use a tool like Hypefury.

Which I use.

Also, you can fill up your draft box with tweets.

When I do check Twitter after my morning routine, I write 16 tweets in my draft box.

And post it throughout the day.

This allows me to enter Twitter strategically.

You can do the same with your platform.

4. CATCH YOURSELF MID DISTRACTION

Awareness is king.

At times, you'll be in the chilling zone for a while.

There will be one dope content suggestion after another.

This is when a 20-minute rest session can turn into a 2 hour one.

Make yourself aware.

Even if you don't want to turn the social media off, turn it off.
This allows the body to become a servant.

Your body and smartphone are similar.
As long as you tell it what to do, it will do it.

MELT AWAY SOCIAL MEDIA ADDICTION

Back in the day, computers were the size of living rooms.
Nowadays, it fits in your pocket.

Why waste this golden tool?
Social media used correctly allows you to freeze your thoughts,
build a media empire & have high-value people come to you.
Don't waste it on petty shit.

When 30 people are going 1 way, be wary of following them.
Most people are not thinking for themselves.
They are letting others think for them.

Use social media to break out of the mental rat race.
Go from a consumer to a prosumer.
A person who consumes, produces & makes social media their
servant.

SOCIAL INTELLIGENCE VS EMOTIONAL INTELLIGENCE: WHAT'S THE DIFFERENCE?

Social intelligence and emotional intelligence are like cousins.

They are similar.

But not quite the same.

Both are crucial in terms of improving soft skills.

However, the differences between the 2 are difficult to spot.

Emotional intelligence is predominantly about improving internal states.

Social intelligence is predominantly about improving external states.

The 2 are not completely disconnected from one another.

Improving emotional intelligence improves social intelligence & vice versa.

It's important to see the difference between these 2 worlds to build synergy.

'Synergy?'

Yes...

When 1+1 equals something far greater than 2.

WHAT IS EMOTIONAL INTELLIGENCE?

Contrary to the popular belief, emotional intelligence is not about being emotional & crying out loud all day.

Instead, it's the opposite.

Emotional intelligence is about building emotional literacy (understanding of internal states) so outbursts are bypassed.

This is when a person behaves in a responsible manner.

'How do I build emotional literacy?'
By going beyond simple words like 'happy', 'sad', 'angry' etc.

These words serve as training wheels for the mind.
But eventually, you need to grow up and let the training wheels fall off.

This is when a person learns to sit with their feelings & understand what the data is trying to tell them.
At this point, the discrete words of 'happy', 'sad', and 'angry' become **blurry**.
A person can experience multiple emotions at the same time.

A great time to build emotional literacy is during dark moments.
That's when the body is highly charged, which allows for deeper insights.
Appreciating the dark moments makes the light moments even more profound.

WHAT IS SOCIAL INTELLIGENCE?

Social intelligence is the etiquette behind social skills:
- Holding conversations.
- Telling jokes.
- Learning the art of empathizing.
- Paying attention.

etc.
Social intelligence is difficult to do without emotional intelligence.

'Why do you think that is?'

It's because humans are emotional creatures first.

Success in social intelligence depends upon emotional literacy.

Let me give you an example.

Imagine a businessman who has a lot of things in order.

A product made; fliers made; potential customers are made aware of the product etc.

However, his business has been losing cash for the past 10 years.

They're down in the hole.

Is he a successful businessman?

'No!'

Why not!

'Because he is not remotely profitable.'

Exactly.

In this context, **profitability** is used as the measurement of success for the business.

Likewise, **emotional intelligence** is used as the measurement of success in social interactions.

Charisma seems like an outwards process.

However, it starts off as an internal process.

HOW TO MASTER SOCIAL INTELLIGENCE & EMOTIONAL INTELLIGENCE

This subheading is an oxymoron.

Mainly because you never master social intelligence or emotional intelligence.

Instead, this is a field where you become a master by remaining a lifelong newbie.

All fields are like that.

The masters often have the most curious approach because they've learned:

- The more they know, the more they have to know.

To improve social intelligence, aim to improve emotional intelligence first.
This is crucial.

It's hard to be an authentic charismatic presence with a fluffy understanding of the internal states.
This is what I call a charismatic person without much substance.

You ever met someone like that?
A guy who is all talk...
Switches positions depending on the person they are talking to...
And lacks depth?

This is a person who is great with people.
However, they themselves are not functioning properly.
This makes you question:

- Are they REALLY great with people?

It's like a subpar laptop trying to access the internet.
Can it access it?
Sure.
But the connection will be faulty.

Nothing is wrong with the internet.
But the laptop can be improved.

Leveling up is the process of understanding how to improve internal states to influence outside reality.
Learn this mindset in the Level Up Mentality book:

BUILDING STREET SMARTS & THINKING IN A NEW WAY

For a long time, the mind has been primed to view the world in a linear way.
Do X and Y is bound to happen!

However, that's not always the case.
In the real world, do X & sometimes Purple will happen.
Unpredictability at its finest.

Therefore, it's smart to get a head start in developing emotional intelligence.
Find a goal & progress forward on it daily.
^That's Level Up Mentality for dummies.

Why is this important?
Because in the process of progressing toward that goal, the internal world will be challenged.

The grander the goal, the grander the internal change.

The grander the internal change, the more social interactions are presented.
In the process of progressing toward this goal, there are going to be random moments when social interactions just happen.

People find you.

That's not to say that you don't break the ice with others.
However, having the paradigm of seeing others pursue you is when you see that others are not the primary goal.
The vision is.

Socially intelligent people have an abundance mindset towards others.
This allows them to avoid being clingy and needy.

When a person dissolves clinginess & neediness, the entire world wins.
That's because now the external world makes eye contact with your internal world.

WAS IT EVER SOCIAL INTELLIGENCE VS EMOTIONAL INTELLIGENCE?

It was never about social intelligence vs emotional intelligence.
These 2 worlds were never enemies.
That's like calling the athletes and referees enemies.
Not quite.
Instead, they are all part of the holistic GAME.

Emotions are feelings with a perception.
Social intelligence is the game of people.
Learning how to manage the internal and external is all a part of the holistic GAME.

It's easy to get brainwashed nowadays.

So much information all around.
Who is telling the truth & who is spreading propaganda?

A person with emotional intelligence is mature for their age.
They speak the language of intent much better than their peers.

So, they can curve the bs.
And they progress forward anyway.

Day in...
And day out...

Negative Visualization 101: Prime Your Mind for Victory

Words cause sensations in the body.
With certain words, the feelings aren't positive.

One of those words is:
Negative.

It's easy to want to shut out negativity & only invite in positivity.
That's much better than only inviting in darkness.

However, negativity has gotten a bad rep.
Without proper usage, this emotion comes in clutch.

Channeled negativity leads to:
–Clearer thinking.
–Creativity at will.
–Thick skin.

To stop being a victim of negativity, one mental tool is:

- Negative Visualization.

I'm not going to talk about this topic from the perspective of Stoicism.
(Although I know they have a profound perspective on the matter).

Instead, I'm going to talk about this topic from my personal experiences.

If you are looking to improve communication skills & better control your emotions, then read along...

PINNING DOWN THE DEFINITION OF NEGATIVE VISUALIZATION

My definition of negative visualization is:

Envisioning a dark moment for yourself & rising above anyways.

The reason we are **willingly** envisioning a dark moment is because of **expecting** something.

'What's the benefit of expecting something?'

When you expect something, you take away its power.

'What happens if I don't expect something?'

Sometimes, nothing.

Other times, rage.

Being caught off guard is something that enrages people.

Imagine a homeowner hired someone to renovate their living room.

The contractor says that it will take 2 weeks to complete the project.

But that's not what happens.

After the 2 weeks are up, the contractor says it will take 2 more months.

The homeowner is caught off guard and becomes furious.

This anger causes the homeowner to act out of character.

Who knows what happens after...

Violence?

On the other hand, if the homeowner was **expecting** that some contractors are full of shit...

And 2 weeks may take up to 3 months.

Then this homeowner could have had workarounds planned.

There is power to looking around the corners.

Strategic negativity expands thinking.

RISING ABOVE DARK TIMES

Just expecting the negative & leaving it at that is dreadful.

That's not negative visualization.

That's called anxiety.

If the homeowner just expected the contractor to be full of shit & left it at that, then anxiety & despair would ensue.

However, if the negative thought led the homeowner to find backup contractors, now creativity & plans would ensue.

2 variables are mandatory for the negative visualization formula:

1. Envision the worst.

2. Envision yourself rising beyond the worst.

These 2 make a deadly combo.

It's something to warm up to...

HOW TO GET STARTED WITH NEGATIVE VISUALIZATION

I view the mind as a muscle.

Just like anything with muscles, it's smart to warm up.

Imagine if you go to the gym & automatically jump into lifting heavy weights.

May hurt yourself...

Instead, stretch.

Have some warmup sets.

Then go heavier.

If you are someone with no mental training, then you may want to wait before doing negative visualization.

Mainly because negative visualization is **advanced**.

Ask yourself:

-Can my mind be controlled at will?

A more detailed version of this question is:

-Can I adjust my thoughts at will?

Think carefully before blindly nodding your head.

Controlling thoughts (negative & positive) at will, requires training & a control of bodily sensations.

Self-awareness is key to answering these questions.

If you answered 'no'... then fear not.

That's what stretching & warming up is for!

WRITING TO THINKING TRANSITION

It's easier to control thoughts when warming up with writing.
- Writing = Frozen thoughts.
- Thoughts = Vapor.

It's hard to grasp the vapor immediately.
So, warm up with writing.

Create a scenario you want to imagine.
Write it out.

Let's say you have a speech coming up.
The speech is going to be hosted at IHOP.

'IHOP?? At least make it realistic!'
I am. One of my Toastmasters clubs used to host their meetings at IHOP.
So, pay attention carefully.
I'm speaking from real-life experience.

What can possibly go wrong at IHOP?
-Loud crowds.
-Crying baby.
-Losing train of thought.

These are some negative possibilities.
What can I do about that?

—Speak louder when the audience gets loud.
-Somehow incorporate the crying baby into my speech.
-Pause when I forgot a point, smile, regroup, then continue.

See the connections?

This is possible with negative visualization.

Now let's go from stretching our muscles to doing a warmup set.

VISUALIZING WITH TRAINING WHEELS

At this point, I listed out some negative possibilities & how I can rise.

Let's connect, shall we??

This is a sample of what I will write:

"I am already feeling a lot of nerves as I see the host about to call my name. My mouth is dry, and my knees feel weak. To make it worse, 2 of the members from Toastmasters kept asking me if I'm nervous. Now I feel jittery. By the time I am on stage, immediately, a baby starts crying. I notice the customers at IHOP are louder than usual. This makes me angry. But rather than letting the anger get to me, I decide to channel it into creativity. I realize that I can incorporate the baby into my speech! Since my talk is about management skills, I can demonstrate how to deal well under pressure. When I incorporate the baby into my speech, the audience is surprised by my thinking on feet skills. They begin laughing. I feel confident when I hear them laugh..."

As I am writing this, my mind is creating the movie.

Notice that I am writing from a 1st person perspective.

Words influence the brain.

If I tell you to envision an "elephant", you will see an image of an elephant.

The brain converts the symbols of the letters into an image.

I discuss the power of words on the brain in my blog about Neurolinguistics.

Don't sleep on writing.

It's a form of visualizing when the intent is there.

Eventually, you can visualize at will, with or without writing.

NEGATIVE VISUALIZATION = BATTLE TESTING THE MIND

A mind that is always expecting negatives will get more negatives.

A mind that is always expecting positives will get wins & disappointment.

And a mind that is expecting positives & negatives will get power.

Become powerful.

Even the 'negative visualization' label is misleading.

Because it makes you think it's only "negative."

Not quite.

Negative **along** with an empowering ending.

Find creative methods to turn Ls into Ws.

The mind is a muscle.

It eventually picks up the workouts that we repeatedly do.

SCARED OF PUTTING YOURSELF OUT THERE?

Imagine you have a great idea.
The only problem is that you're afraid to share it.

Maybe you'll share it with a close peer or 2.
But they don't need to hear the idea.
They just listen because they are your friend.

For the idea to have an impact, it needs to be heard on a global stage.
That's when **useful value** is provided.

However, you're not comfortable putting yourself out there.
That's why content creation suffers.
There is an inhibitory feeling associated with eyes being on you.

Humans have 3 types of feelings:
- Inhibitory – When you feel small.
- Stagnant – When you feel nothing.
- Expressive – When you feel big.

The goal is to feel BIG when you create content, not small....
Never be scared of putting yourself out there again.

WHY FEAR OF BEING JUDGED HAPPENS

It all comes back to the eyeballs.
'Eyeballs?'

Yea.

I used to be the Vice President, recruitment chair & mentor in my Toastmasters club.
This allowed me to see speech anxiety from multiple angles.
I saw smart people who were terrified of speaking in front of a group.

They rationalized the fear.

When I asked them to illustrate why they felt fear...
They got detailed.

That's when many of the responses came back to the eyeballs.
They were uncomfortable with so many people staring at them.

Why???

Because a flurry of eyeballs staring at us indicates to our primal side that something is wrong.
The old school programs buried in the nervous system think we are being ostracized from the tribe.
Which was a reality back then.
It's predominantly an illusion now.

Nowadays, when people are staring, that's because they are paying attention.
It'd be an insult if their eyeballs weren't visible.

IMPOSTER SYNDROME

I see a lot of channels blow out up of nowhere on YouTube.
Their main strategy is:

- Insert a popular person's name & write 'EXPOSED.'

A group of people flocks to those channels.

That's because there is a group of people who love to see others fail.

I think certain *expose channels* are needed.

Because there are scam artists who need to be exposed.

While on the other hand, the opposite problem exists.

Where good people can have their reputations ruined by someone who wants more followers & subscribers.

'What if I don't want to be exposed?'

Putting yourself out there opens up a bunch of possibilities.

Nothing is certain.

You can do everything right, but a shithead can come & use you as a target for their fast come up.

'You're not making me feel confident in putting myself out there, Armani.'

Good...

WHY ONLY A FEW RISE

Want to know something?

'Sure...'

Anything great requires risk.

More importantly, anything great requires preexisting paradigms to be shattered & revaluated.

Let's talk about risk first.

What do you think people who rise in a field get motivated by?
'Beats me.'

It's a compelling vision.

That vision allows them to push forward.
That vision makes their mind 1 pointed & cultivates work ethic.
Learn how to build your vision in the Level Up Mentality:

When the mind becomes 1 pointed, (which means to center itself on a key idea), it goes beyond negative criticism when faced with any.
The desire for bringing the vision to reality beats the fear of being criticized.

That's what allows great people to move forward.
More importantly, that's what allows them to place more importance on character rather than reputation.

Reputation is fragile.

As mentioned earlier, some shithead can come out of the blue moon, make up lies about you & destroy your reputation.
But the character is something that is not fragile (hopefully).

Character beats reputation.
Character also makes a solid reputation a byproduct.

Warren Buffet's mentor, Benjamin Graham, was quoted saying:
"In the short run, the market is a voting machine but in the long run it is a weighing machine."

Funny.

Similar concept with character.

IT'S RARELY THAT BAD

Thus far, I talked about the negative parts of putting yourself out there.

Where your body hates having attention on it.

Also, I discussed how fragile reputation is.

I talked about the negative parts first to weed out the people reading this blog.

I want the few risk-takers to continue on.

Let me talk about the empowering parts now.

It's rarely that bad.

There is beauty to putting yourself out there.

Ideas that lie in the mind, die in the mind.

When an idea is clearly communicated in the public domain, the power of that idea RISES.

Which allows your power to rise...

Each time you complete a content piece, publish it & put yourself out there, the more potential for useful value is added.

'What determines if something is useful?'

When it takes a person from Point A -> Point B.

The transition process can be:

- Turn a sad person -> laughing uncontrollably.

- Turn someone who is ignorant on a topic -> smarter on the topic.
- Equip someone with a process to make their life easier.

All useful information is a byproduct of expressing your idea.

That's when the DM's flood up over time with comments like:

'Whoa, that 1 blog you wrote completely changed the way I look at life. Thanks!'

That's adding value to the world through the creative method.

Where for you to win, others had to win in the process.

This is a skillset of content creation & exercising the articulation muscle.

The most important word is: **exercising**.

Practice makes progress.

MOVE FORWARD OR SLIDE BACKWARD

This is the golden age of creativity.

One-man armies are being formed in real-time.

Experiences are being turned into useful information.

Focus on the great parts of the era rather than being depressed by the bad.

Acknowledge the bad, yes.

Then take away the fear of the bad.

After that, find useful information in the bad & articulate that.

There is a power to words.

Words don't only allow a person to express their idea, but they also allow a person to travel across time.

- Words can be used to make sense of the past.
- Give clarity to the present.
- And propel someone to their future.

Use the words correctly & putting yourself out there becomes a fun process that allows for constant reinvention.

The risk takers rise, while the people on the sidelines will watch with lowkey admiration.

3 TRICKS ON HOW TO IMPROVE EMOTIONAL INTELLIGENCE

Logically knowing something is important.
But only factoring in logic is idiotic.

There are certain questions, behaviors & actions that logic cannot answer.
It's important to be holistic.

Leverage logic & emotions.

Emotions are energy + perception.
We may not always be able to control our energy.
But we can always control the perception.

The ability to control our perception is the staple of emotional intelligence.
I like the phrase **energy intelligence** better.
This is when we make the mind & body friends, rather than enemies.

In this article, I'm going to give you 3 practical ways on how to improve emotional intelligence.
Before I do that, I want to you understand the value of what you're about to learn.

THE IMPORTANCE OF EMOTIONAL INTELLIGENCE

A few years ago, I was the vice president of my Toastmasters club.

This is a global public speaking club that helps all walks of life improve their communication skills.

I couldn't believe that I was the vice president of my club.
'Why not?'
Because a few years earlier, I had massive speech anxiety.

When I say *massive*, I mean it.
I'd lose sleep in the weeks that I had a speech coming up.
My mouth would be dry.
And I felt lethargic.

So now as the vice president (the person who was responsible for getting the message of Toastmasters out there), I knew EXACTLY how to relate to new guests who struggled with speech anxiety.

There was 1 member who seemed like the dictionary definition of a great speaker.
He was a lawyer, easy to speak to, and funny guy.

However, when he got called on stage to do Table Topics (1–2-minute impromptu speech), something happened.
'What??'
He froze...
Didn't end up saying a word.

After our meeting was done, he couldn't put into words what happened.
It's like he logically knew all the words he wanted to say.
But his body was not allowing him to say it!

That's when I shared the concept of working with emotions.

It doesn't matter how well you logically know something if you're scared shitless.

During moments of terror, that's when the importance of energy management starts to click.

Till then, you cannot internalize it.

I wanted to share the story because you never know when you will be **unexpectedly** put in a moment of terror.

No one knows beforehand.

So it's smart to prepare early.

Since you now understand the value, let's learn some tips on how to improve emotional intelligence.

I. BIG BODY OR NO BODY

There are body language superpowers you can use to build more emotional intelligence.

Learn how your body works to the tee.

See how your body moves when you're sad.

Happy.

Confused etc.

Are you jumpy around certain people?

Do you walk with purpose or slow as fuck?

'Why do I need to read my body for?'

Because when you read your body, you read your emotions.

Body language is the expression of your emotions.

The more you understand it, the more you create a remote controller for your emotions.

This allows you to learn how to improve emotional intelligence.

I noticed when I'm nervous, I touch my neck a lot and make myself small.

When I became AWARE that I did that, I decided to do the exact opposite.

- Rather than touch my neck, I put my hands to the side.
- Rather than make my body small, I made it big.

Learn to read your body and see how it works so you can make adjustments as needed.

2. EMBRACE DIFFERENT WORLD VIEWS

'Should I start a random argument with someone?'
No, that's not what I mean.

Just know that you are just a speck of sand in the sea of life.
A person who lacks emotional intelligence has an inflated ego.
They think they are the sea.

The ego is tricky.
I do not believe it should be killed.
I believe it should be tamed.

When it's inflated, it gives an illusion of power and a certainty of fear.
Inflated egos make you grasp for control. The more you want to control everything, the further you program the mind to be fearful.

Someone with a strong ego is terrified of a moment where they are disrespected in public. They entertain this thought a lot.
This fear happens because they want power.

Warm yourself up early to be open to different world views.

It can be something as simple as watching content from a creator that you vehemently disagree with.

Try to see where others are coming from more often.

3. WILLINGLY INVITE PROBLEMS

Here's a life irony.

The further you run away from problems, the more problems you face.

You can take this literally or figuratively.

In a literal sense, the irony implies that nature is wired for us to face problems.

It's not a matter of "if". It's a matter of "when."

The figurative part of the irony is that the mind needs an enemy. That's the ego that we were talking about earlier.

Let's say you lock yourself in a room by yourself for 2 years.

No problem then, right?

Wrong.

Now you will get the narrative mind saying:

'Wow, look at you. What a loser! You lack guts. Who stays in their room for 2 years?'

Problems.

The cheat code is to willingly invite some sort of problems.

We are looking for problems that help us **grow**.

I'll give you an example.

I willingly took off a screw on the left side of the chair that I use when recording my YouTube videos.

This unbalances my body and makes it difficult for me to breathe as I record my videos.

'Why the hell would you do something like that?'

Because by unbalancing myself, I introduce a stressor.

This allows my body to realign & improve my breathing patterns under duress.

Even though this was a **SMALL** problem, that's not the point.

The point was that I **WILLINGLY** introduced a problem.

This changes my **PERCEPTION** regarding problems in a micro sense.

What did I say emotions were?

'Uh....'

It's energy plus perception.

We may not always be able to control the energy that we are feeling.

But we can always control our perception.

Even if it's by increments.

BONUS TIP: TURN FEELINGS INTO WORDS

I want to give you a bonus tip since you made it this far.

This is probably the most important.

'Then why didn't you make it number 1??'

Because I reward people who invest in my content. Rather than the skimmers.

Turn your feelings into words.

Keep practicing that.
It's immature to just say:
'I feel happy, mad, sad, etc.'
That type of surface-level thinking makes you emotionally unintelligent.

Get in the habit of articulating EXACTLY how you feel.
I capitalized *exactly* because I want you to get super-specific.

I used to do this exercise with people who were nervous before they had to give a speech.
At first, they'd be like:
'I'm terrified.'

Then I told them to keep on talking.
That's when they'd be like:

'I don't know Armani. Yes, I'm terrified. But a part of me is feeling grateful. I'm honored that my friend asked me, out of all people, to give his best man's speech. I guess I just want to do a good job so bad that I have been putting more pressure on myself. But I'm not even the star of the show haha. He is! Him and his wife are the stars for the night. I'm just an extra. You know what? I feel calm again.'

Look at how well he articulated his feeling.
The range of emotions he felt included:
- Terrified, grateful, humorous, brave.

You can do the same.
Adding nuance to your emotions is called emotional literacy.

4 Hobbies to Make Money & Improve Communication Skills

Hobbies are activities that someone does in their leisure time.
A good hobby allows you to relax and unwind.

But can it be more than that?
Can the right hobby help you build wealth?
What about help you build your articulation skills as well?

I believe so.

It's been said that the eternal markets are health, wealth, and relationships.
Luckily, communication skills spill over to all 3 of those.

In this blog, I'm going to share some fun ideas for hobbies to make money and build self-confidence.
Increase your value for yourself & in the marketplace.

Why Hobbies Are a Must

Human beings were wired to have hobbies.
Hobbies are acts done to decompress.
'What if I don't actively find a hobby?'
Then a hobby will find you. It just won't be the good kind.

When a hobby finds you, it comes masked as drugs, excessive alcohol, porn, etc.

When you find a hobby, that's when productivity & having fun in your adulthood happens.

There are a range of hobbies to choose from.

Since this blog is centered around communication skills, I'm going to give you 2 suggestions that everything else will be built on.

Speaking & writing.

Rather than making everything complex, be simple.

You are not a YouTuber, podcaster, public speaker, etc.

Your hobby is speaking.

You are not a tweeter, blogger, author blah blah blah.

Your hobby is writing.

By focusing on these 2 fundamental skillsets, it becomes easier to build hobbies.

IDEAS FOR HOBBIES THAT MAKE MONEY

The key to making money is to give something of useful value to someone in exchange for cash value.

This concept holds true for employees.

This concept holds true for entrepreneurs.

Let's get started.

1. BLOGGING

Blogging is a hobby that can easily be monetized down the line.

You can sell your products & services.

If you have no products or services, affiliate for other people's products or services.

Don't want to do that?
Then run ads on your site.

It's important to have something worth saying.
Blogging becomes **mighty** when you realize you have your own newspaper.

This personal newspaper can be read by 1000s of people from different countries.
How dope is that??

This is also a great business card.
If you have the guts to publish your ideas, then you learn where you stand on certain issues.
Others will actively seek you out because they know the topics you stand for.
Fun way to provide value.

2. EMCEEING

There are events consistently being hosted around the world.
Since the lockdowns, things may be a tad bit different where you are living.
Less events do not mean no events.

The emcee is different than a public speaker.
Where a public speaker goes deep with topics, the emcee is surface level.
Don't let surface-level fool you.
The emcee serves as the GLUE guy.

An emcee is the heart of an event.

They breathe life to the random acts of movements.

To start this hobby, download the Meetup app and see if events need an emcee.

Ask a wedding planner to get you connected with an emcee who you can shadow.

Or start your own club & practice your speaking skills there.

Emcees can negotiate their payments down the line.

If you can start building up a body of work, then you raise your value in the marketplace.

3. WRITING BOOKS

One of my favorite hobbies is writing books.

My books are currently sold on Amazon, Audible, Gumroad, etc.

Read by over 1000s of people.

Think about it like this real quick.

I enjoy writing.

Others enjoy reading.

This is when win-win relationships are created.

I write a book once & create 5 streams of income.

'5 streams??'

Yea.

Let's use my book, Level Up Mentality as an example.

- I put the book on Amazon for Kindle AND paperback. **That's 2 streams right there.**
- I put the eBook version on Gumroad. **3rd stream.**

- I get Level Up Mentality converted into an audiobook and put it on Audible. **4th stream.**
- Then I put the audiobook on Gumroad. **5th stream.**

Imagine writing 5 more books and constantly repeating this framework.

The passive income adds up over time!

Know this though...

Writing a book is one of the hardest tasks out there if you do not enjoy it.

It's thinking for a long duration of time.

Tons of people can't even think for little bits of time.

If you can see yourself enjoying writing, the only roadblock is your imagination.

This is one of the lethal hobbies to make money.

4. IMPROMPTU SPEAKING SKILLS

Impromptu speaking skills are versatile.

But let's add a remix.

Impromptu speaking skills on a YouTube channel.

If blogging is you owning your own newspaper.

Youtubing is you owning your own television station.

Each time you record a video, pick a topic...

Then hit record and begin talking.

No form of planning whatsoever.

This hobby is a pain in the ass in the beginning.

But over time, it becomes a joy to practice.

The beauty is that you don't need to make it any more complicated than that.

No need for complex software, freelancers, music, etc.

Just you and the camera.

The more videos you publish, the more you'll see others messaging you and saying:

'Wow, it seems like you are speaking to me & articulating my personal experiences. Thanks!'

That's you building a market.

A market you can always sell products to down the line.

Hobbies to Make Money & Have Fun!

Hobbies are meant to help you unwind.

It's even better when it helps you unwind plus puts money in your pocket.

It's the best when it helps you unwind, puts money in your pocket & makes you more creative.

A great communicator can persuade, inspire, educate, entertain and much more.

Relationships improve.

Mental health improves.

Wealth improves.

3 big markets are tackled when you work on your speaking and writing skills.

When you don't actively look for a hobby, a bad habit comes looking for you.

HOW TO PERSUADE SOMEONE

When you're thinking about persuading someone, you may be thinking about saying the 'right words.'
Better yet, the right sentences.

Here you are, speaking in a beautiful way.
Nice rhythm.
Great body language indicating confidence.

You think this other person is in awe of your speaking skills.
Surely, they are coming to your side!

'Well, are they??'
Nah...

Persuasion is not about showing how great of a speaker you are.
Just like teaching is not about showing how smart you are.

Persuasion done correctly is about being **useful**.
In order to be useful, you need to understand what the other person **needs**.

Talk less, listen more.
Take less, provide more.

PERSUASION VS MANIPULATION

'Yo Armani. Are persuasion and manipulation the same thing?'
Nope.

At a surface level, they seem the same because of the end product. Behaviors are being warped.

But HOW the behavior gets warped is a night and day difference.

Manipulation is about getting someone to do something that only serves you.

Persuasion is about getting someone to do something that serves them & you.

It may seem like a subtle difference.

But a difference nevertheless...

At the core of it all, great persuasion is a positive-sum effect.

Where no one must lose for you to win.

By aiming to be useful to the other person, you prioritize listening more than speaking.

Because how can you address someone's needs when you're only persuading to win for yourself?

'Uh...'

Exactly, you can't.

HOW TO BE USEFUL

Would you give a hamburger to a man who is not hungry?

'Of course not.'

Why not?

'Because he is not hungry. It will be a waste of a burger.'

Bingo.

Likewise, how often are you trying to give someone something that they do not need?

It doesn't matter how much you try to 'persuade' me that your new organic chemistry book is the best text book in the field.

I have no use for it.

On the other hand, if you were to give me a book that pertained to my interests...
Then I'd be all ears.

For me to be all ears, you need to be ALL ears first.
That's step 1 of persuasion.
Find out what the other person needs.

It's something that they want at a core level.
They will often flat-out tell you.
It's your job to help them get to that level.

That's persuasion without tension.
More importantly, that's persuasion the positive-sum way rather than the old school zero-sum way.

HOW TO USE STORIES TO PERSUADE

Storytelling is a great factor in persuasion.
'Why do you say that?'
Because it's subtle.

Humans don't like being sold to, but they love buying.
Humans don't like being taught, but they love learning.

Stories allow you to teach without the other person having a clue.
You subtly sneak in lessons.

View persuasion as teaching opportunities.

This turns the act of persuasion from a task where you need to 'put on a show' to you being a helpful friend to the other person.

When you are teaching a friend, are you giving them a lecture?
'Nah, not really.'
Then what are you doing?
'I tell them stories with analogies.'
Exactly!

Analogies are the language of the subconscious mind.
Analogies can convey what mere facts, data & charts cannot convey.
'Why do you think that is?'
It's because an analogy speaks to the other person's **experiences**.

Every person you are trying to persuade has a big sticker on their forehead which writes:

- What's in it for me?

The right analogy addresses that question.
There is an art to the analogy...

HOW TO MAKE YOUR ANALOGIES RELATABLE

To persuade, we are trying to help the other person.
Rather than trying to sell to them, we are teaching them and let them sell themselves.

Stories are a great way to sprinkle in meaningful lessons that can alter behavior.

For the stories to be successful, analogies are great.

For analogies to be great, it should be:

- Language that the other person understands.

- Examples that speak to their experiences.

You'll know how to use the right language if you were ALL ears before trying to create a story.

Imagine Stacy is a nurse who is thinking about buying new nursing pants.

A bad analogy will be:

"These nursing pants I sell are like the new microchips on an oscillator ray."

What??

The analogy made no sense because it had confusing language that I'm sure Stacy is not familiar with.

A better analogy would have been:

"These new nursing pants are so comfortable, that my last client wears them to sleep. The nursing pants are like pajamas."

I'm sure Stacy sleeps.

I'm sure she understands what pajamas are.

Her subconscious mind will now create an association from the comfort of the pajamas to the nursing pants.

TRUE PERSUASION IS ABOUT YOU WINNING SECOND

Persuasion becomes an anxiety-riddled task when you make it all about you.

*Persuasion becomes a large puzzle when you make it about
the other person.*

You don't need to spend days, weeks, or months creating a
story.
The story creates itself when you are listening to the other
person.

See how you can create value for them.
Then in exchange, how you can get something back.

It's easier to persuade when you prime the mind to see win-win
relationships.
Rather than win-lose relationships.

Win-lose relationships are the byproduct of linear thinking.
Win-win relationships are the byproduct of nonlinear thinking.
Also known as systems thinking.

Think bigger.
Allow your persuasion to be a generous act.

PERSUADERS DRIVE CHANGE

Every great act requires persuasion at one point or another.
Confusing persuasion with manipulation is sad.
This mistake causes great entrepreneurs, artists & speakers to
second guess themselves.

Manipulation leaves a trail of dead bodies.
Persuasion leaves a trail of empowered individuals.

So, persuade.

If you are gifted, great.
But to become great, you need to be gifted.
'Gifted in what?'
Gifted in persuasion.

Be all ears.
And then allow the other person to be all ears.

ATTRACTION MARKETING 101: CONTENT FOR MARKETING PLAN

Don't fix what is not broken.

Don't do something in 15 steps when it can be done in 3.

These 2 sentences will be the theme of today's blog.

Remember the 90s?

The music was so much different than it is now.

One group that was huge in the 90s was Nsync.

They made hit after hit.

However, in this era, only one of them is mainly remembered.

That's Justin Timberlake.

When Justin Timberlake was asked what allowed him to be so consistent...

He responded back with :

"I found my formula and stuck with it."

Discovering our formula is a journey.

We can find and look at other people's content marketing plans.

But ultimately, it will be us who creates the plan that works for us.

This post will help you understand the value of content marketing & will share some tips on creating a plan that you can do....

LONG TERM.

WHY THERE IS NO SUCH THING AS THE PERFECT CONTENT MARKETING PLAN

Let's get one point out of the way.
There's no perfect plan out there.

Some people will swear that video is number 1.
Others will die by written content only.
Some will say, both of them suck. Podcasts are the future!

All these people have fallen into dogmas.
They are heavily biased or are trying to sell you something.
Much love to them.
Everyone needs to make a living.

For your brand though?
The closest to perfect you can get for a content marketing plan is the plan you can stick with **long term.**

So if you are an author, then you may lean towards writing.
This may set you up to start a blog in the beginning.
Maybe you can evolve into podcasts and videos later.

For now, ask yourself this simple question:
'What kind of content can I create for 15 years if need be without it feeling like a hassle?'

This question gets you thinking long-term in this instant gratification world.

FINDING THE PRACTICAL VALUE OF CONTENT MARKETING

Etch 2 words into your mind:

- Traffic + Offer.

These are the basic elements of an online business.

Let's say you're an artist.

You have a YouTube channel where you paint your newest creations.

This attracts an audience.

Then in the description box, you sell that painting in your online shop.

Traffic is the eyeballs. These are the people's attention that you have.

You're my traffic right now as you read this post.

Offer is the product/service that is being sold.

So this artist got traffic on YouTube.

The offer was the painting that they created.

Do you see the value?

'Kind of, but not really.'

The value is the attraction process.

For the longest time, interruption marketing was the main form of marketing.

I used to see it all the time with commercials when I was watching TV.

However, with content marketing, you attract people to you.

When you interrupt, the traffic has the power.

When you attract, you have the power.

This is mind-blowing & should allow you to see value in content marketing.

Something that you work on today serves as digital energy, which serves as a magnet & sparks the attraction process.

The internet ranks content differently.

So have a decent understanding of your market and/or learn some basic keyword research & you'll see why content is king.

START OFF LIGHT AND EXPAND

To work on your content marketing plan, I recommend starting off light.

Let me tell you a bit about my journey and show you how repetition adds up.

I started my journey on Twitter.

Wrote tweets as a hobby.

That's when one of my followers DM'd me and told me to set up an email list.

I didn't see much value in the list.

Until on the same weekend, a well-known Twitter account got banned off the platform.

That's when I realized I didn't own the traffic on Twitter.

But I owned the list.

So I started tweeting & also created a daily email list.

That's the setup I had for some time.

As more time went on, I had a collection of tweets that were very popular.

Plus, I had emails where I'd get a response like, *'Wow, this email was exactly what I needed.'*

The virality of certain tweets and seeing resonation with my emails gave me the PERFECT topics to talk about on my YouTube channel.

It's as though the ideas had been created.

So it was now me articulating the concepts verbally on a different platform.

YouTube played a synergy with podcasts as well.

Some people couldn't watch me all the time. They liked to listen in their cars as they drove to work.

So I practiced my storytelling skills in the podcast format as well.

Which led to what you are reading now.

The blog feature.

Do you see the main principle?

Start off light & gradually expand (if you want to expand).

Don't just expand because others are doing it.

Seth Godin pretty much only touches blogs and books & is a wealthy man because of it.

As I said earlier, there is no perfect plan.

Just gotta start doing some introspecting on where you're trying to go & evaluate where you are.

CREATING A CONTENT CREATION MARKETING PLAN

What gets written gets done.
I've been a big fan of that.

Such a big fan that I decided to create my own planners to organize my time.
Each day consists of 4 basic principles for me.
Consume, create, market, meditate.

When you take a bite at a time of the burger, it becomes much easier to eat.
Rather than shoving the whole thing in your mouth like a pig.

So just have a BASIC plan to get started.
Maybe, just 1 video a week?
'No, I don't want to do video.'
Then maybe 1 tweet.
'Hm..Twitter sounds interesting.'
Sure, find out what resonates.

Then start **atomic**.
In his book, Atomic Habits, James Clear talks about how small increments build up over time.
Same concept with a content creation marketing plan.

My formula is:
- Monday, Wednesday, Friday – YouTube videos.
- Tuesday, Thursday, Saturday – Podcasts.
- Sunday, Wednesday, Saturday – Blogs.
- With daily tweets and emails.

This seems like a lot to someone who is just first starting off.
However, I started atomic before I went macro.
Start off blurry and clarify along the way.

THE GREAT CONTENT MARKETING PLAN FOR YOU

Your content is an extension of you.
If you want to get close to reading someone's mind...
Become fluent in body language or look at their Twitter.

So if content is an extension of you, then you **need** to know yourself to a certain degree.
Aim to do some introspection.

Which topics can you talk about effortlessly?
Which form of delivery makes you feel the most curious?
What kind of content do you consume the most?

From there, it's a game of finding a **blurry** plan.
Just knowing that there is a plan of SOME sort adds tremendous clarity to the mind.

Then, it's repetition.
You'll get better with time.
Traffic will be created.
Now it's a game of getting the offers lined up.

How to Be a More Interesting Person

You want to know how to be a more interesting person?

'How?'

By first asking yourself if you're boring.

This is one of the counterintuitive ways I learned about interesting people.

They know the art of viewing themselves from 3rd perspective.

It was never personal.

Real talk.

Do you consider yourself boring?

Simply pondering on this question will present a problem.

'What problem will it present?'

Difficulty in concentration.

One second, you start asking yourself if you're interesting.

Then the next second, you're wondering what you're going to eat for lunch.

No results to show for it because the mind controls you.

Not the other way around...

Learning how to be a more interesting person will require some work.

The process of answering this question turns you into a **completely** different being.

I want to talk about the role of content creation in the process of blossoming your personality.

DEFINE "INTERESTING"

It's hard to be something when you don't know the definition.

5 people in a room.

4 are wearing white shirts and 1 person is wearing a purple shirt.

Which one is the most interesting?

Answer this in 2 seconds.

If I gave you a lot of time, you'd want to consciously break it down.

However, since I'm giving you little time, I guarantee you'd choose the purple shirt.

Do you know why that is?

'It's because they are different.'

Correct, **different**. That's what makes someone interesting.

A difference is what creates a contrast in the mind.

Without the contrast, a person just blends in with society.

Humans are wired to want to blend in because that requires no courage & minimal risk-taking.

Rules, norms and past habits are presented to you.

Now you just need to implement those moves.

Being a purple shirt in a land of white shirts is something that requires brutal honesty.

Are you different or do you consider yourself the same as the masses?

One life irony is that:

- It is normal to be weird and weird to be normal.

However, the boring boy has taken up the opposite paradigm and wonders why he lacks an interesting personality.

GOOD DIFFERENT VS BAD DIFFERENT

I see a lot of celebrities wear a dress nowadays and call themselves, "different."

If that's for you, go for it.

Lowkey, I think it's corny.

Heck, I think that's the bad kind of different.

It seems like a "try-hard."

A person who is like, *'yo, look at me. You see how interesting I am?'*

That's just the intention that I get from it.

Good difference in my eyes is the byproduct of being yourself.

Being yourself is difficult because personality has layers.

So, telling someone to just 'be yourself' is an ambiguous command that seems like a clear one.

Let's be more surgical with it.

It's impossible to not be 'good different' if you pursue natural curiosities.

A boring person labels curiosities as good **or** bad.

By labeling curiosities, it's hard to find out what comes from within and what has been manufactured with the intellect.

Never label a curiosity as good or bad if you are trying to learn how to be more interesting.

Labeling happens when we fear judgment.

I just made fun of someone for wearing a dress.

That person may be pursuing his natural curiosity.

A guy like will me exist when you are pursuing your natural curiosity.

Someone may be like, *'I question your intentions.'*

Despite it being a natural curiosity.

Live with it.

The dress-wearing man probably does not give a shit that I don't approve.

Nor should you give a shit if someone doesn't approve.

Your curiosities are for you.

Those curiosities turn you into a different being.

The good kind, hopefully.

HOW TO BE A MORE INTERESTING PERSON THRU CONTENT CREATION

The process of writing and speaking follows the T.O.L.D formula.

Which is, Thinking Out Loud.

When I first began writing, I was like, 'whoa, did I really think that?'

Then I thought, 'I don't know WHY I think like that. So why did I have that belief for so long?'

It's because a lot of beliefs are **programmed**.

You could be the strongest-willed person out there, but the environment will still have some role on your personality.

Through the process of content creation, it allows you to kill 2 birds with 1 stone.

1. You learn to focus rather than letting your mind drift off to what you are going to eat later.

2. You learn to see where you stand on certain issues.

In that process, you start to discover whether you're a purple shirt or a white shirt.

Well...?

'Well, what?'

Are you purple or white?...

THE PROCESS OF INTROSPECTING LEADS TO BOLDNESS

It's hard to be swayed when sitting absorbed in the truth.

Think out loud, buddy.

Simply by writing freely and letting the pen, or the letters on the keyboard lead, the authentic personality is created and revealed.

It's not a game about showing others where you lean on certain issues, but more so about seeing where you lean.

'What if I discover that I'm boring? That I have nothing to talk about?'

That's a great problem to have.

Because it naturally forces a growth mind.

Now you are naturally propelled to find activities to do that you never considered.

Rather than doing random activities for the sake of doing it, it's now more a game of thinking,

'Ah, I am doing these activities to become the purple shirt!'

These white shirts are not bad people.

It's just that they don't achieve that higher echelon level of greatness.

Opportunity favors the bold.

Opportunities are found by those who ask the tough questions and commit to finding the answer.

WEIRDNESS SHOWS COLOR

If someone can predict that next thing you'll say, then predictability has shown its face.

A predictable personality is a boring personality.

Learning how to be more interesting is a process of "looking in" more than it is a process of "looking out."

It's about *Thinking Out Loud*, finding holes in the game and filling those holes in with grace.

Write like no one is watching.

Preferably, by hand.

Through this process of writing, is where thoughts slow down...

Where realness is revealed...

Where the tough answers are found...

Turn your life into a story.

And watch yourself become more interesting.

To chronicle your life, check out the *Story Mode Journal*.

A blank book with 365 lined pages to write in every single day of the year.

3rd perspective yourself and see where you stand in the game of life.

How to be Self Disciplined for the Long Run

Self-discipline is a foundational skill set of winners.
It's a muscle that needs to be cultivated.

Plateau's are a strange thing.
At one moment, you are on top of the world.
The next moment, you are struggling to stay afloat.

Did something break??
No.
That's just the nature of the game.

Bulldoze through the plateau through hard work, discipline, and consistency.
That's what allows you to develop a new level.

This post is going to discuss the nitty-gritty details of how to develop self-discipline.
Understand the benefits of discipline so it's easier to implement it into your life.
That's where we will begin.

Benefits of Self Discipline

Discipline is the art of programming yourself.
There is a certain goal and system you want to implement, so you implement it.

The surface-level of discipline seems like a bunch of moments.

However, the essence driving the movements is where the money lies.

To learn how to be self-disciplined requires a strong why.

Why are you doing these tasks when you could not be doing these tasks?

Think about this for some time.

You're on the right track when you can state your *why* in 1 sentence.

-I have fun being disciplined.

-I have been undisciplined before and I hated the outcome.

-My goals cannot be reached without finetuning.

All strong whys.

My favorite is the first 1.

Have fun being disciplined due to the benefits you gain:

-Added confidence

-Less stress

-Completed to do list

-Added skills

And much more.

HOW TO START BEING DISCIPLINED

To learn how to be self-disciplined, it's better to start off with 1 and build your way up rather than trying to do too much.

That's skill stacking.

A foundational habit is a habit that spills over to all other parts of life.

If you can focus on this one habit, all other parts of your life improves.

257

2 foundational habits are starting a business and lifting weights.

'Starting a business is no habit!'
It can be. Especially depending on your business model.

If you're a writer whose business is wrapped around your books, you'll see yourself building discipline in a unique way.
Let's say you're in the early stages so you have to do a lot of work by yourself.
Writing, you do.
Editing, you do.
These 2 acts alone change the physiology of your brain.

If you want to bulldoze through the work, you'll see yourself building writing systems.
The writing systems make it easier to communicate.
The systems allow you to time your breaks and get back to work to meet deadlines.
In this case, you started with one act, and discipline fell out of that.

Another core habit is lifting.
Where starting a business is more advanced, lifting is beginner-friendly.

The mere act of incorporating the gym into your life changes everything.
From lifting weights at the gym to sleeping well at night.
From meal prepping in the weekends to cutting back on alcohol.
Lifting weights allows other parts of discipline to slowly build up.

SLOW AND STEADY WINS THE RACE

Discipline is a lifestyle rather than an act.
When treating it as an act, discipline becomes situational.

'Are you telling me I can never rest?'
Not quite.
I'm telling you to rest because that's a part of discipline.

It's the art of programming yourself, remember?
Therefore, you can have a set time when you won't touch work.
Not even look at it.

It's easier to relax when you put in the work beforehand.
Incorporating rest into your game plan makes it easier to be disciplined for the long run.
Slow and steady wins the race in the world of productivity.
1 can annihilate many in the world of productivity.

Just like complex machines in fortune 500 companies need rest time allocated, so do you.
Without it, you aren't doing slow and steady.
You are doing fast and choppy.

PRIVATE OR PUBLIC?

There are different personalities out there.
Some people like to announce their goals.
Others like to keep it private.

Keeping it private is for the people who don't have too hard of a time being disciplined or are just more lowkey.

That's a strategy.

Another strategy is being public with discipline.
Set a standard for yourself, yes.
But also allow others to set a standard for you.

I have been writing on a daily email list for over 700 days now.
I do it for myself.
Plus, I have accumulated readers who would know if I didn't write on a certain day.

The long streak of 700 plus days will come crashing down before my very eyes if I chose to skip a day.
And my ego doesn't want that.
This keeps me motivated to keep the streak going.

Another example includes 2 friends who set a bet with each other to see who could get a 6 pack first.
In this situation, multiple parties were involved and fitness was set as a target.
The loser has to buy dinner.

Although the bet is friendly, it is highly potent.
This public strategy forces you on track even on the lazy days.

Creating a public streak or leveraging pride through a bet are great ways to learn how to be self-disciplined if you keep straying off track.

WRITE DAILY

How you start the morning influences your day.
How you end the day influences your morning.

To keep your discipline strong, start writing every morning.
This is a cheat code that crystallizes the mind to see clearly.

A clear mind is a happy mind.
A muddied mind is an anxious mind.

Where most people are starting their day off with Instagram scrolling, don't even check your phone!
Get at least 2 hard tasks done before checking your phone.

One of those hard tasks is writing.
'Writing is hard? Any bubba can do that!'
Nope. Writing by hand is not easy.
It takes work.

Work is good because it makes the thoughts stickier.
And it creates a beautiful tone for the day.
This act creates a tsunami of benefits.
'What do I write about?'
Anything. Just try to end it off with a to-do list for the day.
You don't need to get super detailed. The simple act of writing a to-do list helps you think and act differently.

SELF DISCIPLINE OR FADE AWAY

Discipline feels like work until it feels like play.
Do you know what's worse tougher than being disciplined?
'What?'
Not being disciplined.

Hopping around from activity to activity.

Yawning away despite doing nothing..
Little work to show every night...
No thanks.

Learn how to be self-disciplined.
Incorporate it.
That's when the hidden joys speak for themselves.

DEALING WITH REGRETS

Confidence is not built via easy ways.
It's built through pain.

And one of the facets of pain includes regret.
Yes.
What is painful now, leads to joy later.

Hopefully.

Regrets can cause someone into a downward spiral.
Or allow the bow to be pulled back before it is propelled forward.

Are there any frameworks to deal with regrets?
Sure.
But more importantly, it comes down to going **past** dealing with regrets.

And the only way to do that is by having a target for your life.
A vision that forces regrets into making sense.

GETTING THE MOST OUT OF REGRETS

Intellectually dealing with regrets is time-consuming.
And you can make the argument that it leads to more dissatisfaction.

To hit the heart of the issue, let's make it simple.
An empowering vision is a must.

Without the vision, the mind is not compelled to do much.
It's more so walking around in circles.
And has no clue what to look out for.

If I point you to the forest, would you know where to go?
'Not really.'
Why not?
'Because you didn't give me anything. You just pointed at the
forest.'

Okay. But what if I pointed at the forest and told you to go get
me a rock.
Now would you have more clarity?
'Yes, I will.'

This showed that staring at the forest doesn't mean much.
Likewise, looking at regrets for the sake of looking at them
does not mean much.
Need to find the rock.

WHY REGRETS LEAD TO LESSONS

I hate the question:
What would you tell your younger self?

Actually, no, I don't hate the question in itself.
I hate the flaw it brings up about my younger self.

I'm a stubborn guy who doesn't always like to listen.
I rather learn on my own.
Who knows when I'll grow out of this.

Younger me was even more stubborn.
All I know is that younger Armani would not listen to shit the present Armani had to say.

'How are you so sure?'
Because younger Armani was stacking up his regrets.

Regrets lead to stickier lessons because the body gets involved.

I'm sure you've heard that it's not wise to speed on the road.
Intellectually, the lesson was understood.

Then you sped.
The body didn't understand.

And you got caught by a cop.
This is a regret, yes.
But this regret primes the mind AND body to **listen** next time.

Regrets cause lessons to become supercharged.
And now there is a beauty to the pain.

VIEWING LOSSES AS LESSONS

A loss is only a loss when the lesson has not been extracted.
Regardless of how dark it is.

This is tough to imagine when someone close to us passes away & we didn't talk to them enough.
Mainly because we were grinding.

This requires reframing.

The ego can temporarily fool you and be like:
'The other person passing away was a lesson? Get out of here.'

This situation has the ego passing off blame.
No, the lesson was that you should call people while they are here.

It's unfortunate that this lesson needed to be learned in such harsh circumstances.
But now, you're prone to learning it.
Dealing with regrets is not always pretty.

Add a vision to your life, and past lessons begin to make more sense.
Add a vision to your life, and past losses morph before your eyes.

WHY MISTAKES GET REPEATED

'All this sounds good man.'
Appreciate you, bro.
'Let me finish...But what if I don't want to learn from the regrets?'
Then you are living through past programs.

Knowledge and awareness are twins.
Both have 9 letters.

Without knowledge of regrets, the internal world remains dim.
Awareness is lacking.
And mistakes are bound to repeat in a different scenario.

This leads to a rat race in terms of life.

Normally, when the phrase, 'rat race' is pictured, it's viewed in terms of money.

This ridicule is given to someone who gets a job, gets a mortgage, and settles down early.

That's not fully fair.

The rat race is for the **entirety** of life.

When a loop is constantly being repeated.

Different day, same jaded paradigm.

Life Irony:

The more you run away from the regrets, the more the regrets stack up.

CREATING A NEW CHAPTER: DEALING WITH REGRETS

Okay, enough with all the dark talk.

Time to bring some light.

'I was going to say man lol.'

Ey, without scaring someone, they never learn.

Need to milk it while I can.

In reality, there are tons of **regrets** that everyone has.

Even the most 'perfect' person you know.

This makes it much more difficult to spot which regret to begin learning from.

Let me save you some time.

Anyone may have 500 moments they hate from their life.

Yet, they remember 5 of them the most.

And it's 1-2 which take up the most mental bandwidth.

Start with those.

How you learn from it is up to you.

Journaling helps.

Trying to make amends with it by forcefully articulating at least 5 lessons from that dark moment helps as well.

Either way, the name of the game is to turn the:

- loss into a w.

An example is Johnson.

He cheated on his high school sweetheart of 10 years after getting drunk at a party.

She was the love of his life.

And she was never able to forgive him.

She dumped him, rebuilt herself & found someone new to settle down with.

Johnson's ex now is settled down with a family.

Meanwhile, Johnson is a fat, alcoholic, slob who still cannot forget his error.

That's his regret.

He can seek therapy. He can seek the process of articulation.

Johnson is hopefully different now.

And by having one of those 'the one who got away' stories...

Hopefully, he learned the lesson to not cheat in the future.

Or who knows...

If he doesn't learn, he is bound to repeat it.

ACCOUNTABILITY AT ITS FINEST

As the world builds tools, people get softer.
They get softer because they don't know the value of work ethic.

That's why accountability is down.
And finger-pointing is on the rise.

Nature balances this out.

A person can run away from taking accountability in the external world.
But not in the internal.

Regrets are programmed in the mind for a reason.
It's nature's way of showing that you don't run away from accountability.
Run towards it buddy.

Articulate your past.
Learn from your past.
Memories become memories and no longer realities when the lesson has clicked.

Till then, history is bound to repeat itself.
Or at the bare minimum, rhyme.

COCKY VS CONFIDENT: WHAT'S THE DIFFERENCE?

It's easy to get carried away.
Especially when the act of getting carried away is confused as swag.

The 2 words: cocky and confident...
Do they resemble one another?
Do they seem like the same meaning?

If so, then it's time for a wake up call.

This is one of those situations where the words are highly different in terms of one another.
Sort of like quiet & shy.

Sure, for quite and shy, both look the same, externally...
But internally, the 2 people are **different**.

Quiet people don't say much because they don't have much to say.
On the other hand, shy people don't say much because they are self conscious.

Night and day difference when focusing on the internal state.

Likewise, this is the same case for cocky vs confident.
It's the confidence that eventually wins.
And it's the confidence that shines the brightest.

BEST DESCRIBING COCKY

Cockiness is born thru fear.
'What? I know a cocky person & he seems FAR from fearful.'
On the surface level.

- Orange juice is a drink.
- Orange is the fruit.

Which one is the source?

'The orange is the source. It leads to the orange juice.'
That's true.
You spotted the correct fundamental.

When comparing someone on the surface level to the fundamental level, things look different.
No way can a person who is brash, overly talkative & arrogant be nervous?

Yes, they can.

On a fundamental level, there is a level of fear that they are operating with.
This causes a larger desire for attention.
More validation is needed.

WHY FEAR LEADS TO COCKINESS

At the surface level, it's easy to see a whole lot of things.
You may see an attire, jokes, names etc.

At the core level, social skills comes down to an **abundance or scarcity mindset.**

-Abundance is when the opportunities are endless.

–Scarcity mindset is when the opportunities are limited.

The cocky individual works with a scarce mentality.

This person may be hyper competitive & takes another person's win as their own loss.

It's sad though.

Because this character creates more tension in social interactions.

I like to call them the clog.

The person who can turn a dialogue into a monologue real quick.

And no one likes that.

CONFIDENCE

Confidence is born thru an abundance mindset.

An abundance mindset is *always* earned.

The act of abundance seems like a very glittery word.

While it's not meant to be...

It's meant to be a practical word.

This state is normally built thru a lot of reps, focus & compassion.

The last trait is key.

Confident people lead with compassion.

And once again..

Compassion seems like a very glittery word.
However, it's meant to be practical.

Compassion in terms of analogies goes like this...
A computer turning from a computational device to a communication device.

The computer works great by itself.
But when it enters the internet?
It's just one of MANY computers.

And when entering the internet, all the other computers acknowledge their own individual identity...
While remaining perfectly cognizant of the bigger identity.
That's the internet.

In this situation, the enhanced perception of the internet represents compassion.
Just a rough analogy..

COCKY VS CONFIDENT: THE SPLITTING OF WAYS

'So Armani, you were mentioning how shy & quiet are different.'
That, I was.
'For both those, the end products are still a lack of words. Do cocky & confident people share **any** similar traits?'
Sure.
It can be opportunities.

-I used the word 'can be' for a reason.

Because a brash cocky individual can easily create opportunities for themselves.

That's the beauty of speaking up.

However, it's important to not just view that surface level opportunity.

Let's see the **tiered** effects.

What happens overtime?

Did the cocky person still remain in good graces?

Or is there a line of bodies & burned bridges?

A confident person too can create opportunities.

However, these opportunities last.

A cocky person plays a zero sum game.

And the confident person plays the game of synergy.

Where the other person needs to win, otherwise, the confident person does not enjoy their own win…

BEING LESS NEEDY WITH CONFIDENCE

Confidence is not about getting others to like you.

It's more so about not caring if others like you, because you like yourself.

And ironically, this gets others to like you.

There's always a fine line from what I noticed.

Not caring at all about what others think can lead to boorish behavior.

And a lot of political, societal & relationship issues.

So this requires some finetuning.
1 opinion sticks out over the others.

In this case, I show you a dollar & 50 pennies.
And I ask you which is the most valuable?
Immediately, the dollar is pointed to.

It's not like we negate the pennies.
We just put one focus above the other.

That's the way with opinions.
Sometimes, pennies are needed.
Sometimes, opinions give great feedback.

But the confident person doesn't allow a sea of pennies to make it lose value of the dollar.

CONFIDENCE IS GRACE & COCKINESS IS NOT

To build confidence to the core, it always needs to be tied to 2 things:
-Self improvement.
-A grander vision.
Confidence without one of those variables often leads to a cocky person.

Why?

Because improvement serves as a staple.
Improving builds a line of micro skills such as self discipline, a philosophy, cooperation mindset etc.

It teaches you, as the computer, to be the internet.
Rather than the lone computer.

The grander vision is something that is personal & is earned thru iterations.
It's the driving WHY for the self improvement.
And this WHY changes with you.

Without those 2 variables, the mind doesn't have a FORCE.
It starts to become needy.

A nice guy and a cocky guy are very similar in terms of moving with a scarcity mindset at the core level.
Never abundance.

People come and go...

- When you have a scarcity mindset with people, you get tension.
- When you have a scarcity mindset with opportunities, you get competition.
- And when you have a scarcity mindset with people & opportunities, you get a brash arrogant individual who lacks substance.

Cocky vs confident..
The 2 are not the same.
Nor will they ever be.

UNAPOLOGETICALLY ZONING IN ON NATURAL TALENT

'I have no clue what I am going to talk about.'
Why don't you talk about your natural talent?
'My what?'
Your natural talent.

Think about it.

'I don't need to do much thinking. I don't have a natural talent.'
You do.
And we often discover it when we aren't thinking, too much.

Natural talent is something that we all have.

It's something that comes effortlessly for us.

Not only is it easy, but it's fun.
There's a joy when the moves are being executed.
What is this natural talent?
And how can we go on a journey to perfect it?

HARD WORK VS TALENT

There is a problem with the mind.
It loves to compare.
It doesn't like to hold 2 very counterintuitive concepts together at once.
But luckily, this quirk can easily be resolved.
'How?'

By looking at the edge of the coin.

Soft skills or hard skills?
Both.
Quantity or quality?
Both.
Hard work or talent?
Both.

'Both' is the gold standard for the 'edge of the coin' mindset.
And it allows us to go past the mind & fix the natural quirk to compare.

Hard work & talent are joined at the hip.
Both are needed.
Hard work allows us to build discipline, rituals & practices to train the body and mind.
Talent allows us to use that hard work to flow to another level.

Talent is something that we are exceptionally gifted in without much conscious effort.
Not the type of effort where we are thinking a lot.
But there is a level of joy.

Joy can only exist when we aren't overthinking.
Joy comes out to play when we make joy an intention.
And thinking is joy's servant.

SPOTTING OUR NATURAL TALENT

So not only are hard work and talent joined at the hip.
Talent and joy are also joined at the hip.

To find something we are normally good at requires some introspection.

Time needs to be something we put on the back burner.

Don't view it in terms of past, present & future.

Just view your life from the context of your life.

What is it that you are capable of doing very easily & it can provide value to atleast one person?

A great example of this in action is Steve Harvey.

Like him or hate him, Steve has been able to zone in on his gift which is comedy.

At first, the possessor of the gift thinks there is nothing special about it.

Making someone laugh?

What value can that possibly provide?

But rest on that thought for a second.

Because most gifts are capable of adding value to **at least** one person.

- And that one person turns into many.

Steve Harvey was able to zone in on comedy.

He saw that he had a natural talent for turning mundane information from his life into meaningful information for other people's lives.

'How exactly did he make it meaningful?'

He turned mundane information into knowledge plus laughs.

That 2 in 1 punch combo allowed him to add value.

ZONING IN ON THE EASY

The hardest part of zoning in on what's easy is that we feel guilty.

No way can we work on something that feels easy.

It feels like tricks are being pulled.

This mindset of 'tricks being pulled' is what leads to self-sabotage.

Back to the Steve Harvey example.

He is a great proof of what it means to hone a craft.

A craft is not just one thing.

It starts as one thing & gets spilled over to other things.

Through his honing in on jokes, Steve was able to learn public speaking.

Public speaking was a great leeway into learning entertainment.

By learning how to entertain others through laughter, he signed TV deals.

Built credibility.

There were 4 kings of comedy.

Bernie Mac, DL Hughley, Cedric the Entertainer, and Steve Harvey.

By zoning in on one thing, he was able to expand onto many things.

It started off as easy & it went to the wide net.

That's how you learn many topics by zoning in on one.

CREATING CONTENT REGARDING THE CRAFT

When running out of content, the best question to ask yourself is:

- *What is my natural talent?*

Not questions like:

- *What will the algorithm like?*
- *I should ask my audience, right?*
- *Is it over for me? Am I done??*

Just ask for the natural talent.

In the information age, we are living in a unique era. **People are being rewarded for zoning in & focusing.**

The internet age rewards creativity due to the ease of access to information technology.

Anyone can use their phones to start a social media & share their ideas.

During moments of saturation like this, people don't like parrots.

They like the Bald Eagles.

The rare ones who share insights from a completely different perspective.

Steve Harvey is not only a comedian but a motivational speaker now as well.

The insights that he can provide in his come-up will be very different from other comedians.

Although a lot of the lessons may seem similar, the **path taken** to reach the lessons will have a **night and day difference.**

By focusing on the natural talent, Steve is going to have infinite content material for life.

It's just a game of zoning in on the easy.

OVERCOME SELF SABOTAGE WITH NATURAL TALENT

Everyone is good at something.

And joy serves as a great compass for finding that special something.

Self-sabotage is the trait of the ungrateful.

Just because it came easier to you than for others doesn't mean that gratitude should be curved.

The more creative a mind becomes, the more high ROI gratitude becomes.

Mainly because gratitude keeps us grounded and keeps the fragmented mind in check.

You can make the argument that gratefulness is the **antidote** for self-sabotage.

Natural talent rarely gets discovered due to poor work ethic.

That's the norm.

However, what's even sadder is when the *holder* of the natural talent suppresses their own talent.

Hopefully, this post helps you look within & collapse time.

No past, present, or future.

What comes easy to you & can provide value for **at least** 1 person?

It starts with 1.

1 evolves into 2.

2 evolves into 4.

And once you're at 4, there's no reason not to double that.

Keep this formula going for life.

PEOPLE PLEASER: HOW TO STOP BEING SO NICE

Nice.

Isn't that good?

Why would I want to stop being nice?

A couple of months back, I had a discussion with a friend who praised being nice.

He said his entire brand was built around building more nice guys.

Hearing him say that with a straight face had me dying of laughter.

I thought he was joking.

But no.

He wasn't.

He viewed being nice as a good thing.

So this got my curiosity.

As we talked longer, I came to realize he wasn't describing nice.

He was actually describing kind.

Kind and nice are NOT the same.

This is an important distinction to make.

Confusing the 2 for one another leads to a lot of heartache, betrayal & surprise endings.

And not the good kind of surprise endings.

Let me reiterate.

Kind and nice are not the same.

Let's learn how to stop being so nice.

SIGNS OF A NICE GUY

A nice guy is a people pleaser.

That's my nice way of saying it.

Plenty of the most confident people out there have been the nice guy before.

This is when they confused people-pleasing as social skills.

We were rarely taught how to carry ourselves in social interactions.

Therefore, we wing it.

And a part of winging it is us going back to our baseline state.

The fear of confrontation.

The fear of confrontation can create a passive person.

A person who works with the narrative:

'If I just give the other person what they want, maybe they'll like me!'

Pay attention to those final 4 words:

Maybe they'll like me.

^ This is the CORE mission statement of the nice guy.

WHY NICENESS LEADS TO SELF DESTRUCTION

A lot of villains in movies were once the nice guys.
They were playing their 'ideal' role in society.

However, as time went on, society was not rewarding them.
Rather, the exact opposite.

Society started to take advantage of them.
Piece by piece.

The nice guy started to learn a dark truth about reality...
When you give someone everything they want, then they will want more.

Not everyone though.
I don't want to paint such a bleak perception of people.
However, that's the case with **many** people.

Why does this happen?
Because social skills are not led with the conscious mind.
It's led with the subconscious mind.
 'Can you explain what you mean by that?'
Sure.
It comes down to feelings.

SPOTTING FAKENESS

I feel confused about the word: *feelings.*
Especially with being a former engineer.

The word 'feelings' was often seen as a taboo word in my field.
It's too gray.
Too abstract.

Yet, feelings are the core driver of social skills.

You can be putting in all the effort in the world.
Saying all the right words.
Wearing the perfect outfit.

But ultimately, people make a decision on whether they like you or not by analyzing THEIR body:

- Did you make them feel empowered?

OR

- Did you make them feel drained?

These 2 questions will determine likability.

With nice guys, there is a drained feeling.
'Why?'
Because the subconscious mind can spot micro-movements in body language.
The subconscious mind can also spot **intent**.

You ever had a gut feeling that something was wrong?
Yet, you intellectually talked yourself out of it...
All for your gut feeling to have been right?

'Yes, man! That's happened too many times.'
Well, this was a situation of your subconscious mind spotting the intent.

But your intellectually gifted conscious mind talked you into believing something else.

The reason nice guys can accidentally give the wrong impression is due to the intent they are working with.
They aren't often present.
Instead, they are working with the 'what's in it for me' mentality.

Aka: The 'maybe they'll like me' mentality.

LEARN HOW TO STOP BEING SO NICE WITH KINDNESS

Self-improvement and social skills go hand in hand.
Anyone who separates the 2 is a fool.

Why is this?

Because self-improvement leads to a purpose.
A set north star that someone is working towards.

Earl Nightingale once said:
Success is the progressive realization of a worthy ideal.

How **fire** of a definition is that?

When someone is trying to realize a worthy ideal, do you think they have time to impress others?
'Hm...probably not.'
Not probably not.
The answer is no.

This isn't to say they are a jerk.

It's just that their order of values is different from the nice guy.

'Different how?'

The kind guy has an order of values. With their purpose being high up there.

While the nice guy has little to no order of values. Which causes them to be scattered.

The mind needs a target.

And when the mind doesn't have a target, it'll assign itself one.

The target it assigns itself is the approval of others.

We can talk about this for a while.

But the core difference between the nice guy and the kind guy is an ideal.

To learn how to stop being so nice, the mind needs some values.

The ideal can be different for different people.

Starting a business, raising a family, building a dream body, etc.

These are just 3 options.

Any of these 3 options require more real estate in the mind.

And by giving the mind a target, naturally, a charm comes over you.

The more you try to impress, the faster they run.

The less you try to impress, the faster they come.

Melting Away Niceness

If you are trying to learn how to stop being so nice, a great question to ask yourself is:
'What other interests do I have?'

You'll be surprised how this is a foreign question for many.
They just take it day by day.
So their mind drifts from opinions to opinions.

With me, a large part of my life is centered around communication skills.
And that can be broken down into subcomponents like:
- Writing this blog.
- Recording YouTube videos.
- Giving a speech.
- Working with a client, etc.

It doesn't really matter what it is.
Scratch that...
It sort of matters.

Make sure the task is more so based on YOUR competence rather than THEIR approval.

-Are you more focused on writing better for each piece?
-Or are you more focused on what others will think of your work?
This question is more important than it seems.

And this question will determine if you remain a nice guy...
Or you graduate into being kind.

HOW TO STOP BEING JEALOUS OF OTHERS

Jealousy can either serve as fuel.
Or jealousy can serve as a way to self implode.

'Why do others get jealous?'
Well, can you blame them?

We live in a society that encourages competition.
Which is great in many fields.
But not productive in many other fields.

Rather than breeding a competition mindset, it is much more effective to breed a *cooperation mindset*.
With the cooperation mindset, a lot of jealousy melts away.
That's the fastest way to learn how to stop being jealous of others.

That's not to say jealousy isn't good though.
It can be very good.
It is a human emotion, you know.

But let's talk a bit more about this competition mindset.

THE COMPETITION MINDSET

Competing is a gift and a curse.
In the world of sports, you get paid to compete.
So that's a high ROI mindset.

But in the world of social skills, you don't get paid to compete.

In reality, it's a self-imposed narrative that's being implied.

The desire to compete often implies that this person is a 'winner.'

Or on a journey to be a winner.

That's what society says.

However, the weakness of this narrative rises the more one matures.

Competing aimlessly isn't the trait of a winner.

Awareness & emotional regulation are the key traits of a winner.

Competition mindset is fine in doses in regards to social skills.

Like a friendly bet.

But when that's the core narrative running your operating system, it's planting some darks seeds that will eventually grow.

WHAT COMPETITION MINDSET LEADS TO

The competition mindset regarding humans leads to a lot of tiered effects.

What, you thought the mindset didn't have effects?

Fam, everything has a cause & you know what follows the cause....

The competition mindset leads us to resent when someone else wins.

It makes us create the narrative that:

- Someone else's win = Our loss.

This is silly though.

For the most part, that is rarely the case.

Someone else's win is their win.... But the ego tries to slide itself in there.

That's when jealousy is born.

Jealousy happens on its own.

Like a little kid who sees his baby brother suddenly getting more attention.

However, jealousy is amplified when combined with a competition mindset.

That's when a bitter attitude is slowly conditioned to the subconscious mind.

TO ACT OR NOT TO ACT?

Jealousy can fuel a lot of greatness.

Same with competition.

However, after a certain period, a part of someone is like:

'Do I always need to pull down others to pull myself up?'

That's when compassion **is being unlocked.**

A higher form of intelligence that can take years to tap into.

Jealousy can spark action.

Heck, a lot of businesses are started that way.

One person who hates their job may see someone else much younger, thriving in a business.

The person in the job is like 'why can't I do that too?'

The jealousy in this case sparks a motive for change.

I hope that this individual is not setting their entire business plan around beating the youngster lol.

But it's hard to deny that the change that it sparked was needed.

So jealousy comes down to the question of:

Should I act or not?

THE DIFFERENT KINDS OF JEALOUSY

One of the best ways to learn how to stop being jealous of others...

Is by learning all jealousy is not the same.

'What do you mean?'

They are not the same...

Some jealousy is small.

And you'll notice it.

It's something that can happen on autopilot.

Let's say you see someone driving that new Lexus.

A part of you immediately gets jealous.

But after a couple of minutes... you're like:

'Wait a minute, I don't even like the Lexus.'

That's what I call baby-burst jealousy.

On the other hand, the other form of envy is the one that sparks a core desire.

Sort of like the situation with the employee and his anger towards the youngster regarding business.

This jealousy is potent.

It can fuel us to drive massive change.

Or can cause us to act very much out of character.

And this is where different individuals are created.

HOW TO STOP BEING JEALOUS OF OTHERS

I've always found social media unique.

Not because of the content alone.

But the way some people act with the content.

Every now and then, you'll see a very normal guy, offline, becoming a massive hater, online.

I'm not talking about a constructive critic who is pointing out areas of improvement.

I'm talking about a guy who just talks shit to vent.

Paragraphs on paragraphs.

That's just an observation.

Jealousy can easily cause someone to become a hater.

The envy sparked the hidden desire.

And rather than this individual doing something about it...

They decide to tear the other person down.

The dark truth is that this is the case with a lot of people.

I wouldn't be surprised if it was the majority.

And I wouldn't be surprised if the 'always hear both sides of the story' quote stemmed from these types of jealous individuals.

Needless to say, this is the loser way to behave.

The other way to act towards jealousy is to *immediately act*.
The core desire is sparked.

You do a bit of thinking... Not too much.
Otherwise, procrastination will happen.

But then a 'you know what... if he can do it, why can't I?' question will be asked.
This frames you as the go-getter.

At first, it may seem that you're putting the other person down.
Maybe this person worked years for this goal.

But when you look closer, you're actually bringing your potential to the forefront.
Not immediately hating.

If you lack the willpower to carry on and make something happen...
Ignoring is always an option.
But with willpower, the jealousy may have been the best thing to happen.

ENCOURAGING COOPERATION ONE STEP AT A TIME

It's funny how people of power are consistently collaborating behind the scenes.

However, they pass the narrative to those below them to compete like mad men.

This creates a fragmented community.

And when a community is fragmented, these individual nodes are much easier to control.

People of power don't want others to know how to stop being jealous of others.

It may not be something that's perceivable when you are that node.

But for those people high up there?

They know the game they are playing.

Don't let your jealousy play someone else's game.

Play your own game, playa.

Control the jealousy.

Harness it.

And allow it to propel you to new heights.

HOW DOES THE BRAIN & MIND PROCESS INFORMATION?

Data vs information...
Are the 2 different or the same?

'The 2 are different ways of saying the same thing!'
Nope.
Wrong.
The 2 are different.

You can have data without information.
But you cannot have information without data.

By understanding the differences, we'll be able to understand how the mind & brain processes information.
It really comes down to understanding data vs information.

WHAT'S THE DIFFERENCE BETWEEN DATA & INFORMATION?

Data is unstructured.
Information is structured.
- Structured data = Information

Information can take up different roles in one's life.
A book on starting a business may be perceived as information for one party.
Because this party is starting a business themselves.

While for another party...it's data.

It doesn't really register.

The core difference is that information has MEANING.
And that meaning allows someone to add structure to a narrative.
A narrative that will eventually influence behavior.

HOW DOES THE BRAIN PROCESS DATA & INFORMATION?

'How does the brain process information?'
The brain is smart.
'How smart?
The brain is capable of turning the data of the world into something more.

The world around us consists of light & electromagnetic waves.
And the human has a few components.
-Action organs.
-Knowledge organs.

Action organs allow us to interact with the environment.
Hands, legs, mouth, anus & genitals.

Knowledge organs allow us to consume from the environment.
Eyes, ears, mouth, nose, skin.

Knowledge organs take in data from the outside...
Then it's all accumulated in the storehouse of the brain.
The brain gathers the *data*.

THE BRAIN – MIND CONNECTION

At this point, everything is just neural impulses.

How do the neural impulses turn into imagery?

The vivid imagery that allows you to read these words right now?

Well, in terms of Eastern philosophy, the mind is viewed as a body as well.

The mind is not just something that is a passive bystander.

The mind gets the data from the brain…

And that's when we begin the **data to information conversion process.**

The mind is composed of:

Memory, ego, intellect & imagery.

All the data sent from the brain are transmitted to the mind.

And in the mind, one is able to gather meaning…

- Memory is the storehouse of past experiences.
- Ego is the storytelling identity. Who are you & who do you perceive yourself to be?
- Intellect is the capability to make true or false decisions.
- Imagery is all the data from the brain converted into the perception units of space, time & causation.

Overall, the blending of these 4 variables allows one to perceive information.

Not just data.

But meaning.

WHAT IS THE SIGNIFICANCE OF PERCEPTION?

You ever heard someone saying, 'life is one big story'?
Well, this can be viewed in a very philosophical way.
Or it can be viewed in a practical way.

Right now...
I want you to think about something.

You are currently reading what?
'Your words.'
But what are words really?
And let's go deeper....what are you reading the words on?

You're reading the words on some sort of information technology.
Maybe a tablet, computer, phone.
There are electrical signals with certain rulesets that are creating pixels.

Only ONE screen.
But a bunch of different colored pixels to give the illusion that there are differences.
And from the differences, there are words.

Well, the phone without the mind means nothing.
It's just a bunch of pixels colored in a way to represent words.

But when you add the variable of the mind...
Now you have the capability to extract meaning.
Aka information.

What is the predominant factor in terms of getting this information?

It's the story.

The story determines which of the data will be converted into information at an *experiential* level.

UNDERSTANDING THE NUANCES OF PERCEPTION

To understand the importance of storytelling on the mind…

We have to realize something.

This is not to say that we should act self-centered and be like:

Only my story matters.

It's just important to understand how information processing works.

It's important to distinguish the capabilities of the brain from the capabilities of the mind.

The 2 speak different languages.

The brain has a lot of neural connections which signify meaning, yes.

But the mind is the body we cannot see.

It's the world of experience.

And thru this first-hand world of experience, that's when data is converted into information.

This is why there are 1,000,000s of books created.

But only a few are registered by the mind.

That's because only a few are registering with past experiences, future desires & the present-day intellect.

All these variables of the mind create a holistic view of the story.

The holistic view of the narrative.

WHY PEOPLE SEE THINGS DIFFERENTLY

Humans have an objective reality as well as a subjective reality.

The mistake someone can make is applying objective rules to the subjective.

And subjective rules to the objective.

The nervous system which includes the brain, spine, sensory & motor nerves allows us to take in **data**.

Allows interacting with the environment.

But eventually, in terms of the mind....that's when we experience the **information**.

This explains why 2 people can see the same exact thing.

But perceive 2 completely different things.

Mainly because their mind, intellect, ego & memory led to a different story.

A different story that extracted a different meaning.

That's important in terms of understanding the difference between information and data.

PROCESS INFORMATION AT RAPID RATES

Hopefully, now you can understand the difference between data and information.

One is unstructured.

To extract meaning, there is a form of structuring that is required.

The structuring process can happen in a matter of seconds.

The beauty of learning comes when someone internalizes how does the brain & mind process information.

It's a game of:

Learning the instruments of the body.

Learning the language of the mind.

Humans operate on stories.

In order to extract meaning, the mind is needed.

And in order for the mind to convert the data into information, a narrative is required.

Humans are complex creatures.

Many different functionalities.

At the core level of it all, it's the narratives that are our operating system.

And it's the narrative that governs the hidden nuances of our behavior.

BENEFITS OF IMPROV

A couple of years back, one of my friends hit me up & told me to keep the 3rd Friday of the month free.

I asked why.

He said because that was the day of his improv show.

He & his team had been preparing for a long time.

And he wanted me to be in attendance.

I agreed.

On the day of the event, I was nothing short of **amazed**.

Hadn't expected what I saw...

That event had a brilliant display of storytelling, comedy, and fast thinking.

I was hooked.

Afterward, I found the host of the event & asked her how to join.

She said that they were going to be doing their next 6-week program in a few weeks.

I went to my friend & told him that he was going to be re doing his improv journey.

This time, with me.

Improv is everything & more.

In this post, we are going to learn some benefits of improv & decide the next steps.

WHAT EXACTLY IS IMPROV?

Improv is short for:

- Improvisational.

This is when you are improvising different topics to put on a show.

Maybe in terms of comedy, acting, or a bit of both.

2 very famous improv shows were "Whose Line is It Anyway" and "Wild n Out."

Just if you're looking for references.

Improvising is not easy.

Therefore, the classes host exercises & activities to build comfort.

The improv classes are different for different locations.

But the general theme is that a group of people join with a set instructor/s.

All exercises are based on the foundation of thinking on feet skills.

WHAT ARE THE BENEFITS OF IMPROV?

There are plenty of benefits.

But this post is going to discuss a few that pertain to mindset & communication skills.

Let's start with a few.

THINKING ON FEET SKILLS

There is no field or position out there that couldn't benefit from thinking on your feet.

Whether it's law, business, being an HR rep, etc.

Thinking on feet skills gets amplified when there is a group of people watching you or when the red light (recorder of a camera) is on.

I know some improv clubs which record.

But for the most part, all of them have a group of members.

This group helps add pressure, which skyrockets the thinking on feet skills process.

IMPROVED PUBLIC SPEAKING

Toastmasters is normally seen as the first club to go to in order to improve public speaking.

However, improv is a good fit as well.

Toastmasters has a formula that is applied in all clubs.

It's a brand.

Different improv clubs follow different formulas based on the location.

But the core element remains the same:

- You're talking in front of people.

Brilliant way to conquer the #1 fear in the world.

ENHANCED CREATIVITY

Humor & storytelling.

2 of the great traits for content creators.

-No one can turn down a good laugh.
-No one can turn down a good story.

And the beauty is that a lot of the topics that you're improvising on lead to you being funny and/or practicing storytelling.
Call that a 2 in 1.

Just like in the world of muscles...
What you flex becomes stronger.
Keep flexing your content creation muscle & exercise the boundaries of the creative mind.

SOCIAL CAMARADERIE

It's tough to move to a new location.
And it's tough being in the same location with friends who are not willing to grow.

Improv clubs attract people who are looking to grow.
Otherwise, you could be sitting at home watching TV.
Carrying out the same mundane routines as usual.

Improv clubs often have a certain program that will not only build improvisation skills...
But will build a social circle as well.

-It's one thing to go thru an experience by yourself.
-It's another thing to go thru an experience with a group.

Most people who are in these clubs are challenging themselves just like you.

This builds that inner fire & social bond.

These were just a few benefits of improv.

HOW DO YOU JOIN A CLUB?

Google is your best friend.
And I recommend reading the reviews for different clubs.

Just type in "improv clubs near me."
Something like that.

'Is it free?'
The one I did cost money.
But that's because I was in a program.
It was 6 weeks long.

During the 6 weeks, there are different activities & exercises to help build creativity.
This gets you working in a group.
And the group gradually builds chemistry.

The 6-week program is geared towards throwing a big show at the end.
The show has family & friends of the members who participated.

Sometimes the show can go up to 50-60 people.
Sometimes even more.

The audience members on the show day are able to participate with the members.
The improv members ask the audience for topic suggestions.

And the audience members get creative with these suggestions.

Now it's the improv member's duty to bring those suggestions to life.

Overall, if you are thinking about joining, hit up a few clubs and see if they are doing a show.

Go to a show (like I did for my friend's show) & see how you like it...

Assess if you can see yourself making a commitment.

Now the decision is on you.

SHOULD YOU JOIN AN IMPROV CLUB?

Only you can decide if you want to do improv.

But I will tell you this.

It's an experience.

In the world of communication skills, experiences are key.

It's always these experiences that make sense later on in our lives.

And even better, the experiences make sense in the present day.

In that case, we get to enjoy those moments longer.

Overall, an improv club leads to enhanced creativity, faster-thinking skills, the ability to deal with pressure...

Plus, social bonds that will last for a very long time.

Improvisation is an art form.

Sort of like impromptu speaking.

The question is:
Do you want to invest in this art form?

If you do, just know that there will be a myriad of benefits.
Benefits which will make you 6 inches taller.

OUTGROWING PEOPLE & FRIENDS

You ever had that moment where you were super cool with someone...

However, as years passed, things changed?

Conversations that were once fire are now cold.
Topics that would get both of you excited now fall flat.
And there are more awkward silences?

This sort of stuff happens in the social skills world.
The social skills world was never meant to be fixed.
It's dynamic.
Like the changing waves & weather.

There are a lot of similarities between the world of nature and the world of humans.
If you have the right perspective, then a lot of lessons present themselves.

WHAT CREATES A FRIEND IN THE FIRST PLACE?

One of the most important words in the communication world is:
Resonation.

We do a lot of things due to that word.
Resonation is when there is a match in vibrations.

When we resonate with a story, our ears tune in.
When we resonate with a product, our wallet opens.
And when we resonate with a person, the friendship is born.

Resonation can happen quickly.
Resonation can happen over time.

Look at any friendships that you have.
Humans never become friends strictly with the head.
It may start off with the head... but it eventually graduates to the heart.

That's what separates an acquaintance from a friend.

WHAT LEADS TO A RESONATION?

'What are some key components that lead to a stronger resonation?'
Well, there are plenty of variables.
But a few stick out.

-Similar interests.
-Similar social circles.
-Grand visions for the future.
These are just a few.

Once we get to know someone on a deeper level, we get a feel for them.
The feel gives us what we call the **vibe**.

The vibe is the language of the subconscious mind.

You ever had that moment when something just didn't feel right?

'Idk man, something about that dude gave me a weird vibe.'

That's the subconscious mind processing data at a rapid rate, then an interpretation is being assigned.

What's not given enough focus is the exact OPPOSITE phenomena.

Where you don't have much data on the person...

But for some reason, you are DRAWN to the person.

This is the opposite of the creepy vibe.

The subconscious mind can tell that this person has something that you will resonate with.

It's just a matter of finding out.

WHEN RESONATIONS DISAPPEAR

'I've had a lot of friends throughout my life. But many have come & many gave gone. Why?'

Outgrowing people & friends happens due to physical reasons & mental reasons.

Physical reasons are when geographic locations are bought up.

This is when one party moves away from the other party.

Moving neighborhoods, cities, states....country.

When a physical barrier is introduced, more importance is placed on communications technology.

Aka, social media, text messages, phone calls, etc.

Some friends are able to follow up through communications technology & maintain the social bond.

Other times, it's even difficult to do that.

When the parties are not following up even thru technology,
the connection dissipates.

Another reason can be due to mental reasons.
This is when the content of a conversation is changing.

One group is all about leveling up & evolving as a person.
While the other person is still living in the past.

Talking bout how they were the 'man' in college.
There are people who are pushing their 30s, still going to
college parties.
This is a dude living in the past.

When the content of the mindset changes, now a mental
barrier is introduced.
And a mental barrier is what we call the silent killer in
friendships.

WHEN COMFORTABLE SILENCES TURN AWKWARD

You ever noticed the silence?
'Ya. What about it?'
Well, silence has 2 effects.
It can either be soothing...
While at other times, it has the polar opposite effect.
It's hella awkward.

Friends can often be silent around each other for a long time
without it being weird.
While on the flip side, being silent for too long with an
acquaintance has you feeling weird.

Well, when the silences go from soothing to awkward, that's a red flag for friendships.

-One time, it's one thing.

-Multiple times, it's another thing.

The awkward silence is the warning sign for things to come.

This is a sign of outgrowing people.

The content of the mind is too different at this point.

Running out of conversation material.

The vibe feels weird.

Resonation...disappearing?

CAN LOST FRIENDSHIPS EVER BE SALVAGED?

One problem with some people who enter the self-improvement space is that they get carried away.

This is a newbie... Not a veteran.

Saw a dude on Facebook a while back saying that they were going to block a bunch of their friends for not wanting more out of life.

And then saw this person's friend list dwindling away.

He was keeping up with his promise!

Since I was able to see his friend list, you can tell I wasn't one of the guys deleted.

Whew!

But is it really "whew!" ?

This is a person who is quick to cut others off.

This is a person who wears self-improvement like a fashion sense.

'Look at me, I'm improving. You should be like me.'
Ego **move.**

It's better to leave communication lines open unless malice was involved.
'Big word for me bro. What's malice exactly?'
Malice = Bad intent.
Aka: a fake friend.

If the friend you outgrew didn't do anything to backstab you...
Leave the communication lines open.

Friends may outgrow one another.
But no one ever said that they cannot grow back together.

Different experiences shape different people at different rates.
Although the strength of the friendship dissipated.
Content of the minds altered...
And resonation is low...

Leave the communication open.
Maybe one day, you 2 will reunite again.

ACCEPTING THE SOCIAL WORLD & GROWING REGARDLESS

There are a lot of social principles we learn along the way.
It's because the human dynamic is like an everchanging wave.
And each person's subjective experience is different.

But by understanding the lessons from others, it's easier to pick up the lessons for ourselves.

Becoming a social scientist in our life requires precision & practice.

Outgrowing people is just a part of life.
It's not weird.

But beware, there's a big difference between outgrowing people & incessantly burning bridges.

That'll show if you're in the wrong, they are in the wrong or that nothing is wrong.

Always make these decisions picturing the world is smaller than it is.

Because surprisingly, the world IS smaller than it is.

Unless malice was involved, operate with the assumption that you may see this person one day... again.

And hopefully, when you see them again, you can recall the good memories rather than being reminded of what went wrong.

DO AFFIRMATIONS WORK? MY HONEST RESPONSE

This blog discusses communication skills.
And a big part of communication skills includes *words*.

Well, guess what else has words?
'Uh...'
Affirmations.

"Affirmations" is a popular phrase in many self-improvement spheres & law of attraction circles.
Some people know what they are talking about.
And others are using the phrase without proper knowledge.

'Who are you to say what is proper knowledge and what isn't??'
That's a good question.
And a smart question.
And this question will be the theme of what I want to discuss.

WHAT IS AN AFFIRMATION?

An affirmation is a:
Phrase that is repeated in order to lead to a behavioral change.

There can be different definitions in terms of wordplay.
But this covers a core idea of what it means.

'How often is the phrase repeated?'
That depends.

For some people, they do it first thing in the morning.

For other people, they do it first thing in the morning and the last thing at night.

In many Eastern cultures, the affirmation is viewed in a different context.

It's viewed more as a mantra.

And many of those cultures repeat the mantra continuously throughout the day to steady & purify the mind.

So **repetition** is a key factor of an affirmation.

And the second key is that it should lead to a change.

'What kind of a change?'

A **change in behavior** that is meaningful to you.

Initially, I told you that it's a good question that you called me out on saying that some do not have the proper knowledge.

'Why?'

Because proper knowledge is personal to us.

Only we can decide if it works.

FROM OBJECTIVE TO SUBJECTIVE

Objectivity is something that can easily be measured.

Subjectivity is more difficult to measure because of the human experiences which are involved.

In terms of repetition, that's objective.

It's clear to measure how many times you did it.

But in terms of subjective...

The emotions, experiences, changes in behavior, that's more *personal*.

The key to remember is that affirmations are meant to **spark a change.**

And it's difficult (if not impossible) to spark a long-lasting change if your emotions are not involved.

The main reason the repetition is required is because the mind learns that way.

The mind often learns via pain & repetition.

This is when a few problems occur.

'Problems?'

Yea, let me explain.

PROBLEMS SOME PEOPLE HAVE WITH AFFIRMATIONS

Anytime a movement get's popularized, it attracts lazy & uninformed people.

And this group is often the loudest.

Two big problems in regards to affirmations some have are:

1. being too objective.
2. being too word focused.

1. BEING TOO OBJECTIVE

This group thinks repetition is all that is needed.

And they believe repetition alone will take them to the final destination.

Repetition is better than doing nothing.
However, that's not optimal.

It's like going to a 5-star restaurant & ordering a grand meal.
Getting your food delivered...
Just to drink the water & dip..
Food untouched.

Valuing the objective too much does not engage the subjective.
'And how can I exactly feel an emotion? That's hard.'
Exactly.
This is why point 2 is just as important.

2. BEING TOO WORD FOCUSED

Words are just the tip of the iceberg.
It's impossible to truly engage your subjective side without
action.

'Wait, I gotta put in work? I thought I was just supposed to
recite some stuff...'
Nope, not at all.

The work is what engages the subjective side.
That's when the words you were reciting starts to pick up life
IN you.

'But wait. If I need to work...Then what's the point of
affirmations at all?'
-Affirmations are like the steering wheel for the mind.
-Work is the gasoline.

For a lot of individuals, when they work, they are operating with limiting beliefs.

- *I can't do this... but guess I'll show up anyways.*
- *I hate this work.*
- *Man, I wish I was watching a tv show fiddling with my balls just about now.*

They are mechanically doing the work.

However, it's not good work.

Not pure work.

Affirmations get the mind & body in harmony over time.

HOW DO I KNOW IF THE AFFIRMATIONS WORKED?

'Okay, you're saying I need to put in work?'

Yes.

'You're saying affirmations work as a steering wheel?'

Correct.

'Then how do I know if these affirmations are actually working for me?'

Great question.

Here's what I noticed...

When people initially hear about affirmations, their ego gets involved.

A part of them becomes a bit greedy.

Normal.

They make a list of a WHOLE bunch of affirmations.

Like a little kid who is going to ask Santa for a bunch of gifts.

Once again, normal.

As they list out 50 affirmations...they spend days, weeks, months reciting them.
Highly disciplined.

At this point, a few people match the affirmation with work ethic.
And by few, I truly do mean *few*.

As some time goes by...something magical happens.
'What?'
The affirmations are slowly becoming less and less.
'Meaning?'
Meaning that the 50 affirmations are morphing into 3.
Which may even evolve into 1.

This is when the subconscious mind is engaged.
This is when all the excess words are falling off.
You are getting straight to the source.

From the 50 affirmations, now you know 1 is the source.
And all others are derivatives of that.

So at this point, rather than mindlessly reciting 50 affirmations.
You can mindfully recite 1 affirmation, which allows your behavior to morph drastically.

'So were the 50 initial affirmations a waste of time?'
No. Those 50 laid down the groundwork. The infrastructure.
And now those multiple moving parts of the infrastructure is leading to the emergent property.

You needed to go thru the 50 to narrow down…

That's what I noticed for people who did affirmations with work ethic for overtime.

For ~2+ years-ish.

If you find all 50 of your affirmations just as relevant now as you did in the beginning…

Then go with your experiences.

FINAL VERDICT ON AFFIRMATIONS

Fields that require objectivity & subjectivity often say 'it depends' alot.

'Do affirmations work??'

It depends.

If you match the recitation with work ethic…

Then you'll feel the emotions over time.

The emotions are what will be responsible for behavioral transformations.

So in this case, the answer is **yes**.

If you are just mindlessly reciting, and sloppy with your discipline, the answer is a staggering:

Fuck no.

Nope, it will not work for you.

Ultimately, anything that has a subjective element will require you to decide the answer for yourself.

Maintain that work ethic.

And cultivate the faith.

A lot of individuals start something.
Half ass it.
Quit.

And surprisingly, these people are the most vocal.
When you ask them, do affirmations work?
They confidently say 'trust me man, it doesn't work.'

Smart people see thru the noise.
They try it out for themselves.
And then they live with the results.
Like the scientist of THEIR life.

EVOLVING OUT OF
THE VICTIM MINDSET

It feels like victimhood is on the rise.
How so?
Better yet, *why so?*

Look around you...
Information technology is richer than ever.
Books & high-value content are cheaper than ever..
And there are more services that make life easier...

So what's the issue?
A human's personal narrative.

You can fix the outside world with the latest gadgets and technology.
But you can't easily fix a human's personal narrative.
'Why not?'
Because that's a choice on their end.

Can't help someone who doesn't find anything worth fixing.

However, if the victim mindset is on the rise, then it's important to understand that victors are becoming rarer.
If you consider yourself a victor, it's not correct to scoff at a victim.

A better strategy is to learn their mindset.
Understand how to communicate with them if you come across them.

And if you consider yourself a victim, it's time to understand why you move the way you do.

And if you have no clue what is a victor & what is a victim, then continue to read on.

VICTOR MINDSET VS VICTIM MINDSET

'So what's the difference between the 2 groups bro?'

I can explain it in 2 sentences.

-Victims undermine what they can control & amplify what they can't.

-Victors undermine what they can't control & amplify what they can.

This is the core difference.

'How did the 2 groups become so different?'

Due to a decision.

Our childhood indicates that we are wired to be victims.

We come onto this planet crying & whining when we don't get things our way.

Rarely do we show accountability at a young age.

To graduate to victor status, it needs to come down to a decision.

And that's what all victors have in common.

They made that decision.

'How do they demonstrate that decision?'

Thru acts.

Victors consciously practice acts like gratitude, skill-building, lifelong learning, etc.

Victims subconsciously practice acts like whining, finger-pointing & entertaining toxic people to reinforce limiting beliefs.

CAN A VICTIM EVOLVE?

Charles Darwin talked about the survival of the fittest.
That's his understanding of evolution.

Well, it looks like Charle's Darwin's view on evolution is evolving in itself.
We are no longer just a world of survival of the fittest.
We are now a world of survival of the smartest.

Our world is becoming more and more MIND focused.
Especially in the information age.
Yet, very few people are on time for this party.

Victims have to evolve because this is a world of fast-paced change.
The victim mindset may have worked in the industrial age without much repercussions... but it'll be a different story in the upcoming ages.

'Why do you say that?'
Because in the industrial age, a lot of jobs were capable of requiring minimal cognitive effort once learned.
You could bitch and moan as much as you wanted.
As long as you executed the repetitive task, the owners were happy.

Nowadays?
You bitch & moan too much, then owners & smart entrepreneurs will replace you with code.

If there can be procedures made for a job, it may be automated down the line.

Therefore, victims **need** to evolve.

We are transitioning into the era of creativity & the survival of the smartest.

At a faster pace than imaginable.

HOW DOES A VICTIM MINDSET EVOLVE?

Mindsets are malleable.

The mind & our nervous system are joined to the hip.

New research is coming out showing that the brain has plasticity (neuroscience), deliberate practice can rewire our nervous system, & repetition changes our reticular activating system.

But all these studies don't mean shit without one big concept.

'And what is that?'

Accountability.

It's impossible to shift a behavior without accountability.

Accountability is defined as taking responsibility for one's thoughts, emotions & behavior.

And this transition is something that is worked up to.

Therefore, accountability is a PROCESS.

Accountability is like love.

'Huh...'

Let me explain...

Let's say I give you a puppy and tell you to love this puppy...RIGHT NOW.

You will try to... but will not feel anything.
In order to love this puppy, you need some time.

The love will emerge when a certain process takes place.

Let's say you take the puppy under your roof.
The puppy comes to your bed when you are about to sleep, showing human behaviors.
Let's say you're sad one day, and the puppy comes to comfort you....
Slowly, you are seeing the puppy from a different angle, warming you up to this animal.

All these acts of being exposed to the puppy BUILDS loves.

Similarly, accountability isn't something that you just do overnight.
It's a decision that you make...and now you work towards it over time.

HOW DOES ONE TAKE ACCOUNTABILITY?

So now we understand that accountability comes down to taking control of our internal world.
The question is, how do we do it?

It's a game of starting to feed the right narratives to our minds.
I've never seen someone empower their mind by inputting junk into it.

That means detoxing losers & idiots from social media & real life, who just whine all day.
Turn down the garbage on mainstream media.
And start consuming more empowering content.

That's not to say you shut yourself off from the world & what's going on.

Just understand that there's no such thing as a clean 50/50 split in the real world.

It's always ONE side dominating, while we are aware of another side.

Which side do you want to dominate?

The light or dark?

That's the choice.

The next part is to focus on what you can control & undermine what you can't.

This builds **momentum** in changing the personal narrative.

The mind of victimhood is the exact opposite.

This tendency of victims to get caught up on what they can't control has them running their mouth a lot and finger-pointing.

But little is getting done.

Making a difference comes down to priming the mind to focus on what it can control.

This is different for different people in context to their life.

These 2 decisions are how accountability is slowly built.

1. Consume empowering content & detox the negativity.

2. Focus on what is controllable, and undermine what isn't controllable.

These 2 acts will start a tsunami & start rewiring the mind.

Especially in the era that we are headed towards.

Evolution doesn't discriminate.

THE TOP 3%

The masses, unfortunately, perpetuate mainly negative news.

And making a transition from victim to victor will not come without conflict.

Especially if most friends are forcing their personal narratives on you.

However, this is the first challenge towards the life of a victor.

It's time to take the steps to go past the narratives that have been formed from generalized cultures.

To control large masses of humans, media & figures of power give them the illusion that they are powerless.

They feed them the wrong knowledge.

'Why would figures of power intentionally create victims?'

Because the victim mindset is easy to profit from & easier to control.

Victims fuel the consumerism culture.

Only 3% will break out.

But hey, better 3% than 0%.

This is the best era to be a victor.

One who is able to capitalize on the opportunities that are all around us.

Change the personal narrative.

Change personal behaviors.

Call that magic.

HOW TO CONTROL YOUR EMOTIONS

Our emotions have a big say in our life.

It's one of the elements of our internal world that we can never run away from.

I'm sure plenty of us have heard the phrase:

The mind can make a heaven out of hell & a hell out of heaven.

I believe it should be:

The mind AND emotions can make a heaven out of hell & a hell out of heaven.

When you break it down, the memories that we remember are the ones that have a strong emotion attached to it.

We have been thru years & years of experiences in our life.

However, only a few stick out.

That's because those few that stick out had the strongest emotional charge.

You'll be surprised how many people are living in the past.

That's because their memories are fixed in the past.

This is the mind of a victim.

In the life of a victor, emotions are our servant.

Therefore, it's imperative that we control them.

FIXING OUR BELIEFS

'What would you say is the most important part of learning how to control our emotions?'

Knowing that we can.
'Haha seriously.'
I'm serious.

I spent years thinking that emotions were fixed.
Thought that's just the way it was.

However, my perspective started to change as I grew older.
Things that would bother me ALOT slowly started to melt away.

One example was public speaking.
My early childhood consisted of shyness & speech anxiety.

However, joining a Toastmasters allowed me to work past that speech anxiety.
That speech anxiety slowly turned into speech excitement.

Hm... fascinating.
So if an emotion can be switched at one point in life, can it be switched at other points?
Of course.

Stop.

Now take a walk down memory lane.
How many times have you been able to control your emotions?
It can be something big.
It can be something small.

Just find a moment when you didn't react to an emotion, were able to regulate energy levels or...
Stopped yourself from tailgating the car that tailgated you.

IDENTIFYING OUR TRIGGERS

Every human has a different trigger for different reactions.

What is a trigger?

A trigger is a stimulus that we feel before a reaction or response. The trigger serves as a narrative.

It's extremely difficult to control our emotions when we are in the heat of the moment.

What's smarter is to find the trigger that happens in the BUILD-UP to the heat of the moment.

Back to the public speaking example.

During my bouts with speech anxiety, I noticed I had a trigger of:

'What if I fail? What if I forget my speech & the audience won't stop laughing?'

That was a BIG trigger for me. Forgetting the speech.

That was my worst fear.

'What did you do?'

I believe becoming **aware** of the trigger is more than enough.

Trying to logic with the trigger can be a little excessive.

What allowed me to deal with the trigger was to expect it.

So once it would come, I would not react to it.

And if it did not come, then it was a pleasant moment.

See if you can spot moments of feeling angry, anxious or sad.

What is that typical moment when you know you will react?

Now ask yourself, is there a trigger that you feel?

This trigger will be a narrative.

A narrative not in your favor. This narrative tries to paint you as the victim.

Spot that narrative & bring awareness to it.

LEVERAGING THE TRIGGER INTO REGULATION

The next thing to be aware of is that controlling the trigger is no easy task.

It's easy to logically say: 'I will calm down when I notice the trigger so I don't make a fool of myself.'

Easier said than done lol.

You need to realize that learning how to control your emotions is a PRACTICE.

Just like a basketball player does not shoot a dozen free throws & say they will never have to practice again.

That's idiotic.

As a professional, they need to work on their game as long as they are a professional.

Likewise, we need to work on our emotional control as long as we are human.

You see, emotions are wired to be chaotic.

Same with the mind.

The mind & emotions thrive off chaos.

Therefore, spotting the trigger is one thing.

The next part is getting comfortable with the uncomfortable.

Not doing anything is one of the toughest things to do.

Let's say your weak spot is getting sad when someone comments mean stuff on your social media posts.

You feel the trigger of 'this person is trying to attack my character.'

Plus, the trigger has STRONG physical sensations in your body.

The next action would be to do nothing. Ignore the person.

Difficult, right?

'Very difficult.'

Good.

View this as a workout for your internal world.

It's not simple. Just like when we lift weights.

But it gets easier with practice.

So doing NOTHING is one of the most difficult things to do.

But this proves an EQ concept...

'What is that concept?'

That you are in control.

Not your emotions.

ADD ACTIVITY TO NOTHING

What makes great sports players powerful is that they are able to absorb the criticism & channel it back into their craft.

This is what I call *emotional alchemy.*

You don't need to stop at just ignoring the person who wrote a mean comment.

How about you ignore it...

THEN, you get all those uncomfortable emotions & channel them back into your social media content.

You're killing 2 birds with 1 stone:

-Conditioning the concept of being in charge of your emotions.

-Using renewed emotions to channel to your mind. Which unlocks different thought waves.

Haven't you ever wondered what creativity was?
Creativity = Structured Emotions

Therefore, the act of holding & rechanneling is a powerful way to prime your mind to find practical use in uncomfortable emotions.

This can be applied to all contexts where discomfort is involved.

During rock bottom, use the energy to go to the gym.

When getting cut off in traffic, force yourself to remain at speed level. This builds concentration skills during pressure.

In getting mean comments...use it as fuel to keep outdoing your prior work.

Make it a game.

CONTROLLING YOUR NARRATIVE

Communication skills are a game of emotional management.

And it's a game that we are in charge of.

All the training & books out there...
But others cannot feel your emotions for you.

People try to take shortcuts though.
They either bury the pain or find others to distract them.
This is a short term solution for short term thinkers.

The mind & emotions can make a heaven out of hell or a hell out of heaven.

When you are in control of how you feel, that's when your behavior comes under your command.

Not someone else's.

That's how you remain the ventriloquist to your mind and body, rather than being the puppet to someone else's narrative.

Control your energy, control your life.

WHY DO I OVERTHINK?

Overthinking has you creating problems that never existed.
It turns the small into gargantuan.

Our mind can be our best friend or worst enemy.
And unfortunately for many, it is an enemy.

The mind at a natural state is high in entropy.
Meaning, if it is left unchecked, it will resort to chaos.

Sort of like your car.
If you don't maintain your car, give it gas, do oil changes...
Then it will devolve.

Overthinking is a sign of HIGH entropy.

Our goal is to lower the entropy via knowledge & action.

You'll be surprised how much knowing why you do what you do, helps you engineer your future.
Today, you asked 'why do I overthink?'
And today, I will give you a response.

THE SOURCE OF OUR WORRIES

Have you ever analyzed your worries?
What sparks the overthinking in the first place?
Answering that question does a lot of good.

You'll notice a lot of your worries tend to be in RELATION to something.

It is rarely a standalone topic.

'Not sure what you're saying bro.'

Let me explain.

We are not afraid of failing.
We are afraid of being JUDGED for failing.

So your worries are rarely about you failing your speech because you are worried about the speech.

It's more so in context with some figure judging you in terms of your choking your talk.

Other worries are relationally based as well.

You are always comparing yourself to something.

If you are worried about your future, then you are comparing the present with the future.

You aren't just worried about the present.

Something took you out of the present & a comparison is being made.

This allows you to trace back a lot of worries.

When you compare too much, you create potential energy of awkwardness.

Even in social interactions.

You create a figment of 'what is the right thing to say.'

And try to compare it with how you are behaving.

Problems are being created out of thin air!

So what I want you to know is that a lot of overthinking stems from a comparison of some sort being made.

Whether the comparison is a judgment from others, time-based, or how you think you should behave.

WHY THINKING IS OVERRATED

If you were to tell me a few years ago, that thinking is overrated, I'd call you stupid.

I mean...isn't that the LITERAL definition of someone who is stupid?

A person who doesn't think?

Nah.

- Stupid is when someone thinks in logical inconsistencies.
- Peace is when someone can stop thinking at will.

Our problem is that we confuse consciousness as thinking.

That's a BIG mistake.

And this is why we overthink.

Consciousness is our awareness.

Thinking is a faculty of consciousness.

Let me give you an example.

John has a smartphone where he surfs the web.

Surfing the web allows him to learn, grow his online business & network.

With me so far?

'Yes.'

But is it smart for John to ALWAYS be surfing the web?

'No.'

Why?

'Because once he has used the web, now it's time to come back to real life.'

Exactly.

Our thinking faculties allow us to problem solve, imagine & create.

But once we are done using it, we need to turn it off and just exist.

When you see a baby laughing, you feel this level of joy.

You aren't thinking.

When you see a cute puppy, you feel a level of warmth.

You aren't thinking.

When you are talking to your best friend, you feel relaxed.

You aren't thinking.

You are BEING.

Even when the intellect is stilled, you are still awake.

You don't die.

That's when you come alive.

IT ALL BEGINS WITH AWARENESS TO THE ISSUE

So thus far, we understand that we overthink because of some comparison being made.

The comparison can happen in a range of different contexts.

The comparisons, unfortunately, is taking us away from the present.

And with the era we live in, being pulled away from the present has become the norm.

It has become SOO much of the norm, that nowadays, we confuse consciousness as thinking.

Our generation is in hyperdrive mode all the time.

We are a bunch of people always with faces on our screen, confusing the digital world as reality.

And that's the same thing happening in terms of overthinking.

We assume that our thoughts are the real world.

While in reality, they are not.

In order to become more present, you need to realize that presence is your essence.

Overthinking is not natural.

'Not natural? Well, that's mean Armani!'

It's not really mean. It's a statement that helps you spark change.

If I told you that your dirty plate in the sink was naturally dirty, would you have any inclination to clean it?

'Haha, not really.'

What if I told you that your dirty plate was TEMPORARILY dirty. And your goal is to wipe off the dirt.

'Now I would clean it because there is a reward.'

Exactly.

At a natural level, you are conscious & aware.

Your goal is to turn down thinking faculties.

'How?'

With a decision and reminders.

TURNING DOWN YOUR THOUGHTS

Overthinking does not go away on its own.

It would be a perfect world if it did though.

Overthinking melts away the more that you start treating the mind like a muscle.

I told you in the last section that you are naturally present, we just need to get you back to your original form.

Therefore, you need to do some mental workouts.

You don't want to overdo this.

The 2 most popular methods are mindfulness and meditation.

A mix between the 2 is powerful.

But you can just incorporate one.

I recommend starting off with meditation and gradually transitioning into mindfulness.

Meditation is when you pick a target & focus your mind on that.

When you lose focus, make yourself aware & gently bring yourself back to the target.

Mindfulness is when you are actively remaining aware throughout your day.

When you get lost in thoughts, you gently bring yourself back to the present moment.

The key is that we are building your awareness.

The more aware you become, the more your mind self corrects.

Entropy lowers.
And you think, rather than overthink.

But even more beautiful?
You can CHOOSE when to think & when to turn your thinking faculties off.
That's a special kind of peace.

Start off light & work your way up.
2 min a day beats 30 min every now and then.

Go back to your natural essence.
See life in a different way.
No one wins when you overthink.

Think less & be present.

OVERTHINKING A LITTLE LESS EVERYDAY

When you go thru your first-ever breakup, you feel pain.
And a part of you wonders, how long is this going to last?
Give me an exact date man!!

But that's the incorrect question.
The right approach is…you just take it one day at a time.

Take it one day at a time to improve & level up.
And as the days pile up, you realize that you are now stronger than the pain.

That's how it is with overthinking.
You are wondering: 'Why do I overthink and when will it end?'

Just know that your mind is always going to want to hop from thought to thought.

But you are still consistent, day to day, with some sort of mental workout.

You'll realize your awareness is STRONGER than the hopping thoughts.

That's when you'll realize you are not your thoughts.

You are not your feelings.

You are something much more.

And a stilled present life will be a byproduct.

WHAT IS WILLPOWER & HOW TO BUILD IT

There are plenty of types of personalities out there.
Some are determined.
And some give up at the first sight of conflict.

We associate willpower with something complex.
Yet, it's best when we view willpower as something simple.

The willpower of a human will determine whether they become great or fail miscrably.
Quitting showcases the weakness of willpower or sharp judgment.

'How can you bring up 2 polarities like that?'
Well, sometimes, quitting is smart.

Let's say you're a 45-year-old man who is 4 foot 7, dreaming to become a center in the NBA.
This may be a dream you pursue for a while.

Until one day, you come to terms with the ridiculousness of the goal.
Mainly due to physical setbacks.

A lot of goals aren't like that though.
Many times we quit just because we have weak willpower.

Can it be strengthened?
Of course.
And that's what this post is about.

WHAT IS WILLPOWER?

Will power is defined differently by different people.

I define willpower as:

The ability to take purposeful action despite the good and the bad.

That's you extending past duality.

You show up whether you feel like it or not.

It's easy to show up when things are going well.

However, it's difficult to show up when we aren't seeing improvement.

Or worse, when we are seeing negative improvement lol.

During those moments, we may:

1. Quit.
2. Carry out the actions with a loss of enthusiasm.

Both of the acts showcase poor willpower.
Especially part 2.

Quitting means you have thrown in the towel.

At least, there was a commitment.

But doing tasks in a lazy fashion is bad because not only are you showcasing poor willpower...

You are also showcasing indecision.

No thanks...

HOW TO IMPROVE WILL POWER?

Earlier in this blog, I said that will power was about simplicity, not complexity.

So here's my solution for a stronger willpower:

1. Understand that willpower is a muscle that can be exercised.
2. Exercise the muscle by constantly bringing yourself BACK to the task at hand.

Step 1 is the philosophy.

Step 2 is the practical aspect.

Both reinforce one another.

The philosophy aspect is learning the art of a growth mindset.

A growth mindset is when we believe anything worth learning can be learned as long as we have the physical faculties for it.

If you have the physical faculties for it, now it's a game of the mind.

In order to internalize this philosophy, we must put it into practice.

And the practice comes down to utter simplicity.

Just bring yourself BACK to the task at hand fam.

The reason I used the word "BACK" is to illustrate that the assumption is already being made that we will stray away.

It's just human nature.

Let's say you are starting a New Year's resolution to go to the gym.

You may be motivated in the beginning stages.

But there may be a point when you stray away from the goal.

At that moment, you have the perfect chance to exercise willpower.

Sort of like a mental rep.

WHY WILL MANY FAIL WITH WILLPOWER?

Many will fail with willpower because they simply don't understand the concept of bringing themselves BACK.
That's it.

This is one reason why people fail at meditation.
They sit down to count their breaths.

As they start counting their breaths, they get distracted by the mind.
Which is to be expected...

The goal is to just make yourself aware and bring the mind BACK.
However, this is when they start getting too intellectually involved.

- *'Am I doing something wrong?'*
- *'Why am I not figuring this out? I mean I have been practicing meditation for a staggering 3 minutes.'*
- *'Is meditation a scam?'*

Blah blah blah.
Making everything complex.
Just shut up & bring your awareness BACK.

Likewise, we do the same thing with following a task thru.
We get to intellectually involved, making everything complex.

At times, intellect is needed.
However, other times, intellect is meant to be suspended.

And the heart needs to be showcased.

Willpower requires heart.
And anytime you are showing that heart, the less thinking, the better.
Just shut up and bring yourself back to the task.

You strayed...
All good.
We all do.

Just realign yourself BACK to the path as a slightly stronger version of yourself.
That 'slightly' will turn astronomical as long as you stay consistent.

How Long Does It Take To See Improvement?

I believe anything worth doing in life requires an investment time of at least 6 months.
That's the mantra.
6 months or bust.

The reason I don't follow the 21 days to build a habit rule is because it doesn't work for me.
21 days feels too light.

There are a lot of micro bad habits that need to be worked out.
Limiting beliefs, poor lifestyle, poor friends, etc.
21 days does not seem to present enough time.

6 months primes your mind to think long term.

And even though this seems daunting...
It brings out even MORE enthusiasm.

You set into your venture with realistic expectations & feel like you are truly committing to something.

Imagine how many people would have amazing physiques if they committed at least 6 months for their New Years resolution.
Rather than saying 'we'll see how it goes.'

6 months or bust.
For 6 months, just keep bringing yourself BACK to the task.
Do the task with FULL enthusiasm.
You'll be surprised how much stronger your internal motivation becomes.

Once the 6 months are done, you will find it difficult to stop, even if you wanted to...

BUILDING AN IRON WILL

Willpower is a powerful soft skill.
It does not discriminate against anyone.
And can be manifested in any position of life.

Whether you're a home keeper, an entrepreneur, college student, etc.
Willpower is a skill set that anyone should look to improve.

The world has enough lazy bums.
However, the world has a few hard workers with social skills.

If you can exercise your willpower, that's when you adopt a growth mindset.

A growth mindset makes you a pleasant person to be around. Not always being negative or competing with others.

Rather, spreading abundance & becoming a creator.

The willpower of a person is a direct look into their character. And it's that character that will allow them to stand the ups & downs of the game of life.

UNDERSTANDING THE MONKEY MIND

Have you ever had that moment where you were going from thought to thought?

Sort of like a monkey swinging from branch to branch?

There is a name for that phenomenon.

It's called the monkey mind.

If you are WILLINGLY jumping from thought to thought, that's one thing.

But if you are UNABLE TO CONTROL your mind, then it's the jumping monkey.

No fun.

One of the top reasons for anxiety is mind wandering.

Mind-wandering is the dark brother of daydreaming.

When our mind wanders too much, we dwell.

And dwelling is introspection minus the intent.

That's when we are just asking ourselves 'what if' questions.

Time is never wasted when you learn about the mind.

It's information that helps you control your subjective reality.

Your internal world.

This blog will cover the monkey mind on a deeper level.

You will learn about different brain functioning modes and how to tame the inner monkey on a macro + micro level.

Without further ado...let us begin.

THE ORIGINS OF THE MONKEY MIND

Our brain has 2 different modes.

- Default Mode Network
- Task Positive Network

The Default mode network is when our mind is wandering.
Task Positive Network is when we are focused.

As you are reading this blog, I am hoping you are in a task-positive network.
But who knows...
You may be daydreaming & just going thru the words.

No one can fully know which brain mode you are in other than you...
There are ways an outsider may be able to tell though.

Example:
You are having a conversation with someone.
And you go from STRONG eye contact to WEAK eye contact.
In this case, the other person may be able to deduce that you stopped focusing.

Being in the Default Mode Network is not always evil.
At times, it is highly needed.
Aka: rest.

After a long time of focusing & being productive, you need to give your mind time to relax.

My definition of resting is giving yourself time to be mindless.

But when you spend too much time in the default mode network?

That's when you get an abundance of anxiety.

SCROLLING & THE MONKEY MIND

In the information age, the monkey mind issue is on the rise.

Heck, I may argue this can be considered a mental disease if left unchecked.

'Whoa Armani!! you are exaggerating.'

No, I am not. Hear me out.

Distraction is an invisible muscle.

The more that we work it out, the stronger than it gets.

What do you consider scrolling?

'Nothing...I just consider it scrolling.'

Try again.

'Not sure where you are going with this.

I consider excessive scrolling a WORKOUT for your distraction muscle.

Why though?

It's because each content piece you are going thru has a different subject matter.

Let's say you are going thru Facebook.

One second, you are seeing a picture of your friend's new puppy.

The next second, you see a picture of your cousin getting married.

Then your co-worker getting a new job.

And so on...

You're conditioning your mind to hop from thought to thought.
By the time you put your phone down, the effects still remain.
This is a great look into how online reality influences offline reality.

The reason that this is a major problem in our generation is that communications technology is on the rise.
And the ease of access to this technology is almost nonexistent.

In the early 2000s, our definition of using the phone was making calls or playing the Snake game.
But nowadays, the smartphone used incorrectly can make the monkey more vicious.

SIDE EFFECTS OF THE MONKEY MIND

There are a lot of different side effects of the monkey mind.
Some effects are:
-Higher irritability.
-Less focus.
-Enhanced anxiety.
-Impulsive behavior.
Etc.

These are the many ways that the monkey mind can affect our lives.
And our relationship with our internal world influences our external world.
Meaning that our monkey mind will not only harm us.
It will affect our relationships.

It's a sad feeling when you don't feel heard.
Well, guess what?
'What?'
Your monkey mind disengages you from an interaction.
Causing you to be the reason that others do not feel heard.

They see your body.
But mentally, it's as though you were somewhere else.
Dangerous bud.

HOW TO TAME THE MONKEY MIND

The opposite of the Monkey Mind is the Bullseye mind.
The mind with a target.

You see...
Your mind naturally thinks in LINKS.
It tries its best to link from one thought to the next.
Well, the Bullseye mind gives those links a DIRECTION.

To give you an analogy:
Let's say you are looking to get something to eat.

The only problem is that you didn't identify where you wanted
to go to eat.
You just went into the car, hoping to 'figure it out.'

What normally happens?
'I drive aimlessly burning a lot of gas.'
Exactly.

But what if you decide where you want to go and THEN begin driving?

'Then I satiate my hunger quicker.'

Exactly.

Listen.

It's the nature of the mind to go from thought to thought.

So if that's the case, wouldn't it be dope if the mind wandering served you some benefit?

In this case, I recommend working on a grand life purpose.

This may seem over the top to you, but it isn't.

When you have a grand life goal, your monkey mind begins to get disciplined to a certain level.

This is a great macro-level discipline to install.

Let's say you have a business that you are working on.

If you can give your mind a BULLSEYE to be the best as you can be in that business, then the default mode network settles down slightly.

With a life purpose, information takes up a new life as well.

That's the macro level to taming the monkey mind.

Keep experimenting with different things until you find something you want to gear your life towards.

The micro-level way to tame the monkey mind is thru meditation.

This is when you set aside a certain amount of time every day in order to focus on one singular target.

Many people set aside time to focus on their natural breaths.

When they get distracted, they make themselves aware &
gently come back to the breath.

However, the beauty of a life purpose?
Your work can be your meditation.

My grand goal is to keep working on ArmaniTalks & develop
compelling stories that help others with communication skills.

Well, writing this blog, working on my YouTube channel,
Twitter, etc are all forms of meditation to me.

When I am engulfed in the task, I truly am ENGULFED.

This allows me to spend more time in the task-positive network
and settle down the default mode network.

I exercise my focus.

Once I am done, I relax and allow my mind to wander.

To tame the monkey mind, a blend of working on your life
goals & meditation will give profound results!

CONTROL THE MONKEY

The monkey mind is the natural state of the mind.

Our mindset is high entropy when we do not work on it.

Meaning that it is high in chaos.

Which also is another phrase for mind wandering.

Therefore, we need to TRAIN the mind.

We need to train the monkey.

And we train the monkey by developing our will power!

I gave you the macro & micro level adjustments that you need
to make in your life.

By no means is this an easy task.

Which is why it makes the journey fun.

Remember, your mind is a problem-solving machine.

When you feed it the right problems, it will work on hyperdrive to fix the issues.

When you run away from problems, it will create problems nevertheless.

So ask yourself, what is the bullseye of your life?

Work on that specified target.

As you have that, find the daily tasks of that goal.

There will be 3-4 tasks that you will have to daily to move towards the goal.

Do those tasks with FULL focus.

That's your personalized meditation.

And take it a level further with formal meditation.

Have the monkey serve you!

Not the other way around.

Let's tame the monkey mind & gain control!

THE POWER OF PERSPECTIVE SHIFTING IN TODAY'S WORLD

There's a famous saying that goes like:
There are 3 sides to a coin. Heads, tails & the edge.

This is a powerful concept to internalize, especially when it comes to your perception of life.

We have our perspective.
The other person's perspective.

But there is also a mythical edge that exists.

What is contained in that edge?
Hm... Great question.

The edge contains another perspective.
A perspective where we are able to 3rd perspective ourselves, the other person & view the situation as **awareness**.

Awareness does not have any identity.
It just is.
In this post, we are going to be talking about perspective-shifting in-depth, one key benefit of this act & how you can implement this skillset into your life.

Change your perspective, change your reality.

DANGERS OF THE UNTAMED EGO

The exact opposite of seeing the edge of the coin is when we only see our perspective.

We view ourselves as the main character in life & that everything revolves around us.

The ego is not bad by any means.

It allows us to give ourselves an identity in this noisy world.

But an untamed ego causes us to become selfish & violent.

The person with the untamed ego looks at the picture & sees themselves as the entire picture.

The person with the tamed ego sees the picture & realizes that he/she is a pixel in the picture.

Major paradigm shift.

Why is this so big?

Because when you tame your ego, you become a systems thinker rather than a component thinker.

A component thinker is someone who only operates with the 'what is it in for me' mentality.

But the systems thinker is able to understand their role in the sea of other moving parts, aka society.

When the ego is tamed via hardships, challenges & losses, wisdom emerges.

And as we begin our life-long journey towards wisdom, we gain more data points for perspective shifting.

PRACTICAL BENEFITS OF PERSPECTIVE SHIFTING

The major practical benefit of seeing the bigger picture & seeing someone else's point of view is that it slows your moves down.

Remember this:
Emotions come & go. But the consequences can come & stay.

If someone cuts you off in traffic, it's easy to become impulsive.
The ego feels threatened & we can go into tailgating mode.
This can lead to an accident.

But with the perspective-shifting mind, we are able to realize that there are MANY cars in the highway.
This particular fellow possibly cut off many others.

In this case, a part of you may wonder why this person is in such a rush?
Is it behavioral or situational?

If it is behavioral, then this individual probably cuts everyone off.
They are just a reckless driver.

If it is situational, then the person may be in a rush to get somewhere.
Hm... maybe a job interview?

But in both these situations, you have considered the other person's perspective.
This simple act of inquiry slows your movements down and prevents you from being impulsive.

Just picture how many opportunities were snatched away because we lost our cool.
Or how many times we wanted a rewind button?
Those are from moments where we moved TOO fast.

The main practical benefit of perspective-shifting is that we slow down.

At first, slowing down is a conscious act.

Just like anything in life, we need to put in the cognitive effort to learn something.

But the more we practice and learn, the easier it becomes.

The conscious act becomes a subconscious act.

And that's when we embody a slower, smoother behavior pattern.

The trait of an emotionally intelligent individual.

HOW TO PERSPECTIVE SHIFT

Hopefully, by now you are understanding the importance of perspective shifting.

The untamed ego is holding us back.

So how do we tame it & gather more insights?

Well, there are 2 ways.

The first method is tension free.

The second method is with tension.

Both methods need to be leveraged in order to build your perspective.

And that's how we unlock this massive superpower.

METHOD 1: TENSION FREE

In Yoga practice, there is a method known as Jnana Yoga.

The path of knowledge.

When we lack knowledge, it is as though we are living in darkness.

Picture a dark room, no light in sight.
And now I ask you to walk around.
What happens?
'I just keep bumping into random things.'
Exactly.

But if I give you a match to light... you'll notice something.
The room incrementally lights up more.
Not by a lot.
But just by a little.

This is the path of tension-free.
Where you are seeking knowledge from external sources.

This blog post is an example of knowledge.
The fire that is lighting up the darkroom.

In order to get this knowledge, you need to build the habit of self-educating.
This is when you are actively giving yourself more data points in order to draw from later on.
Blogs, books, YouTube videos, podcasts, etc.

This allows you to lower the entropy of your mind.
Don't just consume knowledge... But apply it.

Although I call it the tension-free path, I don't suggest that this path is without difficulty.
All the knowledge means nothing if its isn't applied in real-world scenarios.

METHOD 2: TENSION FULL

For this path, you have no choice in the matter.
Tough times find all of us.
Our interpretation however is our choice.

The only way to reach maturity is thru stages of immaturity.
Immaturity is when we have high entropy in our internal world.
And maturity is when we are lowering the entropy.
Lowering the chaos & connecting more dots.

This is where we are able to gain more perspective because we have been an idiot ourselves.
To put it gently lol.

Imagine that you got drunk & made a fool of yourself a few weeks ago.
And as you were drunk, you said pretty mean things to one of your friends.

The next morning, you realize your mistake & apologize to your friend.
Your friend decides to forgive you.
Water under the bridge.

The next time you go out, your brother gets drunk & calls YOU a mean name.
You're livid.

The next morning, he apologizes.
Immediately, you are able to draw into a data point of you in the past of being an idiot.
You realize how quickly your friend forgave you.

And now it is easier to understand the perspective of your brother who is asking for forgiveness as well.

You get the point.

The main goal of perspective-shifting is gaining more data points for our minds to be able to draw from.

Knowledge & experiences are kings in this atmosphere.

For the world of tension-free & tension full, we can not run away from knowledge & experiences.

Leverage those.

PERSPECTIVE SHIFTING MINDSET

This post discussed the dangers of the untamed ego.

And how we can tame it via our lives with knowledge & experience.

We grow thru hardships & losses.

That's just the reality of the game.

The more we realize that we are a pixel in the picture rather than the entire picture itself, a natural humility comes over us.

Not the humility when you're undermining your success.

You get the wrong humility when you compare yourself to humans.

The right humility is when you compare yourself to the universe.

Only then do you realize that you are a spec of sand on the beach.

This perspective allows you to tame your ego in a much faster manner.

As the ego is tamed, we build knowledge & experiences.

The 2 worlds that allow us to build data points to reference in the present & future.

In the world of humans, you never know when a slowed down approach will come in handy.

Start practicing in any situation you can.

When you want to react, don't.

When you want to get angry, distance.

And when you want to judge, aim to understand.

Perspective shifting is a process.

And a powerful one at that.

DEALING WITH ANGER ISSUES

Accepting your emotions will make you feel human.
Suppressing your emotions will transform you into a monster.

That's correct.
Emotions are never supposed to be suppressed.
'Even when dealing with anger issues?'
Yep, even with an emotion like anger.

Instead of suppressing it, the key is to build awareness & understand it on a deeper level.
When you can do that, you can take the bonus step of transmuting your anger.

'Transmuting my anger?'
Yep. This is when you channel your anger into a creative task.

Each emotion serves as a data point that can bring out our best selves.
The goal of emotional intelligence is to build a strong understanding of our internal world.
With that understanding, we are able to move more gracefully in the external world.

WHAT CAUSES ANGER?

For the most part, anger is a hybrid between fear & shame.
The fear and shame could have stemmed from your past or the present moment.
So if you look close, you'll notice that anger is a **byproduct** emotion.
It's secondary to a deeper cause.

In ancient times, anger served as a form of signaling.

Most animals have a voice.

And behind that voice is a *tone*.

When an animal is angry, they have a sharper, louder, stronger tone.

Indicating they are angry.

Animals feel anger in a different context.

It's a form of survival.

With the case of humans, this anger emotion was often unlocked in survival situations too.

But in the modern days, we aren't often in physical danger.

However, we *believe* we are in danger when something sparks the trigger.

We feel a sense of fear subconsciously that something may cause us harm.

Whether it's physical harm or reputational harm.

The shame part stems from us feeling embarrassed after pondering that this fear has occurred.

Humans are not afraid of failing.

Humans are afraid of being judged for failing.

Anger is formed thru this awkward bridge of fear & shame.

From your smallest bursts of anger to the biggest moments of rage.

HOW TO ACCEPT ANGER

You want to take some time and evaluate which predominant emotion sparks your anger.

Is it fear or shame?

Or is it both?

At first, the ego fights you on this.

Because fear or shame puts you in a weak position.

Your ego says 'Yo dawg, I'm not scared or shameful! What the fuck?'

Then the ego convinces you that you are showcasing anger due to 'power.'

But this is a lie.

This is also why we normally feel embarrassed AFTER our temper tantrums.

It's because we know we were in the wrong.

We don't feel like that if we were showcasing power.

So the beginning of accepting this anger is to try to spot one or both of the **core** emotions.

Fear or shame?

Which one do you think it is?

And if you think it's both, acknowledge it.

No need to get stuck on this.

Just ponder on what the core emotions may be as we move on...

NOTICING THE ANGER LEADUP

Wanna know something?

'What?"

Everyone feels angry at times.

'Even zen monks?'

Yessir.

But the only difference is that they are highly AWARE.

They are able to view their anger as a 3rd party observer rather than identifying with it.

This is a tough process.

The process of detaching yourself from anger.

But the key is to work your way to gradually building that awareness muscle.

There are random things that can irritate you.

Try to notice as MANY details as you can LEADING to the blow-up.

Say you routinely get angry in traffic.

Find a day where you embrace yourself getting mad because you know it's going to be busy on the road.

EMBRACE the anger arising.

As you are in traffic, you'll notice sensations in your body.

Narratives that the mind is creating.

And shallow breaths.

Notice all those details.

Just observe it. No need to say 'yo don't be angry.'

Instead, do your best to observe as a third party observer.

'What am I working towards?'

We are getting to the point where you are able to accept the bursts of anger.

And have a **neutral** attitude towards it.

Sort of like watching a scary movie.

You know those parts in a scary movie where it's super silent…
and out of nowhere, the movie director scares you with this
JUMP scene?

A monster attacks the actress and a LOUD noise is played?

When you don't expect this, you get startled & your heart skips
a beat.

But if you watched enough scary movies & KNOW that there is
going to be a jump scene any second, you have a calmness to
you.

It's because now you are observing the movie as a **3rd party
viewer** rather than the actress who is getting jumped by the
monster.

We wanna do that.

We are just getting you to be the moviegoer who observes.

REDIRECTING ANGER

This part is optional.

But heavily recommended.

What I found out is that with accepting anger & learning more
about it…

You slow down your movements.

Slowed movements slows down your breath, which deactivates
the amygdala (fear portion of the brain).

And a calm demeanor is gradually restored.

But I perceive anger as something more than a destructive
emotion.

I perceive it as a creative emotion.

And it's one of the emotions I leverage with this blog.

The beauty of anger is that it serves as electricity to me.
'Electricity?'
Yes.

At a natural state, copper has electrons that are aimlessly bouncing around.
Serving a minimal practical purpose.

But when we connect that copper with a battery & bulb…
The electrons now have DIRECTION.
That targeted direction of electrons is known as electricity.

My philosophy with anger is finding your battery & bulb.
Aka a creative task.

Using anger and redirecting it into any form of creative task helps you use it as electricity.
Not only do you have a creative task that you improve on, but you become emotionally intelligent as well.

This is a hack to building maturity, thick skin & confidence.
A fun way of dealing with anger issues.
I call it rage transmutation.

DEALING WITH ANGER ISSUES & BUILDING THE EQ

Emotions are physical sensations with a perception attached to it.
That's about it.

But that's not what it feels like.

Emotions often feel real & paint our reality.

When our emotions control us, we can make a lot of mistakes in the communication skills world.

We become impulsive.

But when we control our emotions, there's a level of peace we feel.

We feel like the CEO of something...

Our lives.

Try to trace back to what is causing the anger.

Fear and/or shame?

Accept it by understanding it.

Understand the narratives in your mind and the physical sensations in your body.

If you're feeling up to the challenge, DIRECT the anger into a creative task.

That's how we take control.

The mind learns thru facts, charts & data.
The heart learns thru tension, betrayal & losses.

No one said building EQ & dealing with anger issues was going to be easy.

But it will nevertheless be fruitful.

HOW TO INTRODUCE PEOPLE

One of the easiest ways to build social skills is by learning the art of the introduction.

It comes down to being a connector.

There is a big difference between the connector and the networker.

This is a difference that we will be discussing in today's article.

A connector is a highly powerful presence in the social dynamics world.

When you know how to connect, others are much more forgiving with other communication quirks you may possess.

Let's be real.

We all have certain flaws when it comes down to interaction with ourselves & others.

Social skills is a journey to do our best to fix that.

Learning how to introduce people is learning a game of manners.

If you can pick up the manners part, everything else seems like common sense.

DIFFERENCE BETWEEN A CONNECTOR & A NETWORKER

A simple difference between the 2 groups is:

-Networking is how well you introduce yourself.

-Connecting is how well you introduce others.

Both are needed in the social dynamics world.

But different hats are required for each role.

For the networking role, you need to remain alert & aware of **your** social situation.

And from there, it's a game of finding ways for you to incorporate yourself into social interactions in one on one settings, groups or tribes.

Connecting comes down to putting yourself in the back burner.

Instead, your goal is to be on the lookout for **others**.

In all cases of social interactions, it's great to have social awareness.

But as a connector, since other parties are involved, you need to have a larger degree of social awareness.

All in all, one group introduces themselves.

One group introduces others.

No need to make it more complicated than that.

HOW NOT TO INTRODUCE PEOPLE

Normally, it's good practice to teach someone how to do something rather than how not to do something first.

But not on this topic lol.

In this topic, we often fumble introductions sooo badly, that it's smart to start off with what NOT to do.

What you should NOT do is introduce a person's name to a brand new group & just leave it at that.

That's highly socially unintelligent.

Let's say you are in an event with your friend, Joseph.

You know a good amount of people in the event.

But for Joseph?

He's new to town.

As you enter a new group interaction, Joseph is by your side.

'Hey guys, this is Joseph' you say...

And then you go on about having your conversation with others.

This is a big error because you have not **incorporated** Joseph INTO the group before you moved on.

Always beware of this.

Your job as a connector is not done until incorporation has been made.

HOW TO INTRODUCE PEOPLE

So now we understand that introducing someone's name is just the BEGINNING of the task.

Nowhere does it say that we are done.

Our goal as connectors is to INCORPORATE the new person into the social interaction.

And we can do this by stating interesting facts about the new person that matches the interest of the group or specific members of the group.

If you are familiar with the group, then you will know what sort of details about Joseph will resonate.

This allows you to **warm up** the group to Joseph & vice versa.

Still, stick by Joseph's side as he gets incorporated.

When you successfully introduce a person into a group, they remember…

This is a big moment because it was a case where you turned an unfamiliar territory into a familiar one.

And people enjoy it when others have their back.

The case I described with Joseph is when you are introducing a new person into a group.

But what about situations where you are introducing people who are not in the same location?

That requires a different strategy.

Similar theme though.

CONNECTING 2 PEOPLE FROM DIFFERENT LOCATIONS

In the last example with Joseph, we talked about how to introduce a new member into a group.

But all connection opportunities are not like that.

Sometimes, you are introducing 2 brand new people who are not in the same vicinity as each other.

What then?

In cases like this, you need to be alert for **needs & desires** among humans.

The more in tune you are for needs & desires in humans, the more connecting opportunities present themselves.

Let's say Jeremey has been complaining about car issues as of late.

You know a car mechanic named Timothy who is highly reliable.

In a case like this, you can set up a group chat, group email, or live person meetup between the 2 parties.

Since a need or desire is present, you have successfully passed a referral.

And created synergy out of thin air.

Jeremy gets his car issue fixed.
And Timothy has a new client.

This was a concrete example of needs & desires.

In other cases, a connecting opportunity may be less concrete.

Let's say an opportunity like matchmaking.

A matchmaker is a type of connector.

However, the matchmaker has the role of spotting ambiguous needs such as emotions.

Let's say Mary is single & is currently looking.

And you know that your co-worker is also single & looking.

You can set up a date by warming the 2 up to a picture of each other to see if there is interest.

To further warm up the 2 to one another, you can also give a light summary of your interactions with them.

If there is interest, you can give them each other's numbers.

That's a connection process.

Just remember…

When you are making a connection, you are lending YOUR credibility as well.

So aim to be mindful of the connections you are making by evaluating the character of those in your squad.

THE ULTIMATE ROLE OF THE CONNECTOR

We talked about a few different situations today.
But the ultimate premise holds true.
A connector is great in creating harmony between multiple groups & then creating action from that.

In some ways, you can consider yourself a magician.
Making something happen out of thin air.

Whether you are introducing a new person to a group.
Introducing 2 new people in order to spread business..
Or setting up a date among people in your network...

The ultimate goal is to create synergy.

The world works like a magnet.
When you create value for others, value comes back knocking at your door.
This is the eternal nature of Karma.
Cause and effect.

We often associate a negative connotation with Karma.
But that's only if you've been a shithead in the past.

As a connector, you sow the seeds for GOOD karma to come.
Create value for others without immediately expecting an ROI.
Your ROI is coming...

A value creator is a magnet.
Spread good energy thru your connection ventures.
And attract good energy back.

PERCEPTION VS REALITY

What is reality?
How do you view your world?

Do you see a world outside of you?
Or do you see a world within you?
Maybe, both?

Questions, questions.

And this blog is not meant to provide answers, answers.
Rather, it is meant to help you ask yourself how you view reality.
Simply pondering on the question of reality will guide your mind towards perception.

Why?

Because perception & reality seem to be joined at the hip.
No matter how hard we try to fight it...

It seems like our subjective world & our objective world are more intertwined than we can imagine.
At least, that's what it feels like.

WHAT IS PERCEPTION?

Perception is defined as:
Becoming aware of our senses.
That's the definition on Google.

However, that seems a bit incomplete.
Our senses are just a *part* of it.
'What's the other part?'
Our mind.

Our mind is needed in order to activate the perception process.
We absorb data from our external world thru our 5 senses.
Seeing, smelling, tasting, touching & feeling.

The data is absorbed thru our body as signals.
And our mind is able to formulate that data on the basis of space, time & causation.

Have you ever been in a conversation physically, but not mentally?
Code for, you weren't paying attention lol.

Sure, you were HEARING the words that were being said.
But you're mind was elsewhere.

Therefore, the senses of your ears alone did not complete the perception process.
Being aware of the data of senses PLUS mind is what leads to perception.

WHAT IS REALITY?

Reality has a blurry definition on Google.
It is defined as:
The state or quality of having existence or substance.

That is a vague definition because now it opens up questions of interpretation.

With the definition above, is your dream a reality?

What about the content that you consume on a YouTube video?

Although the figure on the YouTube video LOOKS real…

It is just a jumble of pixels plus audio.

Not the actual person.

Rather, a **depiction**.

When we ponder these questions, we begin to wonder, at what point do we draw the line on reality?

Is it simply the reality out there or do we factor in our interpretations as well?

With the rise of the information age, a lot of intrinsic meaning is being taken away from entities.

One great example is in Traditional media.

Big corporations like NBC, ABC, FOX, etc.

Prior to new media, there was the interpretation that big letterheads were the sole relayers of information.

But with added communications technology, news corporations at smaller scales are coming out.

Picture popular accounts you follow on YouTube, Twitter & Podcast for your information.

In the information age, plenty are ditching the industrial age paradigm.

Information REQUIRES an individual to PERCEIVE the content in order to assign value.

Therefore, we can no longer say if the information has intrinsic value or not.

As technology gets more advanced, reality is being blurred.

THE RELATIONSHIP BETWEEN PERCEPTION VS REALITY

Perception vs reality are 2 worlds we need to understand in terms of improving our communication skills.

Why?

Because communication requires us to control perception.

For example...

I could present a lie to you right now by saying a loved family member of yours tragically passed away.

By using my words, I create a story, framing the perception of your family member dying.

Perceiving the information to be REALITY, you begin crying.

This information suddenly became *real* to you.

Outside of the mode of communication, nothing is wrong with this family member.

Rather, I just lied.

But YOU do not know that.

Which is why you gave a human response.

The relationship between perception & reality is that the 2 worlds are tied to the hip.

And both worlds influence one another.

Perception influences reality to a strong degree.

And our perception colors the information that we receive from our senses.

This is important to learn because, in a Utopian world, we create an objective world where there is no misinterpretation.

But this is impossible.

As community scales, perception is a variable that needs to be incorporated when factoring in what has a state of existence or substance.

This is crucial information to learn in terms of improving communication & avoiding miscommunication.

Your reality is not someone else's reality.

WHY?

Because your perception is not their perception.

WHY SO MANY ANSWERS LEAD BACK TO THE MIND

Watch top performers in any field.

It seems like they give similar responses to their questions on a lot of topics.

But one of the most common answers you will hear them give?

'It's all a state of the mind.'

This is a profound answer because the answer discusses the practicality of what we have been talking about thus far.

Perception and reality are joined at the hip.

This is why top performers became top performers.

We believe that they went thru something highly difficult.

From our reality, this seems like a borderline impossible task.

But in their reality, they perceived everything in a much different *context*.

It's because as they trained in their field, their perception became different than ours.

What we dub impossible or difficult to overcome...
What we view as hard work...

-They view as possible.
-They view as play.

Remember at the beginning of this blog, we talked about perception REQUIRING the mind.
Not the senses alone.

Therefore, with simple logic...
Reality is up to the interpreter.
What 'looks' concrete, gets blurrier the more we zoom in.
What seems like common sense rules, become more polarizing as society scales.

That's because reality involves perception.
Perception factors in mind.
And all minds are different.

Even if we get in similar data from our senses.
Our interpretations will be blurry.

THE FINAL POINT OF THIS MESSAGE

This post was not meant to give you any answers.
But rather, help you question the world around you.

-*Ask yourself questions when you want to ask others questions.*
-*Try to understand where others are coming from when you disagree with them.*

Transitioning from the world of hard skills into the world of soft skills is daunting because of the lack of solidified rules.

That's why a lot of engineers are great with machines, but poor with people.

It's because machines don't argue back.

But people do.

Reality vs Perception.

Was that ever the right framing?

Or is it Reality AND Perception?

Personally, the second one sounds much more suitable...

INSPIRATION VS MOTIVATION

Although inspiration & motivation seem similar...
The two are very different.

Before talking about the differences, let's talk about the similarity.
'What is the similarity bro?'
It's motion.

The beauty of inspiration and motivation is that it leads to motion.
Only if done correctly.

But HOW the motion is created differs completely.

Understanding the ins & outs of motivation vs inspiration will give you an edge in the emotional intelligence world.
You'll see which one powers you up.
You'll see which one puts YOU in motion.

Different strokes for different folks.
I get it.
Let's enhance our emotional awareness by building our emotional literacy.

THE MAIN DIFFERENCE BETWEEN MOTIVATION VS INSPIRATION

-Motivation is when you are getting charged up from an external stimulus.

-Inspiration is when you are getting charged up from an internal stimulus.

'So the main difference is between external & internal?
That's correct.

This is where motivational speakers are different from inspirational speakers.

A motivational speaker comes in with the INTENT to have the audience feeling charged up.
They want to make sure they take the audience from one state to an altered state.

Inspirational speakers are different.
'How so?'
They pretty much share their story. If you feel inspired, cool.
If you don't, all good.
Their intent was not to have you feeling charged up. It was to share their story.

So motivation happens from our external sources.
Inspiration happens from our internal sources.
But we can still delve deeper into this.
So let's do it.

THE POWER OF MOTIVATION

Motivational speakers have a lot of power.
They are able to spark change not only with their words...
But with their personalities.

Every now and then, we humans get caught in a rut.

Things are not working out.

We are feeling depressed, in rock bottom, or feel that we are lacking a purpose.

Motivation from an external source can help out tremendously as long as we comprehend the message.

The keyword is **comprehend**.

We don't just want to feel momentary pleasure & go about our day.

But we want to COMPREHEND the message.

Internalize the message on our being level.

The motivation from other parties should charge us up into motion.

We don't just want to feel good & leave it at that.

We want to feel powerful & take purposeful action.

Motivation engages our emotions & has the power to engage our imagination too.

Emotions AND imagination?

Sound familiar?

It should. Those are the 2 staples of the subconscious mind.

The right motivational talk/s at the right stage of your life can change the trajectory of your life.

THE POWER OF INSPIRATION

Earlier, I said that inspirational speakers are not trying to make you feel charged up.

If that happens, great.

But that was not their primary intent.

'So why do I feel so charged up for?'
Because you RESONATED with their story.

Let's say a speaker is talking about how he overcame shyness.
He is sharing his story.
And since you are shy, you are able to see YOURSELF in THEIR story.
From beginning to end…
This leads you to feel charged up to do something about your shyness.

If you understand that inspiration comes from within, then you'll notice how powerful inspiration is.
There are multiple things to inspire you in all facets of your life.
Even inanimate objects.
'Inanimate?'
Yea.

In my home back in West Palm…
There is a tree that I planted when I was a little kid.
During the time, it was a small little plant with branches & leaves.
Nothing special.

But over time, it has grown into a powerful tree.
One of the biggest trees in my back yard.

That tree inspires me, because it showcased how something great can be born thru something small.
All it takes is time.

If you were lecturing me about trees before I planted *that* particular tree... then it wouldn't have **resonated** with me.

But since I saw my personal tree grow in real-time...

There was a strong resonation.

WHAT DOES THIS ALL MEAN FOR YOU?

What this all means for you is that motivation and inspiration are 2 acts to leverage when you feel stuck.

To get yourself back in motion.

The truth is...

Theory is good.

But theory without motion is pointless.

That's like sitting in a parked car & turning the steering wheel.

You're focused on the direction, but there is no motion!

Motion allows the theory to make much more sense.

Whether you get the spark of motion from motivation or inspiration.

And who knows, both.

Listening to a **motivational** talk in the morning to get your day started & staying **inspired** throughout the day is a powerful combo.

But the point is to find out what works for you.

Understanding the difference between motivation & inspiration also allows you to build your social skills as well.

Some people find motivational videos corny.

All good.

For them, you can let your action do the talking when they are in a rut.

Some people need a quick boost but are not that introspective.
For them, you can give them a motivational talk to encourage.
Encourage is a way to give someone courage.
Powerful.

Inspiration vs motivation can seep into many elements of your life.
Especially when you know how to spot different social and emotional contexts.

AN OBJECT IN MOTION STAYS IN MOTION!

Motion is powerful.
And from motion, you'll gain insights that allow you to control that motion.
To control the flow of your movements.

Ultimately though, inspiration & motivation are 2 powerful tools in the emotional intelligence world.
Our emotions have fluxes.
And when we know how to extract meaning from those fluxes, we feel a level of power.

Social intelligence & emotional intelligence is a game of controlling our energy.
And one of the best ways to control the energy is by building our vocabulary of the energies that we possess.
Words are the truest perception programmers out there.

You understand what motivation means.
You understand what inspiration means.

Which one is right for you?
Or is it both?

It's time to get up & get going.
The human in motion plus momentum is hard to stop.

HOW TO FORGIVE SOMEONE

One of the toughest things that you're going to do in life is to forgive someone.

'Why?'

Because this individual hurt your ego.

Your ego is your sense of identity

And when someone hits it hard, it not only impacts you at the moment...

It may also create a ripple effect that shakes up your world view.

This post is regarding a deep betrayal.

Not something small like a friend eating the food that you were saving in the fridge.

Trust me, I don't like it when someone eats my pizza either!

But today, we are going deeper.

Forgiveness is a soft skill.

One of the intangibles of life.

Letting go is an art.

And unless you learn it, you'll devolve into a bitter soul.

Let go of the anchor that you're holding on to.

This is designed for YOU to win.

UNDERSTANDING FORGIVENESS

There are so many things in life that we are expected to do.

Yet, we lack frameworks on how to execute it.

'Be confident' they say.

But how?
'Be more social' they say.
But how?
'Forgive those who hurt you...'
But how?....

If you're like most people, the word forgiveness is just that, a word.

And you are saying the word in a way where it's a command.

'Forgive.'
That is simply a blanket command that lacks specificity.
Right now, you don't have any MEANING behind the word.

To forgive someone is not a command, it is a process.
If you are having some trouble forgiving, just ask yourself:
What is my forgiveness framework?

When you ask yourself that, you may be shocked to realize that you don't have a framework.
You were just barking 'forgive, forgive...well? forgive.'... to no avail.

When you start looking PAST the word alone, that's when you start building emotional intelligence.
That's when you are ready to adopt the mindset regarding what it takes to let go.

THE FORGIVENESS MINDSET

One of the toughest things to do is to forgive someone who hurt us.
It feels like we are letting them off scotch free.

Why aren't they suffering any consequences?
Are you sure I shouldn't plot revenge?

We all heard the quote:
Holding onto anger is like drinking poison and expecting the other person to die

This is true.
When you have a deep hatred for someone, you attach a STRONG emotion to that individual.

The subconscious mind process's life via **emotions** & **images**.
And when you are plotting revenge, you execute both those 2 variables.

- Rage- emotion
- The other person – image

A combination of these 2 constantly replaying in your internal world rewires your perception for the worst.
You are MUCH more inclined to forgive when you realize it's more for you than the other person.
This is a major paradigm shift.

Growing up, I took pride in how long I could hold a grudge.
I remembered the betrayal with a photographic memory.

That strategy did me a lot of harm.
I became a very angry kid that would get agitated by small things.

There's a lot of ripple effects of holding onto a grudge, bud.
Just not worth it.

How to Forgive

The main thing about forgiveness is detaching yourself from the situation.

Earlier, I talked about how betrayal hurts because it stung your ego.

And when you're identity is personally involved, it becomes VERY difficult to view the situation objectively.

Feels impossible.

The key to forgiveness is understanding why someone did what they did.

Note, I didn't say you have to agree with why someone did what they did.

I said you need to UNDERSTAND.

Whether you want to or not, you need to take yourself out of your ego...and place yourself in the other person's ego.

This is NOT easy.

I laugh when someone thinks you can forgive overnight.

Like it's a magical act that makes all the bad disappear.

That's incorrect.

Forgiveness is more about chipping away on a marble block until you see the statue presenting itself.

In this context, you are using your intellect to keep chipping away from the situation.

You learn more.

You gain more wisdom.

Time elapses.

The more that you understand the other person's perspective, the more you:

- Build patience
- Perspective shift
- Develop emotional intelligence
- Understand human nature

and much more

As time elapses, you have built so much UNDERSTANDING that you now realize you aren't mad anymore.

And if I'm being honest..

You realize you weren't guilt free either.

There are a lot of times where we brought the betrayal upon ourselves.

It's tough to admit.

But oh well, happens to the best of us.

The key lesson that I want you to realize is that you're forgiving by *gradually* understanding the other person's perspective more and more.

And once again, I used the word understand, not condone.

BUILDING A LIFE WHERE FORGIVENESS IS SEAMLESS

A lot of people begin their level up journey from pain.

They were let down by a person or people that they trusted a lot.

And that may be you.

Your fight towards forgiveness has led you to your level up journey.

Good.

You're building a life where it becomes easier to forgive.
'Wait, for real?'
Yessir.

When you are leveling up, your time span to forgive reduces by a ton.
No lie.
This depends on a case by case basis of the depth of the betrayal, of course.

But when you have a goal & you're building good habits, it's easier not to get caught up on the negatives as long.
We still feel it.
But we are able to transition our focus quicker.

And once you've forgiven your first 2 betrayals of some sort, the next ones become easier.
Mainly because you know how to do it!

This is a powerful concept because the art of letting go is a soft skill.
A skill that you can't physically measure.
But it's one of the tangibles that allows someone to become great.

EVOLVING THRU FORGIVENESS

Now the word "forgiveness" is no longer just a word.
It's a process.

It's like your entire life, you kept seeing a picture of the Statue of Liberty.

And that's dope.

But when you actually *see* the Statue of Liberty in real life...
WAY different experience.

And that's how it works with forgiveness too.

When you understand the word, all good.
When you understand how to do it, all good.
But when you actually execute on the steps & let bygones be bygones, that's a different experience.

That's what we are going for.
Betrayal, backstabbing & being let down is a part of life.

Build the thick skin, so the art of letting go becomes a seamless process.
Emotional resilience will follow.

6 WAYS ON HOW TO OVERCOME LAZINESS

Laziness is one of the worst feelings to feel when you want to gain something from life.

It's the mentality of a bum.

The question though is why laziness is a thing in the first place?

When you see little kids, they have such a zest for life.

But then you see some adults with the exact opposite mentality.

Why?

If you look closer:

Laziness is not something that is normal. It is something that is highly ABNORMAL.

'Geez Armani, thanks for putting me down.'

Not really, my friend. When you realize laziness is abnormal, you lowkey feel more empowered to do something about it.

Sort of like seeing a dirty plate. You feel hope knowing that the plate on a natural level is not dirty.

Which gives you more FIRE to clean it.

And one of the ways to learn how to overcome laziness is by noticing that you at a core level are meant to **embody work ethic.**

Just time to scrape of the junk!

Let's learn the mindset of someone with a strong work ethic &
then discuss 6 practical ways to make that happen.

WHAT IS WORK ETHIC?

You ever heard the mantra: *don't work harder, work smarter*.
'Yes.'
It's bullshit.
'Forreal??"
Well, *sort of* bullshit.

The reality is that **you need to work hard so you can
work smart.**
Meaning, working hard allows you to gather the data. From the
data, you will be able to spot what is rubbish and what you
need to double down on.
Once you made those findings, THEN you can work smart.

Soon as you start working smart, it does not mean that you
ditch your working hard ways. Now you just work with full
conviction on the tasks with the highest ROI.
You are doing a combination of working hard AND smart.

The reason I'm telling you this is because a lot of lazy people
are born from overthinking.
They are chasing perfection.

They are so obsessed with the idea of working 'smart' in the
initial stages that they keep on consuming and consuming
more information.
To a point where they are TRICKING themselves into thinking
that they are working.

In reality? That ain't the case champ..

The work ethic we are going for is a blend of hard work & smart work

A combination of those 2 create beautify synergy which melts away laziness.

Get yo' mind right!

6 WAYS ON HOW TO OVERCOME LAZINESS

There are different reasons as to why you are lazy in the first place.

When you can spot these reasons, you'll often solve the root cause, which allows you to alter your behavior.

In the following list, I want to give you a few of the TOP reasons why people are lazy & don't take action.

Let's begin.

I. THE GOAL IS TOO BLURRY

It's hard to chase any goal when you have no clue what you are chasing.

And here's the conundrum...

At the beginning of starting anything, you never fully know what you are chasing.

You just need to be patient & put your reps in.

The key phrase is PUT YOUR REPS IN.

The more reps that you put in for the skill set of choice, the quicker the target goes from *blurry -> clarity.*

- The conscious mind always wants to move and grow.

- The subconscious mind wants to chill and keep things the way they always were

In order to take action, your conscious mind NEEDS to overpower your subconscious laziness.

Keep taking incremental action towards the right direction.

The targets will clarify. And the clarified targets lights a fuel to your fire.

2. YOU THINK YOU HAVE TOO MUCH TIME

This is what plagues the masses.

They think they have too much time. Which makes you go into the 'I'll do it tomorrow' mentality.

Big mistake.

You don't have too much time.

In reality, *time is something we never have too much of.*

A second lost is a second never returned.

Not to sound morbid, but here it goes:

People who died young...do you think they had a clue they were going to die?

Nah. Unless it was a case of suicide, they were hit unexpectedly.

You should be grateful that you have another day to live. But don't be so grateful that you are sitting on your ass doing nothing.

Gratitude overdone, just like anything in life, can make you content.

Be grateful, yes.

But acknowledge that tomorrow is never guaranteed. Take action and move G!

3. YOU'RE CHASING SOMETHING YOU DON'T DESIRE

For me, I would always hate studying for class exams.

I had no clue why exams were even a thing. The real world rarely has these little tests to prove whether you can memorize a bunch of stuff or not.

Therefore, I would feel lazy when I would have to study for these exams.

With subjects that I desired learning?

I would never be lazy. I'd be the first one in studying & creating my own schedule.

In the real world, we don't always have a choice on what we want to do. Sometimes responsibilities require us to take care of business.

Other times, we **do** have a choice.

It's easy to want to do something just because others are doing it. But ask yourself, is this what YOU want?

If it's something that you truly want, then laziness is an illusion. It just melts away.

Why? Because you are having FUN doing the task.

But when you are forcing yourself to do something because you feel like that's what you have to do, then laziness will always creep up.

Ask yourself if what you're doing is something you feel like you were put on this planet to do?

If the answer is no, then find the task that was meant for you.

When you find it, it will feel like your chest got hit with a sack of bricks (in a good way lol).

You'll feel alert. And doing the task is fun, not a dread.

4. YOU'RE SUFFERING FROM ANALYSIS PARALYSIS

Procrastination will never get you started.

Perfectionism will never get you finished.

In both cases, the results are the same.

Analysis paralysis is when you are suffering from perfection.

Because if you look close, you know that there is a desire to do the task.

You want to become better.

The only problem?

You keep waiting for the 'perfect' moment.

- Maybe you're looking for the perfect time to being.
- You're probably looking for the 'perfect' mentor to guide you.
- Or you may be looking for that perfect blog post before you KNOW, you have all the information.

Let me save you some time.

- There is no perfect time to begin.

- You are the perfect mentor for you.
- And you'll never know all the information.

Got it?

Now begin.

Analysis paralysis no more.

5. YOU HAVE A FEAR OF FAILURE & EMBARRASSMENT.

Let's say you do begin.

What if you gave it your all, but it still wasn't enough?

That registers as a failure in your world.

So your subconscious mind chooses to sabotage your conscious mind.

Here's the thing...

If you go ALL in on a skill set, you never lose.

You come out with a bunch of micro-skills that you could never get from reading a book.

- The ability to discipline yourself.
- Knowing when to be patient.
- Emotional intelligence.
- Focusing.
- Setting targets.

These are micro skills that allow you to make your entire life easier.

What is failure?

'Uh...'
Exactly.

We have this blob of failure that we never clarify.
As cliche as it may sound, **you only fail when you quit.**

Other than that, you never lose. The micro-skills continue to build up & you change your world from inside out.
Keep goin'.

6. LOSER FRIENDS

Toxic people are not always those with a negative intent towards you.
Sometimes the most toxic people are those who love you the most.

The old school friends who have mailed it in for their self-improvement will want you to mail it in as well.
They want you to remain the same.

This group is not malicious.
Yet over time, they start to make you feel drained. Especially, if you want more out of life.

With friends like this, I don't tell you to cut them off.
I tell you to love them from a distance.
The friend circle you have does play a big role in how you move in life.
And it's difficult to not be lazy when laziness is all you know.

Love them from a distance by staying true to your goals first.

Not saying you can never have fun with them again.

But when you hit the goals first, having fun with them will kill 2 birds with 1 stone.

One of the harsh life lessons we learn is that toxic people often weigh down the ambitious person rather than the ambitious person inspiring the toxic people.

OVERCOME LAZINESS FOREVER

When you become a winner who TAKES ACTION, you will find it comical how you used to be lazy.

You are back to being the clean plate who took away the dirt of limiting beliefs, emotions, and tendencies.

The main thing that I want you to take away from this post is that the way to learn how to overcome laziness is with the **art of action.**

Action will allow you to toughen up and become a pit bull.

You were never born lazy.

You were conditioned into that due to some ill decisions.

But the ill decisions can always be overturned.

And it will be overturned.

You've learned how to overcome laziness.

Now overcome it.

THE MAGIC OF EDUTAINMENT

In school, I hated the whole process of learning.

I used to have this boring-ass biology teacher who would literally plop her butt on her seat & read off the Powerpoints.

High school hurt my image of learning.

It made me think learning was *supposed* to be dry and stale.

Truth be told, I couldn't imagine how anyone enjoyed learning if they didn't need to.

I thought this around the same time I had a strong passion for basketball.

Your boy was **learning** a lot regarding the sport, I just wasn't aware of it.

The irony simply passed my younger self.

Around college, students are given more freedom.

I heard this phrase that said 'college is the place where you pay to teach yourself.'

Hilarious & somewhat true.

But still, in college, there is a curriculum.

Therefore, even though you have more control, you still have restrictions.

'Why do you tell me this Armani?'

I tell you this because once we get into the real world, 2 groups will form.

The group who ACTIVELY likes learning & the group who still hates learning.

'I'm assuming you still hate learning as you did in high school, right?'

Nope, the exact opposite.
'What?! What changed?'
The delivery.

Education was never meant to be boring.

Heck, it was meant to be entertaining.

When education meets entertainment, you get *edutainment*.

To level up your storytelling, you need to be knowledgable AND fun.

Let's take an in-depth look into the world of edutainment & see if you have what it takes to unlock your inner teacher.

IS EDUCATION AN INTERNAL OR EXTERNAL PROCESS?

Let's go back to the high school example.

We are often taught in a very external format.

Meaning we sit in class, absorb a lot of information & then take a test.

This is cool & all.

But may not hit the true definition of education.

Education stems from the Latin word Educare.

And Educare means to 'draw out.'

Have you ever had that moment when you REALLY learned something?

A part of you feels it in your chest.

It's as though you knew the information all your life, but you're just bringing awareness to it.

So if you were to ask me, education is a mix between external AND internal.

But internal is where the money is.

Memorizing stuff & not being able to apply it in the real world is not education.

It's just memorizing bud.

WHAT CONSTITUTES AS ENTERTAINMENT?

I used to be a big fan of the comedian, Russell Peters.

In one of his bits, Russell's dad points out his son is in the entertainment business & implies that everyone in the entertainment industry is flamboyant.

This got the audience laughing.

But why did the dad say 'entertainment business?'
Why not say the Comedy business?

It's because entertainment is an umbrella.
And comedy is simply one of the metal lines.

Entertainment is defined as:
An activity that holds the attention and interest of an audience.

There are multiple ways to hold that attention.
And typically, it can be done via the 5 human desires which are the desires to:

1. Feel
2. Learn
3. Defend
4. Protect
5. Bond

When we think of entertainment, we mainly think of Desire #1.
We consume entertainment to FEEL.

Whether it be a comedy show, a horror movie, reality tv, etc.
All those have components of *feeling*.

If you look closer at the list of human desires, you notice the *Desire to Learn* is also present.
Dope, isn't it?

Humans have a DESIRE to learn.
We can feel a strong urge inside when we are curious about something.
Curiosity is primal.

Guess what happens when you combine the 2 human desires to LEARN & FEEL?
'What?'
You get Edutainment.

ENTERING THE WORLD OF EDUTAINMENT

Yep, edutainment speaks to 2 core human desires.
Which is why it is a booming industry.

And just like entertainment is an umbrella that has comedy as a field...
Edutainment is an umbrella that holds a lot of subsections as well.

When I was in high school, I used to be obsessed with the Food Network.
Strange, I know.

But I loved seeing the recipes & how dishes would be made.

One of my favorite shows was Emeril Live.

He was this pudgy dude with a bunch of charisma who was always creating something dope.

His personality was what carried the show.

Yet once you were done watching, you learned a ton about cooking.

Edutainment is not a new subject by any means.

It's been around for ages.

However, with the information age & global technology, edutainment is taking up a new twist.

Edutainment has been very popular in the video game industry.

But as platforms like YouTube, Twitter, Instagram continue to grow, edutainment is going to continue to soar in the new media industry.

Edutainment, in a nutshell, is defined as:

The ability to educate in an entertaining fashion.

This is HUGE.

'Why do you say that?'

This is big because the term teacher & storyteller are sort of blurring the lines at this point.

Humans have the storytelling gene engrained in them.

If you don't believe me, watch how you tell a story of the guy who cut you off in traffic.

'You won't believe it! Here I was having a great day & this thug began tailgating me...(story begins).

We are telling stories all the time whether we are aware or not.

Heck, we even dream in stories!

Why not tell stories about your skillsets & knowledge rather than whining?

If you're ready for that, then read on.

PARTICIPATING IN THE EDUTAINMENT WORLD

Here's a creativity insight for you:

-If you lead with the skill & sprinkle in your personality, then it will feel like work.

-If you lead with your personality & sprinkle in the skill, then it will feel like fun.

That's it.

If you can adopt this mindset, you'll realize that the world of edutainment is not too far away from you.

What skill sets or knowledge do you have?

Think about something that holds your genuine interest.

Topics that you do research on without anyone telling you to.

The beauty is that there is a niche for everyone.

When I started ArmaniTalks, I didn't know if there was much of a demand for communication skills.

I didn't even view it like that.

Instead, I viewed it as sharing what I was learning via real-life experience.

As I was sharing my journey with public speaking, writing a book, telling stories, I discovered a niche from there.

Ask yourself what intrigues you.

And just create content with that.

Avoid being too technical. No one cares about the technicalities...yet.

K.I.S.S.

Keep it SUPER simple.

The more simple that you are able to explain your skillset, the more your authentic personality shows.

You will flow seamlessly with practice.

When you try to make something complex to show that you're a 'subject matter expert', then you may be educating.

But you are not partaking in the entertaining portion.

That's not edutainment.

And if you want to partake in edutainment with a group, then just remember the core fundamentals.

-The topic that you are teaching: **Education**.

-How you can make the audience feel: **Entertainment**.

This combo hits the brain & the heart.

When you hit the brain & the heart of the audience, you officially have won them over.

Influence will follow.

MAKE LEARNING FUN AGAIN

Learning was always meant to be an enjoyable process.

Not one where you are dragging your feet.

When you get out there in the real world, you realize how important it is to learn.

The world is constantly changing.

Dragging your feet hoping for it to stay the same will have you taking L after L.

As Eric Hoffer said:

"In times of change, learners inherit the earth, while the learned find themselves beautifully equipped to deal with a world that no longer exists."

Find a way to make learning fun.

If you don't see content around your area of interest with entertaining material, all good.

Find ways to learn that topic & make content yourself.

Stories create perceptions.

Stories make the world move forward.

Combine your stories with education & you'll be a force to be reckoned with.

WHY AM I SO SENSITIVE?

The communication skills world is a jungle.
And all jungles come with the good and the bad.

When you first think jungle, you think a savage area.
A place where you can get your head bitten off.

But no need to be so negative, my friend.
Look around you.
The jungle has a lot of beauty to it.

The sounds of nature.
Pretty scenery.
The beautiful water.
Bird chirping.

Now that we talked briefly about the beauty, we need to also talk about the things that can bite your head off.
Yep.
The lions, tigers & other animals that see you as food.
Communication skills have beauty to it.
But the wide array of personalities out there has room for entropy.

Entropy is Chaos.
You can never fully predict humans.
Therefore, being too sensitive can make your life feel difficult.

You'll dwell on small things & overlook the big things.
Results?
Getting your head bitten off.

Today, you are going to learn about sensitivity.
Why does it happen and how you can navigate around it?

Your mindset & your emotions are highly linked.
Influence 1 and you'll find yourself influencing the other.
Let's begin.

THE CAUSE FOR SENSITIVITY

Are you someone who wonders:
Why am I so sensitive?

Well, let's talk about that.
What is sensitivity exactly?
According to Google, sensitive is defined as:
A quick to detect or respond to slight changes, signals, or influences.

If you ask me, that seems like a GOOD thing.
Right?
Seems like the definition is defining a very astute person.

When would a strong level of astuteness like this be needed?
Use your imagination.

If you answered:
"Well Armani, astuteness like this would be needed by my ancient ancestors. You know, those fellas who could have gotten their head bitten off by a sabretooth tiger!"
Then you'd be right.

Sensitivity is needed for humans to absorb data from the external world.

You take up data via your 5 senses:

-Seeing

-Hearing

-Feeling

-Tasting

-Smelling

With these 5 senses, you are able to INPUT data into your internal world.

Once the data is inputted into your internal world, that's when you can process the data via your past experiences & present-day perceptions.

That's what it means to perceive an event.

'So question bro. What you are defining seems cool. But how come I feel so bad with my sensitivity?'

Because you have overdone it, my friend.

Time to fine-tune your mindset.

HUMANS ARE NATURAL CREATURES OF CHAOS

We are born into this planet crying.

And as little babies, if something seems to alert us, we will cry.

Crying was never taught.

It was something that was ingrained.

At a baseline state, we are creatures of chaos.

Very high entropy.

The goal of maturing is to LOWER our entropy.

Which means, lower the chaos.

This requires a **reactive -> responsive** transformation.

Reactivity is when you are impulsive.

An example is when someone cuts you off in traffic & you go on road rage mode.

Responsiveness is when you are more well thought out.

Someone cuts you off in traffic, you say 'oh well' and go about your day, unbothered.

Let me reiterate:

The point of maturing is to lower your entropy.

Being sensitive isn't bad perse.

But being too sensitive is very bad.

It can make your life feel like hell.

Like a jungle where you are constantly being hunted.

You know what they say:

A mind can make a heaven out of hell & a hell out of heaven.

WHY BEING TOO SENSITIVE IS BAD

'Why is being too sensitive bad?'
Doing anything too much is bad.

The gym for example.

Overall, the gym is a great place to workout & get healthy.

But if you are someone who goes there 10 times a day & lifts weights till you vomit, then even the gym becomes bad.

Your nature programmed sensitivity in you to be aware of your environment.

However, you've gone past that.

Nowadays, things that are not in your immediate danger, is PERCEIVED to be in your immediate danger.

'Any idea why this is?'

Because of the blurring of reality...

Our ancestors didn't have to deal with sad movies.

Sad movies have the capability of feeding your 5 senses an illusion of an environment that causes you to perceive something.

That one scene from Fresh Prince of Bel-Air where Will is sad that his dad doesn't want him....made the strongest people feel weak.

However, sad movies aren't the only reason for over sensitivity.

The reason is the blurring of realities.

The information that you consume, plays a big role in your reality.

And in our era, information overload, mixed in with a lack of challenges causes overly sensitive individuals.

Back in the days, you didn't have the time to cry if someone hurt your feelings.

You were to busy trying to stay alive.

With today's era, many survival issues have been mitigated.

Which opens up more bandwidth in our mind to dwell.

If someone hurts our feelings, then we have the time to magnify it.

And as I stated earlier, mind controls emotions & emotions control mind.

You are no longer someone who is aware of their environment.

Rather nowadays, you have the tendency to overdo it.

Getting offended by tweets of strangers, someone cutting you off in a convo & being called mean names.

Getting offended is normal.

But causing it to disrupt your behavior makes you adopt the life of a victim.

A victim finger points, make excuses & lists out 100 reasons why something won't work out.

Bottom line?

Being overly sensitive can make your life feel like hell.

LOWERING YOUR ENTROPY & TOUGHENING UP

I'm not telling you not to feel emotion.

Instead, I am saying the opposite.

I am telling you to acknowledge your emotions and THEN make a responsive decision.

Remember, your senses are meant to SERVE you.

Want to know something?

'What?'

Greatness is fine-tuned sensitivity.

'Hm...mind giving me an example?'

There is a story about a time when Kobe Bryant was practicing his jump shots.

He was known to be a BEAST when it came to practicing.

Well, this particular day, things were different.

His shot didn't feel right.

After some time, he felt that the rim was a quarter of an inch too low.

And once he had someone check it, his intuition was right.

The rim happened to be off from the traditional standard.

That right there is FINE-TUNED sensitivity.

When you put in your reps for a certain craft, you notice your sensitivity sparks intuition.

Even great music producers exhibit this trait.

When they hear a song, they can FEEL when something is right or if something is off.

Once again, FINE-TUNED sensitivity.

That's what you want as well.

Rather than crying nonstop about things out of your control, gain more control.

COMBINE YOUR MINDSET WITH THE HEART FOR A DEADLY COMBO.

Be emotionally intelligent rather than just emotional.

This just requires you to slow down your life a little.

Having that hobby that you are leveling up on will aid your journey.

But before being impulsive, just take a **pause**.

That space will give you more insights than a book ever can.

Look around your living room, or wherever you're reading this blog from.
Most of your environment is EMPTY.
Yup, it's just space.
Space is POWERFUL.
Embrace it.

The more you embrace those spaces, the more you slow down your moves.
Not slow in a boring way. But slow in a dynamic way.

Instead of taking 50 dribbles to get to the rim, you take 5.
That's because you're well thought out.

Your ancestors didn't have the luxury of being well thought out.
Because around then, the human intellect wasn't as evolved as it is nowadays.
The intellect can be your best friend or your worst enemy.

Rather than using the intellect to make yourself a victim, use it to slow things down.
Absorb the data from the external world, yes.
But then process it like an adult.

There is no cheat code for this.
Maturity is an arduous process that requires effort.
Embrace that effort.

We come onto this planet crying.
We are overly sensitive.

If you are overly sensitive as an adult, then no one feels bad for you champ.

Instead, you just come off as a nuisance.

The world isn't always going to be able to give you your 'trigger warnings' and safe spaces.

Toughen up.

And you can toughen up thru your own choice or the world will do it for ya.

However, maturity isn't a choice.

And we learn that at one point or another.

PUT OVER SENSITIVITY TO A BACK BURNER

If you were wondering 'why am I so sensitive?'

Then hopefully you got some answers.

Too much of anything good turns bad.

But luckily, us humans are magnificent creatures.

We can always rewire ourselves when we feel like something is off.

In this case, just slow it down.

Embrace those spaces more.

Try to channel your mind into a task and go ALL IN.

You'll develop fine-tuned sensitivity.

Your emotions are nature's way of telling you to **wake up.**

If you can channel your emotions, then a part of you feels limitless.

The beauty?

You can always channel your emotions via the power of your mind.

Use your mind to grow.

And make your internal world stronger than the world around you.

That's the magic formula.

THE PSYCHOLOGY OF NITPICKING: WHY DO PEOPLE NITPICK?

You ever met that one person who always criticized you?
They always looked for what was wrong in the interaction.

Truth be told, the phrase 'nitpicking' seems a little ambiguous.
In reality, a better way to view it as is 'fault-finding."

Either way, it's **annoying**.
You'll realize how annoying it is if you know some nitpickers yourself.

It can be a friend, your boss, a family member, etc.
Or worse...
It can be you.

We often notice when we are being mistreated.
But our ego blinds us from when we are mistreating others.

Either way, it's a low social intelligence move.
If you want to build your charisma, then it's time to leave nitpicking ways behinds you.

Unfortunately, even if you aren't someone who finds faults in others, others may still find faults in you.
There's no set blueprint on how humans should act.

However, if you understand the PSYCHOLOGY of nitpicking, then it becomes much easier to understand why these people operate the way they do.

Rather than feeling rage towards them, you feel a sense of empathy.

Let's see if you can make this transformation today.

CHILDHOOD CATCHING UP TO ADULTHOOD?

Old school teachers said that if you gave them control over a child up to age 7, then they knew they had the child for life.

That's because these old school teachers understood what the subconscious mind was like.

Whether they were aware of it or not.

Our childhood can often influence our adulthood.

If you had overbearing parents or a mean teacher who were always dissecting your moves, then guess what?

You may be doing these moves in adulthood.

Emotions are pretty funny & unique when you look into them.

You see that a human's child side never goes away.

It simply becomes buried within logic & social norms.

Watch a person get cut off in traffic & you'll notice them act similar to a kid who just got their toys taken away.

Frustrated & highly animated.

This is one of the first things you want to look out for.

Is your past catching up to your present?

If so, you definitely wanna make yourself aware.

Understanding how childhood influences adulthood is a major key to learning the psychology of nitpicking.

WHY NITPICKING IS ANNOYING: THE PSYCHOLOGY

Nitpicking is annoying because humans are gray creatures.
'Meaning?'
Meaning that they are hard to predict.

We THINK we can logically predict them.
But we are never fully certain.

The incorrect way to handle gray creatures is via black & white thinking.
Black & white thinking is when you think in right or wrong.
Highly linear.

In the black & white model, 1 + 1 = 2.
In the gray model, 1 + 1 = ?

MAJOR PARADIGM SHIFT.

However, a large part of our education system mainly enforced black & white thinking.
We were measured with how powerful our intellects were.

Intellects are great at dissecting things.
But when it comes down to dealing with humans?
The intellect can be an enemy.

That's why a lot of academically gifted individuals can make poor leaders.
Machines don't argue back.
But people do.

Having black & white thinking regarding gray creatures has you always analyzing if they are behaving right or wrong.

But by which standard are you measuring the right or wrong?

'Uh…'

You are measuring the standards via your ego.

That's when you fail to understand the psychology of nitpicking.

You are basing other people's decisions based on how YOU live your life.

That's why that shit gets annoying real quick.

Just like no 2 thumbprints are the same.

No 2 personalities are the same either.

We all had different experiences leading up to who we became today.

And that's why using your experiences as the baseline for how others should act is a losing strategy.

Charisma melts…

THE CORE OPERATING BELIEF OF THE NITPICKERS

Our decisions are predominantly based on 2 emotions:

Fear or Love.

You may notice a major paradigm shift as you evolve.

You ever seen that angry young adult mature into a compassionate adult?

That's because their consciousness rose.

As consciousness rises, you go from fear to love.

And love allows you to see the bigger picture.

When you can see the bigger picture, a byproduct is patience & a strong level of understanding.

Love allows you to understand the psychology of nitpicking and humans.

HOWEVER, WHEN THE CONSCIOUSNESS IS LOWER, YOUR MAIN FOCUS IS ON THE PHYSICAL BODY.

You are trying to survive...

And this level of survival has you operating with a basis of fear.

What's sad is that the CORE operating belief of fear doesn't doom you towards a poor material life.

You may operate in fear, but be a very loving individual.

'Hm... the 2 seem contrary Armani, mind giving me an example?'

Sure.

Imagine an older brother who views the world in a very dark negative light.

His name is Timmy.

Timmy has been backstabbed many times and is jaded.

His little brother is Johnny.

Johnny thus far has had betrayals too. But overall, he still is a realistic optimist.

Timmy's CORE operating belief of fear alters his behaviors on the macro level.

He loves his little brother. And wants him to be safe.

So he criticizes Johnny anytime he thinks Johnny is being too open with others.

His criticism spills over to micro analyzing Johnny's moves outside of the social world as well.

Timmy thinks he's is looking out for his lil bro.

While in reality, he is just annoying Johnny.

So yea, you can nitpick the people you love the most.

Because that's mainly due to your core operating belief being fear-based.

Let's say you won the lottery for 1 billion dollars.

The LAST thing you have in your mind is to point out what others are doing wrong.

You may give advice.

But nitpicking? Nah...

WHY NITPICKING NEEDS TO BE DITCHED

The reason nitpicking needs to be ditched is because it becomes a subtle drug.

And this subtle drug soon starts to gain a stronger grasp of you.

It FEELS good when you are nitpicking.

It makes you feel like a virtuous being.

'Look at me looking out for this low IQ individual. Thank God I am here to guide them' you think.

That's false talk right there.

It's the ego screaming in your ear.

While your intuition is whispering that there may be another way.

The more you nitpick now, the more you wanna do it in the future.

Constantly fault finding.
This leaves a trail of resentment along the way.
The energy you put out there boomerangs back champ.

Your intention may not be bad.
You may love the people you are nitpicking.
But you're making enemies.

The beauty is that you can stop at any time.
'Even now?'
Yea, even now.

'Uh.. I feel like there's a catch though bro.'
There is.
It WON'T be easy.

Your ego does not like giving up power.
It finds it very annoying.
So when you DO find a fault in someone & don't point it out,
the ego feels annoyed.
It wants to bark.

The main goal is to do **nothing**.
Just let the other person make the fault.
And unless it's a DIRE situation where you need to correct the
behavior, then don't.

The ego get's slick though.
It tries to justify why you need to get involved.
But after building more maturity, you start learning when to
get involved and when not to.

At the beginning of your journey, just ask yourself how you would feel if someone else is correcting you for making the same mistake.

Then also analyze the other person's personality.

ASSUME MOST HUMANS ARE MORE SENSITIVE THAN YOU CAN IMAGINE.

If you go in with this assumption, you move with more grace.

One thing you learn as you grow up is giving others the GIFT of making their own mistakes and learning from it, themselves.

No need to point out faults so much.

And if you do find the dire needs to do it, then do it in a polite manner.

Mind your tonality.

Sandwich the criticism. Ex: *What they did right, what they can improve, repeat what they did right again.*

And just keep it moving.

Hounding someone doesn't do you any favors G.

'Gotcha bro. And what if someone is constantly nitpicking me?'

First, understand why they are nitpicking.

As discussed so far:

- It can be their childhood manifesting into their adulthood.

- They love you & want the best for you.

- It's just a personality trait.

Next, bring it up.

That's about it.

You don't want to start nitpicking the nitpicker.

They may be quick to change or may not see any need for change at all.

But be sure to communicate their behavior traits in a gentle way.

Don't think they'll read your mind.

We often make pissed-off motions with our bodies when we are offended hoping others will pick up the clue.

But that will not do the trick.

'And if they still don't listen?'

Then you need to distance from them or just use them as an opportunity to build a thicker skin.

The route you choose will be based on your own levels of introspection and judgment.

SEE THE GRAY IN THE BEAUTY OF LIFE

When we think of the color gray, we think bland and boring.

But when you THINK in gray, you see the color of life.

That means, quit breaking everything down so much.

Thinking is not like breathing.

You can stop thinking & still be alive champ.

Just imagine how you behave when you are with your best friend cracking jokes.

You're not thinking all the time.

You are just BEING.

Learn to BE more.

And you'll do that by doing less.

Every time you point out flaws, the more that you want to keep on doing it.

So break out of that loop NOW.

Just put that side of you in the back burner.

Fight through the ego's grasp.

And rise above anyways.

That's what makes the charismatic person shine.

Bulldoze through the psychology of nitpicking via the power of acceptance.

That's the magic insight.

THE FEELING OF ANXIETY

The feeling of anxiety is debilitating for many.
And it causes a loss of enthusiasm for life.

When you picture your life, you recognize when you are
enjoying it & when you aren't, based on your enthusiasm.
Low energy & a feeling doubt cripple that.

Anxiety is not just mental...
It is not just emotional.
But it also physical as well.

When you break that part down, and digest it, there is some
clarity.
During feelings of low energy, we have a lot of doubt regarding
the task.

Our ego doesn't like to feel embarrassed.
So whatever task is causing us anxiety, will be stamped by the
ego. And that act will have tension in the future.

You gotta realize one big part.
Anxiety can get the best of you unless you become AWARE of
it.

*It's as though anxiety and awareness cannot coexist with one
another.*
One always overpowers the other.

If that's your option, then let's choose awareness.
But you don't get awareness willy nilly.

You get it via pain & knowledge.
In today's blog post, you'll get a little bit of both.

You may feel the pain. Good.
Embrace it.
Allow the knowledge of the feeling of anxiety to clarify your understanding of the internal world.

Emotional intelligence gives you depth.
And the depth you gain gives you confidence for your future.
Let's begin.

WHY DO WE GET ANXIETY?

We get anxiety based on perception.
Perception is our interpretation based on our 5 senses.

We input information, and process however we do.
The processing depends heavily on our belief systems.

Humans have developed an ego over generations.
An ego gives us our sense of identity.
A tamed ego can be your best friend.
But an untamed ego can make your life a living hell.

Anxiety is born via an untamed ego.
'What do you mean by an untamed ego bro?'
It's when you make yourself the center of everyone else's world.

'What's the difference between an untamed ego and a tamed one?'

- With a tamed ego, you see the FULL picture and understand your place within that picture.

- However, with an untamed ego, you just see the pixel (yourself) & mistake it for the full picture.

Your untamed ego leads to the **Spotlight Effect**.

In summary, the Spotlight Effect is when you feel as though there is an imaginary spotlight over you.

This makes you extra cautious of your moves.

When you are extra cautions of your moves, the next psychological phenomena kicks in...

The **Illusion of Transparency**.

The Illusion of Transparency is when you THINK that your emotions are leaking out to the public.

Also known as those times when you wonder if you look nervous or ugly.

A combination of Spotlight Effect and Illusion of Transparency has you terrified of making mistakes & being judged for it.

Which causes you to ignore the **Pratfall Effect**.

'The Pratfall Effect?'

Yep... The Pratfall Effect states that humans like humans with imperfections & flaws.

These people are easier to relate too.

However, your chain of fears has created an imitation version of you.

A fake perfection persona which causes you to meet what you were trying to avoid:

Judgment.

How to Break Out the Feeling of Anxiety Loop

Anxiety as a whole isn't a bad thing.
It can actually be good in many ways.

There was a portion of my public speaking journey where I had gotten a little cocky.
I began thinking I had it 'all figured out.'
That couldn't have been further from the truth.

One speech, I ended up going in unprepared.
And ended up bombing.
The speech was very low energy & seemed to lack enthusiasm.

I realized that day that the nerves I normally felt leading up to a speech allowed me to attain a hyper-focus level.
And that focus is what allowed me to bring out my best self.

In the real world though, too much of anything becomes bad.
- A little bit of anxiety allows you to feel ENERGY.
- But too much of anxiety makes you feel crippled.

'Why does this happen?'
It happens because you suppress rather than make yourself aware of your feelings.

Remember earlier how I said anxiety and awareness cannot exist at the same time?
'Uh.. yea.'
Well, then you need to become more aware.

You'll never become FULLY aware.

Nothing personal.

But awareness is a lifelong journey. That's what keeps it fun.

However, the more aware that you DO become, the more you feel in control.

'Gotcha bro. But what do I become aware of?'

You become aware of your internal world.

That's the first step in breaking out of the anxiety loop.

BRINGING CLARITY TO DARKNESS

A lot of anxiety is caused by ambiguity.

Your brain doesn't like ambiguity.

And when it does have ambiguity, it begins to overthink.

Imagine you start clicking a bunch of buttons on your microwave.

That's not a good usage of the tool...

Your brain likes clarity.

If you want a quick little trick... try this:

Next time you feel anxiety, write in 1 sentence why you feel the way you do.

I encourage 1 sentence because it forces you to be succinct.

And I encourage you to write because it forces you to bring WORDS to your FEELINGS.

Try it & you'll notice your anxiety melt...

There are a lot of principles behind this little exercise.

But the main principle is that clarity is what you are going for.

Any thought that you get in your mind generates a FEELING in your body.

Rather than focusing so much on the thought, focus more on the feeling.

You'll notice something.

'What?'

The feelings don't hold any narratives.

Thoughts hold narratives. But feelings are completely neutral.

The mind and body are connected.

Body influences the mind & mind influences the body.

But since your body is capable of understanding via your 5 senses, it's much easier to influence.

FEEL the physical sensations associated with the thoughts.

This allows you to surprisingly bring clarity to the darkness.

Understanding your body allows you to understand your mind.

Rather than multiple thoughts floating around...

You are now more grounded & have a FILTER to which thoughts matter and which don't.

BUILDING YOUR EMOTIONAL LITERACY

One of the main reasons a lot of people suffer from the feeling of anxiety is due to lacking emotional literacy.

Ambiguity causes a lot of anxiety.

And when you don't have the right words in your toolbox, you are unable to make sense of your internal world.

Language allows us to slice up reality into bits that apply to our perception.

I can't even imagine life without language.

Language is primal technology.

Once you have gotten to know your body, that's when you need to assign WORDS to the FEELINGS.
That's emotional literacy 101.

Rather than just feeling 'happy, 'mad', 'sad'.
You now have more depth.

Now you can feel:
Happy & confused.
Anxious and excited.
Mad & contemplative etc.

Having enhanced emotional literacy allows you to feel more grounded rather than a bag floating in the wind.
You become more like a tree.

The more you get in the habit of FEELING your sensations & using your mind to assign WORDS to the feelings, the more confident you become.
Awareness expands.
Anxiety melts.

That's when you start realizing 'anxiety' and 'excitement' have a lot of the same physical sensations.
Almost identical in many ways.

Realizing this insight for yourself allows you to choose your words more carefully.
Instead of just going with what your environment implies you should think.
Things are different now.
Your internal world holds the power.

OVERCOME ANXIETY & TAKE CONTROL OVER YOUR LIFE

The feeling of anxiety in doses can keep you alert.

But unfortunately, most have an overloaded amount of this feeling.

In the most technologically gifted era of human history, we seem the most emotionally out of it.

So change your story.

We have a lot of material possessions in the external world.

But now it's time to look within.

Emotional intelligence is a game of what is within, not what is outside.

Learning to understand your emotions allows you to control your emotions.

And learning to control your emotions allows you to make sense of your reality.

Overcome anxiety, & build your confidence.

Once you get your enthusiasm back for life, that is when you KNOW that you are back on the right track.

IGNORING SOMEONE WHO HURT YOU

One of the strongest signs of social intelligence is learning the power of ignoring.

Social skills by doing absolutely nothing.

This seems counterintuitive at first, until you realize...

All strategic decisions are normally counterintuitive.

If it wasn't, then it would be a no brainer. Everyone would be doing it.

One of the first things we want to do to someone who hurt us, is to hurt them back.

We go on revenge mode.

But is this strategic?

Well, look around you. That's what everyone does.

Heck, that's what you are probably doing now.

However, use this blog post to adopt a new perspective.

Why get revenge? It feels good.

But long term, it doesn't lead to much else.

However, with ignoring?

It's a life long skill that allows you to control your focus at will.

Ignoring someone who hurt you is a cornerstone habit that leads to many more dividends.

Let's break it down.

REVENGE MODE

Revenge is a short term pleasure for long term pain.
Why?

Because you are giving the other human what most humans cherish:
Attention.

Believe it or not, the person who hurt you is lowkey happy that you are plotting revenge against them in the first place.

It gives their ego a certain feeling of power.

They feel like they have control over you without them even needing to be present.

But revenge takes it another level further.

It affects YOU.

Your subconscious mind controls roughly about 95% of your life.

And this part of your mind is highly influenced by pictures & emotions.

All your moments of revenge rewires your subconscious mind for the worst.

You are daydreaming about making this person pay for their sins.

And stamping those images with feelings of hatred.

Over time, you are just playing yourself.

Let's not forget the opportunity cost.

All the time you are plotting revenge, you could be learning a new skill, trying to bounce back from the betrayal, building a side hustle, etc.

WHY IGNORING IS POWERFUL

Ignoring is powerful because of this thing called attention.
Humans crave it.
Heck, BEINGS crave it.

If you have a pet, then you know that it wants your love from time to time.
Why? You are a human and your pet is an animal.
That doesn't make any logical sense.

It doesn't need to.
Attention is a driver of action in a lot of our moves.

The reason ignoring is powerful is that you take away what this individual lowkey desires.
I said earlier that most toxic people are lowkey happy when you plot revenge.
You are giving them attention.

'But it's not the good kind of attention though!'
It doesn't matter.
Low lives don't care if its good attention or not.

People with integrity and high valued individual have tiers to their attention.
They clearly don't want negative publicity.
Because that just hurts their reputation.

If they are going to get publicity, then they will opt to get it the ethical way.

Much more effective long term.

But low lives?

It doesn't matter. Any attention is good attention.

You ever met that person who is like 'I hate drama...OMG.'

But is ALWAYS surrounded by drama?

This is an example of someone cherishing attention.

No filters needed.

Ignoring is powerful because you take what they desire, away.

Lowkey, this ends up turning into a form of revenge without you even trying to do so.

To take it another further, invest in yourself.

Know that you are better off without the snake in your life.

Then act like it.

First, you opt out of revenge mode.

Then, you opt in to ignore.

Finally, you decide to make yourself better?

You're on a roll bud.

WHY DON'T MORE PEOPLE IGNORE?

'So question bro. If this is all the case, why don't more people ignore?'

Because it's hard.

At first, you think doing nothing would be the easy route.

But doing nothing is actually WAY harder than doing something.

That's why they call it 'taking the high road.'

It's tough because your ego is invested.

Your ego is a very sensitive thing, especially when it is untamed.

The ego hates to feel threatened or disrespected.

And when you are betrayed, the LAST thing the ego wants to do is just sit down and do nothing.

Therefore, it is a painful process, physically, mentally & emotionally.

'Physically too??'

Yea. Whenever your mental & emotional faculties are engaged, you **physically** feel it.

This is why you can feel your skin crawling at the sight of not doing anything.

Just ignoring.

As goofy as this may sound, you become tougher for it.

There is short term pain, I get it.

But in the long run, you build a thick skin.

Building thick skin is an investment for your future.

Not to scare you, but there are no shortages of snakes in this world.

People you trusted betray you.
Friends turn into enemies.
And haters emerge.

But the person across the mirror will always stay the same.

Each time your skin toughens, each time you unlock a new level.

Plus, opinions begin to take less of a hold on you.

Most of your life problems come down to what others will think of you, when you look closely.

If you can overcome the fear of judgment, then you have just overcome a large part of your problems.

IGNORING SOMEONE WHO HURT YOU CAN BRING THEM BACK

What's funny about all this ignoring talk is that it often makes the person who hurt you....come back.

They feel like you robbed them of their attention by not seeking revenge (as sick as it sounds).

So they try to make amends.

Once you ignore them for some time you will have the perspective to forgive them.

So the weight will fall off.

But even if you forgive them, do you allow them back into your lives?

Eh...

Always be wary when someone claims they changed overnight.

Humans do not change overnight.

They change over time.

And if they did change, it's up to you to decide whether you want them back in your life or not.

The ball is in your court.

However, the main takeaway is that you learned a SKILL.
Ignoring someone who hurt you is a cornerstone habit.

You get your time back to invest in yourself, toughen your skin
& grab more control over your future.
It's this small decision which allows you to be strategic

A strategic mind often takes the road less taken.
But it was less taken because it was meant for those who chose
to be different.

FLOW STATE THRU JOY: WHAT IS FUN?

When we think of fun, we think of something that is light.
Nothing too serious in the real world.

Sure, having fun is important when you are a little kid.
But when you are older?
It's time to change.
Time to tuck away fun in the closet where it belongs.

But how true is this?

I've often found it fascinating when seeing patterns in interviews of legends.
The legends can range from industries such as sports, art, acting etc.

You know what is something they said that allowed them to be great?
They said that they had fun.
Truth be told, they loved their craft.
And it never felt like work.

This is often why we see some legends take TOO long to retire.
We often think 'You have done so much. Now go relax. '

But they think: *Fool! I am relaxing. And you're trying to get me to retire from that?*

Fun is very practical.
And it alters how you perceive time.

In today's blog post, we are going to be talking about fun, it's connection to flow state & what it means to have a tension free life.

'Tension free!! Yea right?'

Subjective is always your choice.

And we will see why.

THE MYTH OF WORK

Traditionally, when we think of work, we think of it in a negative light.

Uhh...I have to work today.

This simple attitude alters lives.

There are people who spend most of their adult life hating what they do.

And they wait until the weekend to take a reprieve.

Worst, they count down the YEARS until they can retire.

This sort of attitude spills over to other parts of their life.

People who hate what they do often have a sour attitude about them.

Not always, but you can sense it from the way they move.

Typically, what they touch has a sense of death.

I often see this when I'm in a restaurant.

There are some waiters who are SO full of life.

They make it a priority to take care of their customers.

However, there are times when you go to the restaurant and the waiters are dragging their feet.

Fucking up your order.

Never checking up on you.

Huh??

Now I'm not saying that the enthusiastic waiter wakes up in the morning getting ready to wait tables.

Maybe they are..Idk.

But ultimately, one is viewing it as work.

While the other is viewing it as play.

Whether they are aware or not.

WHAT IS TIME REALLY?

You ever had that moment when you were counting down the clock?

And typically, when you count down time, it goes by very slowly.

Sometimes you gotta check if the clock is working properly.

Flip that with when you are having a good time.

That's when the seconds just seem to fly on by.

How real is time?

Time is real in the external world.

In the internal world, it is a subjective experience.

Einstein used to illustrate his relativity principle by making you imagine 2 completely different scenarios.

- Imagine if you put your hand on a hot stove for 1 minute.
- Now imagine a pretty girl sitting on your lap for 1 minute.

Objectively, the time is the same.

But subjectively, time is on a separate plane.

When you have fun, you **warp** time.

You get into the flow state.

The state that allows great artists, athletes, musicians to produce magic.

Let's talk a little bit about flow.

DOES FUN LEAD TO FLOW STATE?

I often found it funny that some people take hours to prepare a speech.

Truth be told, I was like that.

Back when I hated public speaking, I would have to prepare a lot.

As I gained experience, the amount of time to plan the speech began to dissipate.

That's when I was able to create speeches quicker.

The act of speech was the same.

But my ATTITUDE had changed.

Flow is defined by Wikipedia as:

the mental state in which a person performing an activity is fully immersed in a feeling of energized focus, full involvement, and **enjoyment** in the process of the activity.

The phrase 'enjoyment' is the most important part.

And I can go back to the public speaking example.

When I had massive speech anxiety, I had one foot in and another foot out in terms of speech building.

One foot was actively trying to prep for the speech.

And the other foot was filled with worries about fucking up & getting booed off stage.

As I gained experience, the fears began to melt away.

And even if the fears were there, they were quieter.

More of the mental bandwidth was put on the task.

Fun is a cheat code to flow state.

Some people spend a long time reading a ton of books on how to reach flow.

They do a bunch of rituals.

And practice with all these tactics.

While in reality, the trick is to make the activity fun & begin.

WHAT DEFINES FUN?

Fun is defined as different things by different people.

I personally have fun when writing.

Others hate that.

Fun is a subjective experience.

So rather than looking for a definition.

Look for a feeling.

The feeling to be alert for is *tensionless*.

It's a mode where your body feels light.

One definition of meditation I loved was:

- The best meditation is the relaxing meditation.

And it's so true.

Initially, when I pictured meditation, I viewed it as work.

And the whole act was full of tension.

My head would hurt, body would keep tensing up & I felt angry.

When I went in with the intention to relax, that's when I began to enjoy it.

If you don't know what the feeling of light even means, observe yourself when you are relaxing.

Just as your day is winding down after a long day & now you are just chilling.

How do you feel?

Physically, mentally & emotionally.

Observe that.

That's the traits of fun.

And those were the feelings you used to have when you were a little kid playing with your action figures or dolls.

Those are the feelings you want to bring to your task.

TURN BORING INTO FUN

Look, I get it.

We live in a world where everything is not fun.

There are some responsibilities & obligations we must do that we don't want to do.

But if that is the case..

Would you want to do those boring tasks with an agitated attitude, or one with some joy?

The agitated attitude will turn a bad situation into a worse one.
A trained joyful attitude will turn a bad situation into a not so
bad one.

There are certain tasks which legit are bad. Like a funeral. So
you don't want to be joyful for that.

But something like taking out the trash.
Practice conditioning the feelings of joy in the act.

You have to take out the trash anyway.
So, turn it into an emotional intelligence workout.

By simply doing this little rep, you see the power of finding
ways to add joy in your own unique way. And you are
conditioning yourself into a new paradigm.
An evolved perception will follow.

If you have NO clue how to add joy, the bare minimum you can
do is do the task with a smile.
You'll feel some tension melt.

Over time, you want to unlock your inner child.
Just like you used to create storylines for the action figures &
dolls.
Do the same with the storylines for your life.

No one taught you how to be imaginative as a kid.
It just happened.

We are imaginative by birth. It's just a matter of rediscovering
that.
That's what fun is about.

FUN IS A MODERN SUPERPOWER

A lot of people who have fun & eventually condition that as a baseline state discover their hidden power.

This is what I call self-amusement.

Learning how to have fun allows you to condition negative vibrations out of a neutral task.

Remember, nothing is good or bad, only our thinking makes it so.

But to take it a level further.

Our emotions stamp the experience.

Thinking & emotions are a lifelong bond.

Control your thinking by controlling your emotions.

You control your emotions by unlocking your inner child.

That's when you wake up and reach a level of productively that you could never have imagined.

SPEAK YOUR MIND

The core of communication skills comes down to one thing.

If you could understand that, then you will become a better communicator over time.

'What is it Armani??'

Can you handle such simplicity?

'Yes yes, I can!! Tell me.'

Communication skills comes down to turning your mind visible via words.

'What?? Yea right!'

I had a feeling you couldn't handle such simplicity.

Simplicity often scares people. They feel like they are 'missing out' on some information.

But in reality, there is a power to simplicity.

It's all that was important all along.

We always hear the phrase 'speak your mind.'

But it doesn't quite sink in with us.

Speaking your mind is the ESSENCE of communication skills.

Grammar, tonality, posture are all extras.

They derive from you speaking your mind.

'If that's the essence of communication skills, how come more people don't speak their mind?'

Fear.

It's time to dispel some limiting beliefs.

Rather than spending years trying to improve your speaking skills. Cut your time.

Speak your mind.

Let's figure out how to do that.

THE NUMBER 1 REASON YOU DON'T SPEAK YOUR MIND

Earlier, I said that fear holds people back from speaking their mind.

But where does this fear stem from?

The fear stems from multiple situations.

But the core of it is an untamed ego.

Your ego is your sense of identity.

And it loves to analyze, feel powerful, and create narratives.

One habit of the ego is to create an enemy.

Your ego loves enemies.

It's sad because our world has a lot of people in power who possess untamed egos.

Countries go to war because the ego created enemies out of thin air.

Behind the tendency to create enemies is another cause.

'Which is?'

Fear.

When you have a *'it's me against the world'* attitude, sure you can be bold a lot of times.

But ultimately, you'll always be operating with a small or large residue of fear.

That's when you become unaware of the present moment & become more locked into the narrative of the ego.

The narrative of the ego has you worrying about saying the wrong things.

Rather than focusing on the essence of communication, which is to speak your mind.

You start focusing a lot on the words & how to put on a persona.

Ultimately, the inability to express yourself with swag comes down to the feeling of power which ultimately leaves you feeling hopeless.

Leaving you feeling scared to be the real you.

WHAT IS RIGHT AND WHAT IS WRONG?

One of the worst parts of our society is that it places way too much focus on thinking.

'Well, isn't thinking like breathing?'

Not necessarily.

Imagine you are speaking to your best friend.

Are you thinking a lot?

'Not really.'

Then what is going on?

'I am just flowing.'

Exactly!

Communication skills come down to just flowing.

Being in the moment.

The ego cannot exist in the present moment.

It only exists when you are stuck in dualistic thinking.

Past/future, right/wrong, good/bad etc.

Charismatic people are often not thinking a lot.

They are in the present moment & in tune with their deeper intelligence.

'Deeper intelligence?'

Yea. The carefree mode that you exhibit when talking to a best friend.

Thinking is just a tool.

But learning WHEN to think is the key.

'And how do I do that?'

You get rid of the 'it's me against the world' mentality.

The whole Survival of the Fittest concept by Charles Darwin made people fearful creatures.

Always making humans wonder when they will lose it all.

That sort of attitude may have worked in the past, with animals, or lower consciousness creatures...

But in the communication skills world?

- Others aren't your competition.
- You are your only competition.

Declaring a friendly competition with your prior day self LOOSENS you up.

Allows you to focus internally.

When you do this, you aren't as fearful of what others will think of you.

This is the core philosophy of the Level Up Mentality.

You quite frankly don't give a fuck what's the 'right thing' or the 'wrong thing' to say.

That's because you are only focusing on evolving for yourself.

When you take the focus off the external world & put it into your internal world, you begin the journey to speaking your mind.

THE POWER OF SPEAKING & WRITING

The beauty of communication skills is that they are interdependent.

Meaning, each of the skills plays off of one another.

- *Being a great listener will improve your speaking.*
- *Improving your speaking will improve your writing.*
- *And improved writing surprisingly works wonders for your listening.*

What you need to do is **practice**.

The world has conditioned you for FAR too long to be an egotistical creature.

Making you over think.

And making it seem like others are your competition.

What's ironic is that some of the most powerful people who are out of the spotlight actually collaborate.

Whether it's for ethical or unethical reasons is not the point.

The main takeaway is that they collaborate, pass off agendas, and then they tell the rest of the people below them to compete.

Hm... something doesn't seem right.

But that's a topic I'll discuss another time.

Ultimately, you need to unlearn a lot of junk.

And the best way to do that is to discover the real YOU.

WHO ARE YOU PAST YOUR JOB TITLE, NAME &
ETHNICITY?

This question confuses a lot of people.
Which is why you need to find out for yourself.

Thru the vehicles of speech and/or writing, you will discover
who you are.

Talk about topics that interest you & communicate on it.
You can do it thru multiple vehicles.
- Journaling
- Starting a YouTube channel
- Joining a Toastmasters and giving a speech
- Writing on Twitter

etc.

Find a space where you can just be you.
No strings attached.

Remember what I said earlier, communication skills is about
turning the mind tangible via words.
That's it.

Therefore, you need to understand HOW your mind operates
when it's not in a fearful state.
That's the magic.

Choose any vehicle. Don't get caught up in the small details
about whether you should begin with writing or speaking.
I'll save you some time.

Begin with whatever you can see yourself being the most consistent with for a long period of time.

You can always add more later on.

I began with writing thru a Twitter + blog & eventually evolved into a YouTube.

Pick your path and be consistent!

COMMUNICATE WITH PURE AUTHENTICITY

Once you go on a journey to discovering who you are, you realize something.

'What?'

That your internal world dictates your external world.

When you authentically submerge into unlearning fear-based beliefs & actively writing/speaking, you become more confident.

You feel looser in social interactions.

Rather than thinking away on how to say the 'right thing.'

You just flow.

You're in the moment.

That's when you're tapped to a MUCH higher energy.

An energy that the ego couldn't even dream of.

And that's when you start learning communication skills was much more than the surface level portion.

You learn that its a lifeline journey for self-realization.

WHAT'S SOCIAL ANXIETY?

I've been seeing a lot of those Masterclass commercials recently as I wait for a Youtube video to load.

Normally I skip all ads once the '**skip ad**' section comes up.

But there was one ad that was different.

It was this ad with Chris Hadfield.

He is a former astronaut.

'What made this particular ad different?'

Well, I was always into space. So that part caught my eye.

But what kept me hooked was this one line that he said.

The more you know, the less you fear.

It was such a powerful line.

And so true as well.

It hit home because this was coming from an astronaut who has literally been in space.

The home of the unknown.

The more you know, the less you fear.

'Why is this important for social anxiety?'

It is important because we often fear social interactions due to not knowing much about it.

We have no clue why we feel fearful in the first place.

This causes a level of reactivity rather than responsiveness.

Today, I am going to give a very basic understanding of social anxiety.

This blog post isn't meant to be an in-depth discussion on social skills.

Rather, the exact opposite.

(If you want recommended social skills books, I did a blog post here.)

Instead, I am going to talk about the fundamentals of social anxiety, so you have more clarity on the topic.

With the knowledge, you can gain frameworks to dissect your own life the next time you feel social anxiety.

Without further ado, let's begin.

SOCIAL ANXIETY DEFINITION

There are plenty of definitions for the word out there.

But one of the definitions for social anxiety which stuck out was:

A chronic mental health condition in which social interactions cause irrational anxiety.

I like this definition because it has one keyword that sticks out.

And that word is '**irrational**.'

Typically when you feel social anxiety, you are sort of annoyed with yourself.

'Get over it, why do you feel so nervous?' you ask yourself.

But remember, it's typically difficult to logic with emotions.

Emotions are more so meant to be experienced & understood, rather than hit straightway with logic.

Logic has its part in the world.

But with social anxiety, the real logic is intuition & introspection.

You gotta feel the emotions from within.

But you don't know how to exactly do that yet.

'Why don't I?'

Because you don't know WHEN you get social anxiety in the first place...

Let's change that.

WHEN DOES SOCIAL ANXIETY HAPPEN?

You ever had that moment when you were at an event that you were initially dreading and thought:

'THIS is the event that had me soo nervous? This event isn't bad at all! It's actually quite enjoyable.'

I'm sure you can think of a handful of moments like that.

This happened because your imagination got the best of you leading up to the event.

Read the last sentence again.

LEADING up to the event.

In the social world, social anxiety is formed leading up to an event, not so much during the event.

But we are often oblivious to that.

We think that this event is going to be so scary.

Picture you got a wedding coming up on Wednesday.

And it is a Friday the week before.

Well, you are gonna go from Friday, Saturday, Sunday, Monday, Tuesday & the especially the beginning of Wednesday dreading this event.

You spend soo many days feeling fearful to only notice that the event that you were dreading so much was pretty fun.

'Why does it matter if I feel social anxiety before the event rather than the actual event itself?'

Because that allows you to realize that you are fearing an illusion.

And it allows you to know WHEN to tackle the solution.

Most of anxiety happens when we are anticipating something in the unknown.

But when you finally WAKE UP and realize that you are already going thru the 'unknown', that's when you have more power to do something about it.

Which leads me to my next point.

2 WAYS TO DEAL WITH SOCIAL ANXIETY

Once you spot that your social anxiety happens leading up to the event rather than the actual event in itself, that's when you have more control.

You realize that you can go thru the days before, experiencing your emotions rather than trying to bulldoze it with logic.

Also, you feel a sense of calm knowing that you are technically going thru the worst part now.

In the safety of your own home.

Yep, most of social anxiety happens in the mind.

In your home.

Not in front of others.

Now with that out there, let's try 2 mind hacks.

1. Social Anxiety = Social Excitement
2. Body Meditation

SOCIAL ANXIETY = SOCIAL EXCITEMENT

I like this social mind hack because of the importance of words.

Words were created to communicate our ideas.

But words serve more purpose than that.

In my eyes, words are a form of technology.

And if you aren't aware, words influence your perception.

'Anxiety' what a yucky word.

No beauty to it.

 'Excitement' what elegance.

I like the word excitement.

When you analyze your body, you realize the physical sensations of anxiety and excitement are virtually the same.

- Picture yourself going up on stage to speak in front of 500 people. **Anxiety**.

- Picture yourself at the TIP of the roller coaster before it's about to plunge. **Excitement**.

Same physical sensations.

Different perceptions.

During the lead up to the social event, focus on using words that aid you.

'I am feeling a lot of social excitement right now.'

This seems like a small trick. But does wonders for your perception long term.

BODY MEDITATION

Earlier, I said that you cannot logical your way into building emotional intelligence.

Gotta FEEL the emotions.

Put on your big boy pants and look IN rather than finding ways to distract yourself in the outside world.

When you feel a lot of tension for the upcoming event, FEEL the sensations.

Bring conscious awareness into it.

And be detailed too.

Which body parts do you feel sensations?

Where exactly within the body parts?

How does the sensation feel?

Is your body warm?

Etc.

Being detailed with the sensations allows you to build your emotional literacy.

Rather than just using basic words like 'happy', 'mad', 'sad' etc.

You are able to delve much deeper.

Body meditation is just sitting and being aware of your body.

After doing this for some time, you'll realize it's pretty therapeutic.

THE ELEPHANT IN THE ROOM

As this blog winds down, I want to address one last thing.

WHY exactly does social anxiety happen?

In this beginning of the blog, I gave you the WHAT (the definition) of social anxiety.

But were you curious about the why?

I was always curious myself.

And after some introspection, I realized it was because I was putting too much spotlight on myself.

Then I did some research and found out there was a psychological phenomenal for when you place too much attention on yourself.

It's called the **'spotlight effect.'**

The spotlight effect is one of the MAIN reasons humans put a ton of pressure on themselves.

We trick ourselves into believing that we are the main character in someone else's world.

But that isn't the case.

We are the main character in our worlds & an extra in other people's worlds.

This doesn't seem like rocket science.

But when you can truly internalize this concept, you begin to realize the ROOT cause of social anxiety.

I gave you this section last because this is a concept that you need to meditate on.

You aren't the main character of other people's worlds... You are an extra in other people's worlds.

To illustrate this, picture that one time you saw someone slip and fall in public.

In their world, they were mortified. Probably spent their entire day thinking about their fuckup.

But in your world? You probably had a good laugh & went about your day.

Learn this simple, yet profound concept.

You are the main character only in your world & an extra in the mind movies of others.

When you digest this, social anxiety weakens its holds over you.

SOCIAL ANXIETY MELTS LIKE ICE IN SUN

The more that you equip yourself with the right knowledge & take the right action, the more resilient that you become.
Like the astronaut stated:
The more you know, the less you fear.

But knowing isn't just about reading books.
It's about legit applying.

The emotional intelligence world is different than the world of school.
- In school, you got the lesson and then the test.
- In the real world, you get the test & strive to find the lessons.

Emotional intelligence isn't something that you can just learn about.
It's something that you need to experience.

This blog has given you the knowledge.
Now it's up to you to channel the knowledge to come out taming the beast known as social anxiety.

What makes others terror will simply be light work for you.
Now go & level up.

FIXED MINDSET VS GROWTH MINDSET

Look around you. There are multiple different types of personality.

The different personalities of others can play a role in your life.

'Why will someone else's personality play a role in MY life?'

Because we are an interconnected species.

Always communicating in one form or another.

Even tasks that you *physically* do alone, can be *mentally* connected to someone else.

For example: reading this blog.

With this blog, you may be reading it solo at your crib.

But as you are engaged with it mentally, you and I are officially in communication.

Therefore, my personality has some effect on your reality.

The question is, what kind of personality do I have?

Fixed vs growth mindset?

These 2 mindsets are fundamental in defining the personality of a human.

And if you often find 2 people not getting along, you'll typically see a lot of answers based on the mentality they possess.

In this article, I am going to share the differences between fixed mindset vs growth mindset & who the future belongs to.

WHAT IS A MINDSET?

A mindset is simply a word.

And when you first think of it, you probably think of it only entailing the mind.

Let me clarify what mindset means by sharing what it DOESN'T mean.

What it doesn't mean is someone who is intellectually gifted.

That is only one facet of mindset.

In reality, a mindset consists of 3 factors.

- Thoughts
- Emotions
- Behavior

And when all these 3 are congruent towards a higher goal, you end up elevating your consciousness.

Consciousness is always a part of us.

But you build a stronger connection to it as your mindset elevates.

'How do we define what is a strong mindset & what is a weak mindset?'

Unfortunately, WE can't.

Only YOU can.

The life goals & desires you have for your particular life will dictate your perception regarding a mindset.

However, I just wanted to give you the 3 elementary components of a mindset.

Ask yourself if you are in control of your thoughts, emotions & behavior to a certain degree or if those elements control you.

The mindset of a human creates their personality.

And the personality creates personal reality.

WHAT IS A FIXED MINDSET?

This is the sort of individual who believes everything is set.
From their level of intellect, skillset, beliefs, etc.

You can spot fixed mindsets from a mile away.
They believe self-education is a finite process.
Which means they have stopped learning.
And when you stop learning, you begin doubling down on preexisting beliefs.

It's hard to change this group's mind once they have a belief about a certain field.
And since their mind is closed off, they refuse to get new information on the topic.
A lot of their beliefs are tied right into their ego.

So if you DO prove to them that they were wrong about a certain topic with facts, then they will often feel like you are attacking their character.
This isn't always the case, but often is.

Fixed mindset individuals also happen to be a victim of their circumstances.
They do not place much priority on the effect of their habits & free will.

WHAT IS A GROWTH MINDSET?

A growth mindset is the mentality of individuals who have delved into the self-improvement journey.
They seek new information, habits & thought patterns.

If you see someone with a growth mindset, you'll notice them constantly evolving.

How they were a month ago is a distant past to who they are now.

And this is a GOOD thing for the person with a growth mindset.

They take pride in their habits.

And I mean a lot of pride.

They understand that small changes in habits in the right direction have the ability to lead to an emergent property of a **winner's personality.**

You'll notice that this group is typically more poised than their counter, the fixed mindset.

They constantly seek out new information and modes of thinking.

But despite actively studying more than the fixed mindset group, you'll never hear this group act like they know everything.

Because they have learned that the more they learn, the more they can still learn.

FIXED MINDSET OR GROWTH MINDSET?

'Fixed mindset vs growth mindset ...So which one is better? '

It's a no brainer which mindset is better.

Growth, obviously.

But truth be told, I sometimes wonder why so many humans became a fixed mindset?

And that's when I traced back to school.

During school, they passed off this shitty exam known as the IQ test where they tried to imply that your intellect was fixed.

Complete bullshit.

Neuroscience states that your brain is plastic and is capable of installing new neural pathways and weakening old neural pathways.

The 2 key components of lifelong learning?

Desire & repetition.

I don't think it's natural for humans to be a fixed mindset.

It's very abnormal.

You don't see a little child who thinks they have it all figured out.

Instead, they are curious beyond measures.

The curiosity fuels imagination, and the imagination fuels action.

HOW TO ADOPT THE GROWTH MINDSET

We used to hear:

- You become what you eat.

To add onto that, I would also say:

- You become what you consume.

The information that you consume plays a big role in your life.

And the consumption of information isn't just the type of books that you read.

It's also the people that you hang out with.

The thoughts that you entertain.

And content that you feed your attention to.

If you want to start your journey towards leveling up, then you need to get the right information.

You don't know what you don't know, I get it.

But in the Information Age, ignorance is a choice.

My recommendation?

Begin with the free resources.

You have blogs, YouTube videos, podcasts.

If you don't know where to begin, just follow one of your self-improvement curiosities.

For me, I got really curious about mediation one day.

And little did I know, I started a journey towards learning about other topics like neuroscience, emotional intelligence, storytelling, public speaking, etc.

You never know where the path can take you.

But don't just be consuming away.

Apply the knowledge that you are gaining.

If you are going to learn about meditation, then meditate as well.

Start small & work your way up.

Once you have installed 1 new habit that you self educated yourself on, that's when the game changes.

That's when you WAKE UP from the mindset of a fixed individual & realize your true potential.

When you gradually come towards the mindset of someone who is a growth mentality, you start wondering what took you so long.

But no need to judge, my friend.

Unfortunately, some people never find their way to the light.

GROWTH MINDSETS PAY IT FORWARD

One of the biggest things to realize is that someone with a growth mindset doesn't get complacent.

That doesn't mean that they are always hustling away.

Instead, they constantly strive to improve while enjoying the process.

The second that you think you know it all is the second that you begin your journey to lose it all.

Once you have learned & adopted a new mindset, pay it forward.

'How?'

Start teaching others or spreading your information out.

Show others the light as well.

The more that you teach others, the more that you are able to solidify pre-existing growth neural pathways & install a few new neural pathways as well.

Teaching others is a workout for your brain.

And a challenging one at that.

Luckily, the growth never stops.

Good habits compound.

And you become unrecognizable for the best.

Ditch the ways of the fixed mindset.

They will realize the error in their ways by witnessing the growth in your ways.

WHAT LOVE REALLY MEANS

One word that I never fully understood growing up was the word 'love.'

It seemed like people used it in so many different contexts.

Some would use love to define an affection for their partner.

Others would say 'I love you' to their kid.

And some used love to define their intense desire to play a game.

One person who used the word love in a unique way was Kobe Bryant.

He would say that he LOVED basketball.

But I used to wonder... hm... it's just a game though?

However, there was one game in Kobe's career where he tore his achilles against the Golden State Warriors.

And rather than get carried off in the stretcher due to the dire pain... he was able to temporarily play through it.

He had 2 free throws that he had to shoot.

And Kobe came back to the game, with a torn achilles & drained both of those free throws.

That was one time I saw love signified through the game of basketball.

The bottom line, **love is a noun and a verb.**

You can have a state of love.

But unless you show it as well, then the words do not match the actions.

In this blog, I am going to give you my practical definition of love.

I think it's something that is wired in all of us.
We all just have a different way of expressing it.

WHAT IS LOVE?

My definition of love is **the ability to see past dualities.**
It's about acceptance.
When we transcend the ego.

Imagine that you love your business.
You began building it from the ground up.

There will be times when you are struggling financially & are having bad times.
But that doesn't bug you enough to quit.
You understand the action that you have to take & execute regardless.

Despite the waves of emotions, you persevere anyway.

You also see this with a relationship between parents and a child.
Around the 11th grade, I was going through my rebellion phase.
Getting in fights, collecting referrals & getting suspended.

Most of the adults in school despised me. To make it worse, I was in the IB program.
The IB program is a collection of the top students for the curriculum.

My series of troubles were bringing a negative light to the IB program.
A lot of the instructors secretly (but not so secretly) wanted me kicked out.

However, despite all of that, my parents stuck by me.

They knew that this was just a phase in my life & that I would outgrow it.

Truth be told, they didn't have to think that.

It didn't logically make sense.

But rather, it delved into the faith territory.

Faith doesn't always add up logically.

It's a concept that often transcends logic & the material world in itself.

AN ANALOGY FOR LOVE

Picture the sea.

From the sea, there are waves on the surface level.

The surface is often volatile.

It is subject to change due to the changes of wind pressures.

But the depth of the sea?

That is safe from the winds.

There is a level of stillness when you start diving DEEP into the sea.

It's a force of being grounded.

In the context of emotions, the waves represent duality.

If you analyze your personality throughout the day, you notice yourself constantly changing.

Constantly being volatile like the winds.

At one point, you are happy.
At another point, you are frustrated.
Sprinkle in a bit of anxiety...

And so on.

But there is a level of awareness to you that can observe all of these emotions without connecting to them.

Its the depth of the sea that is not bound to change by the wind.

The deep part of you is awareness.

And that level of awareness does not change due to the volatilities of the human emotion.

It just is...

When you begin identifying with the depth of that side to you, you start unlocking your inner love.

You begin accepting your shortcomings & the shortcomings of others.

This doesn't mean you settle for mediocrity.

But instead, you are able to see past the ego alone.

Which brings me to my next point.

LOVE = EXTENDING PAST EGO

At the core level, humans have 2 different operating systems:
-Scarcity
-Abundance

Scarcity is when you feel like something is running out.
-You are leading with the competition mindset.

Abundance is when you feel like there is plenty to go around.
-This is when you lead with the cooperation mindset.

It's hard to love when you are always competing.

A part of you begins to make yourself discrete from the universe.

The untamed ego will have you believing that you are apart from the universe.

That you are on an island by yourself.

But the tamed ego will have you realize that we are all in it together.

We are all incorporating planet earth & the shared universe.

The tamed ego represents constantly striving for a better life, without violating the rights of others.

When you showcase love, you begin extending past your needs alone.

This is when you unlock a Super Saiyan mode.

A person who is ONLY fighting for themselves may do great in a field.

But eventually, they fizzle out.

However, those who are playing their unique role in the universe?

There is no saying how far they can go.

2 WAYS THAT WE OFTEN UNLOCK LOVE

There are plenty of ways to unlock love.

I like to view it as the inner fire.

The ability to see past dualities alone is not an easy feat.

It requires a high level of patience/practice.

Or....

A certain level of trauma.

2 Ways of Unlocking Love:
-Sudden
-Cultivated

SUDDEN

This can happen from trauma or a BIG life moment.

Say that your brother suddenly dies in a car accident.

Your brother was your best friend. You guys did everything together.

This moment will tear you apart from within.

You are going to go through a long grieving process & have 2 potential scenarios.

One road is coming out of this moment more bitter.

Another road is learning the art of acceptance & living a life that your brother will be proud of.

I've seen an individual who went through a moment like this.

A very bitter fellow who learned the art of becoming more accepting as a few years had passed.

He came out of the situation as a more empathetic individual.

Trauma can teach us more about life than a book ever will.

CULTIVATED

This path requires constant practice of connecting with the heart.

The heart has a level of intelligence that transcends the brain.

The brain has a left & right component which can often lead to dualistic thinking.

But the heart is grounded.

In order to connect with the heart, you need to train the mind to connect with it.

Gratitude is a great option.

Acknowledge all the wins in your life (big or small).

One of the best ways to define gratitude is by being your own hype man.

Don't be humble when you are practicing your gratefulness exercises.

Be cocky in your own presence.

FEEL the sensations in the heart.

That's when you know you are doing it correctly.

LOVE IS THE LIMITLESS FIRE

Fire has the power to spread warmth to the world.

When our ancient ancestors discovered fire, the WHOLE game had changed.

The discovery of fire ushered in a new level of creativity.

It allowed the ancient ancestors to stay awake even when the sun went out.

Also, it allowed them to melt items which created cave art.

Fire produced magic.

The beauty?

We have an internal fire within us.

An that is held within the heart.

Going past dualities of good & bad, sad & happy is not easy.

But the more you train yourself to see the silver lining in things...

The more you unlock your inner love.

We all express love in a different way.

How are you expressing yours?

PERSONAL BRANDING FORMULA: ATTRACTION MARKETING

I've always found it funny that people think you can't be authentic with a personal brand.

There are limiting beliefs that cause people to give up even before they begin.

Say there is an individual who is a gifted chef.

And he has a strong **desire** to want to create a YouTube channel to share his recipes.

And you suggest that he *should* start a channel.

Automatically, the individual blurts out 'well, I don't want to pretend to be someone that I'm not.'

Now look..

If you don't want a personal brand to share your insights, that is completely fine.

But if you have a strong desire to share your message, but you stop yourself because you think you have to put on an 'act,' then you want to reevaluate the scenario.

What makes you think that you have to be fake?

In reality, the best personal brands are *genuine*.

They are themselves & others are simply drawn to that.

Those who present to be someone who they are not, eventually get tired of putting on an act & quit.

But for longevity?

Authenticity wins.

Today, I'm going to share with you why authenticity is key.
Why authenticity is the key driver of attraction marketing.

'Attraction marketing??'
Yes, you ever heard of the law of attraction?
'Ya.'
Well, picture a digital version...

WHAT IS ATTRACTION MARKETING?

Content in the digital world can be created in a multiple amounts of ways.
You can do videos.
Podcasts are popular.
Something like this blog etc.

But content is something DEEPER than videos, podcasts, and blogs alone.
'What is it?'
It's energy.

Content is an encapsulated version of your energy that you are about to relay throughout the internet.

Attraction marketing is when you provide content into your communication technology of choice & attract an audience with your value.

The different types of communications technology (new media) include Twitter, YouTube, Snapchat, Instagram etc.

- Content (energy) + Communication Technology =>
  Message is dispersed to the world.
- From there, you attract like energy & repel opposite
  energy.

This is a HIGHLY simplistic summary of the concept of attraction marketing.

But hopefully, now you are understanding the game.

WHAT MAKES ATTRACTION MARKETING DIFFERENT FROM OTHER MARKETING?

When I was in college, my friend had become an affiliate marketer.

When I asked him how he marketed, he would often get quiet.

After a few weeks of probing, he finally invited me to join him one day at work.

I saw how his game operated.

He was the type of affiliate marketer who bought traffic from a website & would overload it with a fuck ton of pop-ups.

The goal was to get A LOT of traffic & hopefully convert a handful of them to make a profit.

He initially got quiet when I asked him about his job because he felt like he was just taking & not giving.

Typically, when we think of marketing, we think of someone sleazy.

There are many honest marketers with high integrity though.

With attraction marketing, you **bring them to you** vs the other way around.

And you are bringing them to you with VALUE.

This is the concept of giving first & receiving later.

Don't expect to post a bunch of nonsense and expect to attract a herd of high quality individuals.

Rather, provide value & then share.

'Gotcha bro. But how exactly do I provide value?'

Great question...

HOW DO YOU PROVIDE VALUE?

In the product world, the goal is to typically find a niche & sell a product to that market.

In the personal branding world, the game is the opposite.

You don't find a niche.

YOU are the niche.

Your genuine personality is your unique advantage.

And I'm sure your genuine personality has a lot of interests as well.

In order to provide value via attraction marketing, it's best that you stick with your hobbies, skillsets and/or expertise.

If you choose your genuine passion, then you will be in the game for the long term.

Here's a disclaimer:

Attraction marketing is a long term game.

- It's not something that you will just build overnight.
- It's something that you will build over time.

If you are looking for quicker data/results, I recommend you play around with paid traffic.

It took my ArmaniTalks Twitter page almost 2 years to generate 30,000 followers.

But when the followers came, they spread throughout my blog, YouTube, Podcast etc.

And the authentic tribe members stayed while the rest left.

At times, you'll have haters who are attracted to you.

But pay them no mind.

Focus on getting the people who like you, to love you.

Rather than getting a hater who hates you, to feel iffy about you.

WHICH COMMUNICATION TECHNOLOGY SHOULD YOU PICK?

'So what should I do bro? Should I do YouTube, podcast, or blog?'

That's a question that only you can answer, my friend.

My best advice comes in 2 forms.

-Pick something you are already good at.

-Pick something you want to get great at.

At the end of the day, communication skills come down to writing or speaking.

The 2 skills just take up a different form.

Writing: blog, tweet, emails.

Speaking: podcast, videos.

Pictures such as graphics & visuals are popular.

I don't know much about that lane so I don't speak on it.

But if that is your interest, then go for it.

Ask yourself what interests YOU.

And then picture what you can do for at least 1.5 years plus.

'1.5 years??'

Ya. As I said, the attraction marketing route is much longer than typical marketing routes.

But it's great in my opinion because you get a chance to sharpen your skills in the communication world.

THE ATTRACTION MARKETING MINDSET

The final point that I would like to make is that attraction marketing is a game of mindset.

Don't focus so much on building a personal brand.

Rather, just **view it as sharing your story.**

This mentality shift allows you to keep your peak creative state.

I see a lot of people who rush the game and end up selling out.

All their content is just a way to make a quick buck rather than leave a long-lasting impact.

Focus on the latter.

Also, when you are just focused on sharing your story, you are much more giving.

You are much more social.

This allows you to build relationships behind the scenes with other players in the game who you are interested in connecting with.

Rather than just asking them for a retweet.

When you build a genuine connection with others, they will happily promote you & give you shoutouts.
Your brand will grow from there.

The key is to focus on being you & encapsulate your TRUE energy into each piece of content.
That's the energy that will one day be attracted back to you.

THE REWARD IS IN THE PROCESS

One of the saddest things nowadays is that people are WAY too focused on getting things quickly.
They want quick money, a quick personal brand, quick connections etc.

But be the rare few find joy in the process.
The intent that you choose from the beginning influences your behavior for the middle.
And the beginning + middle play a big role in the end.

From the very beginning, ask yourself if you want to do this.
If not, all good. Go about your day.

But if you do want to build a personal brand & take up the attraction marketing formula, then ask yourself what your genuine curiosities are.
Zone in on them.

Once you identify them, pick a social media app/s and begin recording your process.
Be yourself.
Easier said than done, I know.

But the more you practice on creating content, the more the initial nerves melt away & the more your authenticity shines.

Karma homie.
The energy that you put out will one day return.
Even in the digital world.

WORK HARD AND SMART

Have you ever heard of the phrase, *work smarter, not harder*.

'Yea, I've heard that phrase many times before! What do you think of it?'

I think its cool, but not fully accurate.

One common phrase in the communication skills world is:

It's not what you say, it's how you say it.

And although this seems like a great punchline at first, in reality, it's not the full picture.

Its what you say AND how you say it.

If you just say something with a nice tone & don't back it up with substance, people will eventually catch on to you.

That's why it's important to speak with substance (the what) and deliver it in a beautiful way (the how).

In the real world, it's about **working hard AND smart.**

- You'll realize by working hard, you learn how to work smart.

- And by working smart, you learn how to correctly work hard.

It's a loop.

Today, you are going to learn more about this loop & why it's crucial to leveling up in the real world.

Don't be ones sided now champ.

Be fluid like water.

Let's see how.

THE IMPORTANCE OF WORKING HARD

When you are first learning something, you are a very unaware individual.

There are a lot of blind spots.

Sure, you can read books to fill in the gaps for certain blind spots.

Books serve as great potential energy.

But eventually, you are going to have to turn that potential knowledge into kinetic energy.

There's a beauty of learning to mentor yourself in the beginning stages.

When you go seeking mentors from step 1, you often lack experience.

And lack of experience leads to very GENERAL questions.

Questions that waste a mentor's time.

Experience comes from collecting data.

And collecting data comes from taking action in the skillet that you desire to improve on.

The more data that you have, the more precise your questions become.

The movements are super sloppy at first.

You keep falling on your ass & wonder if you should be working smarter.

But the unfortunate truth is that you don't currently have the data to work smarter.

Working smarter isn't just about book knowledge & the words of a mentor.

Working smarter happens after you **build awareness** from your own experience.

These experiences will serve as puzzle pieces later on.

For now, keep showing up & showing out, even though your destination seems SUPER fuzzy.

THE IMPORTANCE OF WORKING SMART

After a few weeks/months, your brain is going to thank you.
'Why is it going to thank me?'
Because you have fed it data.

From the data + introspection, you are going to notice a few tasks which stick out.
Those are the levers.

For example, with YouTube.
When I was first starting my YouTube channel, I was focused on all the wrong shit.
Constantly going to different venues, angling the camera, fixing my mic stand etc.

After 100 videos, I realized all that matters is the message.
Normally communication breaks down to:
- Message (what you are saying) + Medium (where is the message being relayed thru).

Since I was doing YouTube, the medium was taken care of.
The MOST important part was WHAT I was going to say.

That 'aha' moment got me to buy a strong mic stand & create a studio.
Now, rather than focusing on all the other nonsense, it was a FULL intention on the message.

The working smart stage is all about spotting the 2-3 tasks which everything is built upon.

And doing your best to harness all your energy & channel it on those tasks.

WORKING HARD AND SMART

If you couldn't pick up on it, the 2 acts mainly come down to:

- Working hard = Going all in + Collecting data
- Working smart = Understanding/simplifying Data + Going all in

The goal is to keep the loop going.

A beautiful synergy of working hard and working smart is the cornerstone of self-improvement.

'And how much am I capable of improving?'

You can improve as much as you want.

The thing with learning a skill is:

The more that you learn, the more that you realize that you have more to learn.

Try saying that 5 times out loud.

You think LeBron James is ever like "I learned basketball, time to go take a nap!'

No.

He realizes that he can keep on getting better as long as he has the desire.

The thing with basketball is that there is a cap.

Eventually, father time does catch up preventing a player from playing after a certain age.

But in terms of communication skills?

There is no cap.

You can keep on improving as long as you want.

Heck, with communication skills, you age like fine wine.

The game is mental.

YOUR CHALLENGE

1. FIND OUT WHICH SKILLSET YOU WANT TO IMPROVE IN.

Consume some content on it.

I recommend different sources, from different creators.

And look out for patterns. The patterns which keep popping up are the core concepts.

Consume enough JUST to begin. If you get stuck on consumption, then you'll get analysis paralysis.

Once you have an understanding of the fundamentals, TAKE ACTION.

2. WORKING HARD.

During your learning journey, you are going to keep straying away from the fundamentals.

We all do.

There were tons of YouTubers who kept telling me the main fundamental was to just create videos.

But I got caught up in a bunch of busywork.

However, the more action you take by *working hard*, the more you keep coming back to the fundamentals.

Whether you are aware of it or not.

3. WORKING SMART.

As you are gathering more and more data, I recommend reading the books or watching the videos you watched at the beginning of your journey, AGAIN.

This time, with your added level of experience, you'll feel like you're consuming new content.

It's the same content, but a different you.

Reinforce the fundamentals again.

Allow your raw experiences to lock in with the words and concepts from consumption.

The locked concepts will now allow you to *work smarter*.

You found out the LEVERS.

4. WORK HARD AND SMART.

With your awareness of the levers, guess what you're going to do?

'What?'

Work hard!

Go all in all those simplified tasks.

Show up with intent & leave with intent.

Follow this simple framework & you'll figure out any skill that you're physically capable of.

Grind Time.

LEVEL UP JOURNEY

The beauty of the level up journey is that you can keep leveling up.

There are many physical tasks that allow you to age with grace.

But mental tasks have infinite ROI.

Tasks like storytelling, creative writing, making Youtube videos, are hard to slow down on once you have the momentum on your side.

The goal is to create momentum for yourself G.

Do you best to work hard AND work smart.

A big part of the level up journey is about finding balance.

When you are too much on one side, make yourself aware & go to the next side.

And sometimes, you gotta be unbalanced for a while to balance yourself out.

Life is a game.

Start playing it.

MULTIPLE INTELLIGENCE THEORY BY HOWARD GARDNER

Have you ever felt as though the IQ test was limited?

If so, then you are not the only person.

Growing up, I was not too confident in the IQ exam.

The first time I took it as a little kid, I asked my teacher how to improve my score.

She looked at me like I had 3 heads.

'This will be your score for a very long time Armani. Not sure it will change' she responded back.

But even she wasn't too confident in her answer.

As a few years passed on by, I wondered if the IQ exam was an accurate depiction of our intelligence.

Was intelligence really fixed??

Well, there was a psychologist named Howard Gardner who was not pleased with the stiffness of the IQ exam.

He believed humans were dynamic creatures.

And that it was time to propose a new theory regarding intelligence.

Since then, The Multiple Intelligence Theory was born.

The Multiple Intelligence Theory includes 8 branches of intelligence which are:

1. Linguistic – Good with words.
2. Intrapersonal – Self-aware.

3. Interpersonal- Good with people.
4. Logical – Good with rationale.
5. Spatial – Good with visualizing.
6. Kinesthetic – Good with the body.
7. Auditory – Good with music.
8. Naturalistic – Good with nature.

Now, this seems much more dynamic!

If any of the intelligence resonated with you, then you may be smarter than you gave yourself credit for.

Just were looking at it through the wrong lens.

So let's go through each of the intelligences & talk about the characteristics.

Then you can see which boat you fall in.

PS: You are capable of being intelligent in multiple of the groups, not just one.

I. LINGUISTIC INTELLIGENCE – GOOD WITH WORDS

These people are great with words.

Linguistics intelligence is broken down into 4 components

Consuming:
- Reading
- Listening

Production:
- Writing
- Speaking

If you are someone who loves words and use it as a vehicle for content creation, growth, learning and much more..then you may be gifted in terms of linguistics intelligence.

This group makes great at public speaking, creative writing, YouTubing, etc.

2. INTRAPERSONAL INTELLIGENCE- SELF-AWARE.

This party is capable of strategic introspection.

A lot of people THINK they know how to introspect.

But in reality, they don't have a clue.

They just sit in silence & give themselves an ego-stroking session.

Imagining why they were right & others did them wrong.

The individual with high intrapersonal intelligence is highly self-aware & able to self correct their behaviors.

This group does not need you to point out their flaws.

They are already 10 steps ahead of you.

3. INTERPERSONAL INTELLIGENCE- GOOD WITH PEOPLE

Have you ever met someone who can make friends in any event?

Even if they are walking into a room full of strangers, they leave with a bunch of handshakes & phone numbers.

This group is good with people.

They know how to listen, show genuine curiosity towards others & ask the right questions.

Interpersonal intelligence is a soft skill that has other factors which include:

- Emotional Regulation
- Focus
- Thick skin

Look out for the local charismatic individual near you.

4. LOGICAL INTELLIGENCE- GOOD WITH RATIONALE

Typically when we think of intelligence, we think of this type.

The good ole fashioned logical individual.

This is the ability to have an analytical mind that can connect the dots in a systematic way.

You won't often see this group getting their emotions played with so quickly.

Very well thought out & loves getting all the data before making up their mind.

They are not only logical with the world around them, but also have the capability to be logical with the world within them.

Aka: past experiences & future desires.

5. SPATIAL INTELLIGENCE – GOOD WITH VISUALIZING

I hated school because I am naturally a visualizer.

Rather than being flooded with Powerpoints, I needed to be able to see the pictures of the major concepts for me to get my brain running.

In the real world, individuals with high levels of spatial intelligence are not only able to visualize...

But they are also able to use pictures in their minds to solve problems.

These are the individuals we think of when we say 'Billy has a VISION.'

While the world is focused on the tiny pixels, the spatially gifted individual is looking at the bigger picture.

Your mind is a natural picture producing machine.

However, this group knows how to use it for practical purposes rather than to be overwhelmed with anxiety.

6. KINESTHETIC INTELLIGENCE- GOOD WITH BODY

Have you ever met that one person with 2 left feet?

Couldn't dance even if you paid them to.

Well, picture the opposite.

Kinesthetic individuals are good with their bodies.

You'll typically see them be in shape, athletic, good dancers etc.

This group believes the body is an intelligent entity.

Not some dumb sack of tissue that blindly follows the commands of the mind.

The mind controls the body and the body controls the mind.

Many don't fully believe in the latter part of this statement.

This group is certain of it.

7. AUDITORY INTELLIGENCE – GOOD WITH MUSIC

Individuals with high levels of auditory intelligence are able to use their ears very well.

They can notice the distinctions between melodies, songs, vocal tonalities.

The famous producer Dr. Dre is a genius when it comes to auditory intelligence.

He can listen to a song & dissect it into the nitty-gritty details.

You know you're around the presence of someone with auditory intelligence when they are seamlessly picking up the lyrics of a song they just heard.

8. NATURALISTIC INTELLIGENCE – GOOD WITH NATURE

I once went camping with a group in college.

Most of my group had no clue how to set up a tent or work their way around nature for a few days, including myself.

But my friend Shane?

Complete opposite.

He led the pack that weekend.

Shane was able to maneuver effortlessly around nature, crating fire, fishing, setting up the tent, etc.

Some people have this talent.

Their childhood may have played a big role in this form of intelligence.

Maybe they had a lot of family trips in nature.

WHICH INTELLIGENCE TYPE ARE YOU?

The beauty of this theory is that you are not just bound to one form of intelligence.

You can fall into multiple boats.

And in several cases, some of the intelligences are more interdependent rather than independent when mastering a skill.

Say you are great at communication skills.

- Well, then you will have a strong skillset with words. **Linguistics intelligence.**

- You may have a musical voice that allows you to seamlessly alter tonalities. **Kinesthetic intelligence.**

- The ears are always alert for listening to the context of other people's tonalities. **Auditory intelligence.**

3 forms of street smarts for the price of 1 skillset.

If you were not fully fulfilled by your intellect level in school, then don't mail it in so quickly.

Humans are creatures that always has the power to surprise one another.

See which one of the multiple intelligence theory by Howard Garner you are.

And doubled down on your gifts.

Its never too late to reach the genius level.

5 STEPS TO IMPROVE SELF AWARENESS

Have you ever met an intellectual individual with very little to show for it?

They knew so much data.

But their lack of awareness had you scratching your head.

I have a friend like this.

He is the first to give others great advice on how to lose weight & maintain a healthy lifestyle.

But he has been heavy & out of shape for as long as I have known him.

If he bothered to apply his own tips, he'd be shredded.

We all know his advice works.

The question we have is, how come he doesn't apply it?

Truth be told, my overly heavy friend is **unware**.

In his mind, he doesn't see much of an issue.

He thinks he is in shape or often tells us 'he's getting to it...'

But the results are non-existent.

We know plenty of people like this.

And if you don't know someone like this, then you are probably that person.

A know it all with low self-awareness.

And these are the type of characters to have trouble in the communications world.

Self-awareness is a staple of street smarts.

And street smarts is a staple of dealing with people.

A life without self-awareness is like driving a car with only a view of the windshield.

But no rearview, side mirrors, windows to the side.

A life with self-awareness opens up your vision & allows you to become more patient.

You are on the process of taming your ego & building your empathy.

In this article, I am going to give you 5 tips on how to improve your self-awareness,

Learn these 5 tips, and you'll see WHAT to fix before giving others tips on HOW to fix it..

I. LISTEN TO COMMON CRITICISMS

I don't like haters.

Think those who are jealous or don't have much going on in their lives have the time to talk shit about others.

But a key component of dealing with other humans is being able to distinguish between haters and constructive critics.

The difference boils down to this:

1.   Hater = Points out flaws.
2.   Constructive critic = Points out flaws & offers feedback.

Unfortunately, a lot of people don't have the social intelligence to fall into the constructive critic boat.

Which is why you'll notice a lot of people who come off as haters.

My tip is to listen to haters & **use them.**

They will often bring awareness to common personality traits that you were unaware of.

And haters will tell you what your kind-hearted friends may often leave out.

Look out for repeat criticisms and meditate on it.

If it's something you dub as a nuisance, then push it aside.

But at least check it out.

2. HAVE GRAND GOALS

A lot of people lack self-awareness because they aren't striving for much.

They have the same routine that they carry out on autopilot.

The only conflict that they have is anxiety due to a LACK of problems.

Your brain is a problem-solving machine.

And if it doesn't have any problems to solve, then it will create them.

Small issues will be blown out of proportion.

Grand goals force you to come to terms with character deficits.

And character deficits don't necessarily mean a bad thing.

It simply is a PRODUCTIVE goal for your problem-solving brain to work towards.

If you're going to have problems no matter what...

Might as well chase a grand goal to at least have problems that help you grow.

This brings me to my next point.

3. EVALUATE WHERE YOU ARE NOW

Creating a grand life goal allows you to evaluate where you are in life right now.

But you know what's funny?

A lot of people don't evaluate where they are.

That's like me dropping you off in the middle of nowhere, and asking you to pick me up from Disneyworld.

You have a destination in mind.

But you have 0 clue which city you are in.

Let alone, continent.

A polarity between your BIG goal & evaluating where you are now, improves self-awareness.

If you want to become the best public speaker in the world, then at least ask yourself if you are a beginner or intermediate.

4. FOLLOW YOUR CONFUSIONS

I used to hate when I was confused about something.

Thought it meant that I was dumb.

Then I realized which era that I was blessed to be living in.

Your boy is living in the **Information Age.**

Anything I want to learn, I have access to it.

Nowadays, confusion is not a bad thing.

But rather a *compass.*

Your gut instinct is primal for your body.

Your confusion is primal for your mind.

No one is born knowing everything.

When you can accept that, your confusion becomes a compass rather than a life sentence.

This is what allows you to build self-awareness, curiosity, and intellect.

5. JOURNAL

Journaling is huge in terms of building self-awareness.

What journaling does is that it allows you to detach from your ego.

My pro tip is to write your journals down & re-read them.

What I noticed is when I read a journal entry from a month or 2 ago, I feel more open to providing myself constructive criticism.

This is when you are able to detach yourself from making it personal & analyze the situation for what it is.

You are able to analyze who you are for what you are.

The writing by hand technique allows you to freeze your personality in moments & come back to it later.

Understanding where you are coming from allows you to understand where you are.

Understand where you are & the improved self-awareness will lead you towards your destination.

BONUS TIP: MEDITATION

The common misinterpretation with meditation is that it's about clearing your thoughts.

While in reality, it's about learning to sit with your thoughts.

MEDITATION IS A WORKOUT TO BUILD SELF AWARENESS.

Now that I think about it, this should have been step 1.

But since you made it so far into the blog, this is my gift to you.

Meditation is all about giving your mind a target, and making yourself AWARE when you have gone away from the target.

You can choose any target: your breath, body sensations, a vision, candlelight etc.

A breathing meditation simulation goes like:

1. Focus on your natural breaths.
2. When you get lost in thought, make yourself AWARE and bring yourself back to the breath.
3. Repeat.

Don't be hard on yourself for losing focus.

Making yourself aware is what you are going for.

That's a rep for your mind.

The more reps, the more you improve self-awareness.

GET TO KNOW YOURSELF LIKE A BEST FRIEND

The mind can either be your best friend or worst enemy.
This is what emotional intelligence is all about.

EQ often gets the reputation as emotional management &
regulation.
But think about it...
Can you really manage & regulate what you don't understand?
Nah..

It's a game of building self-awareness so you learn to enhance
your maturing.
The more self-aware you become, the less impulsive you are.

Getting to know yourself is a lifelong journey.
A journey that will constantly bring about new levels.

If you improve self-awareness, then you will be kinder to
yourself.
And once someone is kind to themselves, they become much
more pleasant to be around.

Strong communication skills will simply be a byproduct.

OVERCOMING SHYNESS

Being shy is not an easy feeling.

And you won't know how difficult it is until you have been or are shy.

Constantly being asked '*why are you so quiet?*' can get super annoying.

If it's done enough times, it can have a strong impact on your identity.

The tough part of being shy is that others can't quite empathize with your feeling because YOU can't even put it into words.

All you know is that you feel self-conscious to speak.

As social creatures, humans have a strong desire to want to be heard.

They don't have to talk a lot.

But they want to be able to speak with confidence if need be.

I spent most of my life being shy.

Moved to the US from Bangladesh at an early age.

Could barely speak English which caused me to get mocked for my accent.

My hesitancy to speak due to my accent caused me to close up & avoid the spotlight.

Spent **years** like this until I had finally enough.

So I can empathize with shy people.

In this article, I am going to discuss the difference between quiet & shy, whether shyness is a problem & 2 practical tips for overcoming shyness.

It's never too late to change.

Just a matter of deciding when you had enough.

Now let us enter the world of social dynamics.

THE DIFFERENCE BETWEEN QUIET & SHY

Quiet & shy are often confused with one another.

But the 2 are VERY different.

Even though the 2 look the same from the outside, the 2 are different from the inside.

In a nutshell:

Quiet people can speak more if they want to, but they choose to use fewer words.

Shy people use fewer words because they feel like they have no other choice.

All in all, quiet people are not self-conscious.

They are just precise with words or often like listening more than talking in a conversation.

Shy people are self-conscious.

They feel uneasy getting their words out because they feel as though they are being judged.

The fear of being judged sparks a self-fulfilling prophecy in the future.

Pretty sure they were told multiple times in their life that they were 'too quiet.'

This causes them to adopt a shy role for future interactions.

Shy people now enter new interactions THINKING that others assume that they are shy.

This alters the shy person's behavior to be more reserved.
Which makes them more prone to getting called out for not saying much.

Toxic loop in the social world...

WHY ARE PEOPLE SHY IN THE FIRST PLACE?

People are shy for many reasons.
It depends on their life upbringing.
But here are a few reasons that people are shy.

-THEY WERE MOCKED FOR IDEA/S GROWING UP

If you are constantly being put down for your ideas, then you will be less likely to express them.
Especially, if you are an impressionable little kid.

This causes them to TRIPLE check before expressing thoughts in the future.
Overthinking causes people to stay quite.

-THEY LOST SELF-CONFIDENCE AFTER A TRAUMATIC EVENT

You'll be surprised how many people became shy after they were once confident.
Something very bad happened to them & the memory stuck.

Imagine if you said something very 'stupid' in an interaction & everyone laughed at you.
Most people will let the laughs roll off.

But some people hold onto the memories.

The level of importance that they assign to the mockery may be enough to speak to their subconscious mind & cause significant character changes.

-BULLIED

I became shy because I kept getting clowned for my accent.

Left & right, people would make fun of me.

This was annoying because I was known as the talkative kid in my home country.

But in the US, I became quiet because I thought my accent was a huge detriment to my social success.

In reality, it wasn't.

Only a few out of billions of people on the planet thought it was.

And I was the one who assigned a lot of importance to those few.

-SHY HOUSEHOLD

Some people were raised in a very reserved household.

Their guardians weren't avid talkers in social settings.

More so observers.

This caused them to adopt a similar behavior pattern as well.

They feel out of place speaking up too much in social interactions themselves nowadays.

All in all, these are just a few reasons.

You want to do your best to trace back the memories which caused YOU to be shy as well.

Finding the root cause helps significantly in overcoming shyness.

IS SHYNESS A PROBLEM?

Hm…
Depends.

'Depends on what?'
Depends on the type of person that you are trying to become.

There are PLENTY of people I know who are happy & shy as well.
And truth be told, they often say that their shyness is what allows them to be happy in the first place.
This group hates the spotlight being on them.

Shyness is only a problem if it makes you feel uneasy.
Allow your feelings to be your compass.

For me?
I hated being shy.

I always wanted to be an amazing communicator, public speaker & an individual who freely expressed my ideas.
In the context of my life, shyness was absolutely a problem.
Therefore, I decided to do something about it.

Before doing something about it, ask yourself **how much** of a problem shyness is in your life.
List 10 reasons if you can.

This step is important because overcoming shyness is not an easy task.

It requires patience, grit & adaptablity.

If you don't have a strong desire to change, then you probably won't.

Pain is a great motivating factor in the beginning.

OVERCOMING SHYNESS: THE 2 PATHS

So you have traced the root cause (or have a rough idea) on why you are shy.

You have assessed that it IS a problem in your life.

The next step is to **commit**.

You have to realize that humans are dynamic creatures.

We can change anytime that we want to.

Our brains have insane neuroplasticity.

This means that we can strengthen new neural pathways & weaken old ones.

Neural pathways are the cornerstone of our nervous system & play a large role in our minds.

Our mind influences our reality.

2 Ways to Overcome Shyness are:

-Incremental Social Skills

-Public Speaking

INCREMENTAL SOCIAL SKILLS

This is more of an exposure therapy approach.

Rather than being the center of attention in the VERY first interaction, ease your way up to it.

Start off with a 1 on 1 conversation and aim to talk more than you normally do.

Just get your feet wet.

Do this for a week. Use this segment to talk to people that you know.

Next, have a 1 on 1 conversation where you tell a story.

A story requires creativity & flexibility.

So challenge yourself to tell a story.

If it's a humorous story, then it will put you in ease.

Keep working your way up the social skills ladder.

You are just climbing 1 step at a time.

And give yourself a pat on the back after each interaction.

Eventually, get in the habit of being the first person to introduce yourself.

Breaking the ice is a major weapon in terms of confidence.

Less is more when it comes to breaking the ice.

A simple 'Hello' goes a long way.

Keep on building your social reps with the INTENT to speak a little more for each interaction.

Go from 1 on 1 convos to groups & keep the momentum going.

Each interaction won't go well. But all good.

Have a laugh over it with yourself. This is a journey, not a final destination.

PUBLIC SPEAKING

Public speaking is a fast way to overcome shyness.

You are pretty much getting a crash course on human nature.

Public speaking forces you to speak to MULTIPLE people at once.

And if you couldn't tell... this is more of a tackling the beast approach.

If you are super shy, then the last thing you'll probably want to do is speak in front of a crowd.

And I get that.

But every so often in our life, we need to show MASSIVE amounts of courage & have faith that everything will work out.

Public speaking to overcome shyness is the perfect opportunity to seize that moment.

Join a Toastmasters.

This is a club filled with other people who were once shy as well & are now looking to become better communicators.

I've been to multiple Toastmasters in my life.

And each time, I noticed that the groups were very supportive.

Commit to the club & keep participating in the events.

It's a 1-1.5 hour meeting every week.

A very small amount of commitment for a lifechanging gift of overcoming shyness.

If you can speak in front of 20 people, then 1 on 1 & group conversations will feel like light work.

Book it.

GAINING YOUR VOICE BACK

We came onto this planet crying.

When we are first learning how to speak, we couldn't stop talking.

Yapping away.

Noticing a pattern?

We were not born with shyness.

It was taught at one point or another in our life.

Whether we are aware of it or not.

All good though.

Overcoming shyness is one of the best ways to build self-confidence.

If you can overcome shyness & rewire your personality, just imagine what else you can do??

Plus, you will have a perspective of the former shy guy, which will allow you to be understanding towards other shy people.

You won't be harsh.

You'll be empathetic.

This is a journey, my friend.

A journey that you were born to conquer.

If you made it this, far, then now is the time to go on your personal hero's journey.

Overcome your shyness for good.

CONSCIOUS AND SUBCONSCIOUS MIND

It would have been amazing if we had a few classes on mindset growing up.

Especially since so much of our lives are dictated by the mind.

There are 2 minds to be specific.

The conscious and the subconscious mind.

It took me up until my early 20s to learn about the 2 minds.

But when I did, my reality shifted.

So many things are in our awareness & out of it.

And we have so many factors which are done subconsciously that it seems cool & spooky at the same time.

Your 2 minds will play a big role in the world of communication.

Which is why it's crucial to make sure you develop a strong understanding of the mind.

In today's article, we are going to be talking about the 2 minds & how it can impact you.

Time to shift your future.

Let's begin.

THE CONSCIOUS MIND

The conscious mind is the critical thinking mind. The mind that is in your awareness.

Right now, you are using the conscious mind to read this passage.

This mind has the power for thought, imagination, filtering situations and much more.

Conscious is being aware.

Consciousness is being aware of being aware.

4D stuff.

When you break down humans, our power for thought is surreal.

This is why we have been able to rise among the ranks on the planet in terms of innovation.

When breaking down your conscious mind, there are layers.

But the 2 most influential layers are:

- Positive Task Network – Ability to focus.
- Default Mode Network – Mind wandering.

You are using the positive task network to read these words.

Or you may be in la la land, pretending to read with your default mode network.

Who knows....

SUBCONSCIOUS MIND

The subconscious mind is the database.

It has no ability to think. It simply absorbs & stores.

When you're young, your subconscious mind is highly programmable.

Which is why little kids can learn languages & new concepts so easily.

It's because their mind is storing all the data.
The subconscious mind sees life through images & feelings.

Humans are naturally visual creatures.
The first-ever form of story was not created in words.
It was created via images, also known as cave art.

But another way to speak to the subconscious mind is through repetition.
Think about driving for example.
At first, you were terrified of driving, right?
'Ya.'

But nowadays, you are able to do it in autopilot.
That's because repetition allowed you to store the movements in this magical mind.

There are 2 layers to the subconscious mind:
- Individual subconscious – These are the traits individual to you & your life experiences.
- Collective subconscious- These are the traits that all humans share at our core level.

THE RELATIONSHIP BETWEEN THE CONSCIOUS AND SUBCONSCIOUS MIND

These 2 minds are purely connected.
Your conscious mind pulls data from your subconscious mind to gather its thoughts.

This is why the people you surround yourself with & the content you consume plays a big role in your reality.

If you are constantly watching junk, drama, gossip…

- Then you have repetition.
- You have images.
- You have physical sensations.

ALL SPEAKING TO YOUR SUBCONSCIOUS MIND.

Do you think in your day to day life, that your conscious mind will be thinking like a winner?

Not a chance.

You'll just be worrying all the time & feeling more anger.

But just like the subconscious mind plays a big role on your conscious mind, the opposite is true as well.

You can use your conscious mind to reprogram your subconscious mind.

The conscious mind has a magical power to imagine.

Visualization is known as guided imagination.

Your subconscious mind cannot tell the difference between imagined & reality.

And remember, I said that it thinks in pictures?

Well, then you can strategically imagine images that make you FEEL with repetition to rewire your subconscious mind.

We are the only known creature who has this power.

But very few truly utilize it.

BUILD AWARENESS

Awareness is the bridge between the conscious and subconscious mind.

You ever saw 2 people presented the same exact information?

But they execute very differently?

That's because the awareness level plays a big role in the learning process.

An individual with minimal levels of self-awareness will just see words & information.

A highly aware individual will see a blueprint.

You can build awareness in multiple amounts of ways.

But the best way to do it is by:

1. Evaluating where you are in life.
2. Creating a grand goal for yourself.

1. EVALUATING WHERE YOU ARE IN LIFE.

Evaluating where you are in life is hard as fuck.

Because it forces you to look into your flaws. Something no one likes doing.

But if you don't get to know yourself, then no one else will do it for you.

Get a journal & begin jotting down memories from the past.

Write freely & try to make sense of your past mistakes.

Carl Jung had a process known as individuation.

Basically, where we bring the dark sides of our subconscious mind into awareness.

Simply bringing it into awareness so you can learn the lessons is key to changing your narrative.

'Loss' is a man-made word. If you want to use it, you can.

But if you are able to build awareness, then you either won or learned a lesson.

Make sense of your past & it will be easier to make sense of your present.

2. CREATING A GRAND GOAL

A grand goal does not just happen.

You sort of get flashes of the idea in your mind.

Then you capture it & begin working on it.

In the initial stages, the idea won't make much sense.

But that's because it's a baby.

Need to give it attention by constantly working on it.

Working on your grand goal targets your mind.

A targeted mind begins creating filters for how to make the goal possible.

You start getting curious about random topics to aid the goal, can spot strategic relationships & become aware of positive habits you can incorporate into your life.

Clarifying your past & aiming for a big goal expands your awareness for the present day.

And added awareness consistently bridges the 2 minds.

MAKING YOUR MINDSET WORK FOR YOU

The mindset is the most potent force on this planet.
It's time that we start learning to use it.

It's sad when I see many people going about their day to day
life with little awareness.
2 disjointed minds.
And that will always lead to anxiety.

Understand your mindset.
Become best friends with it.

You can't always control what's going on in the external world.
But you always have a better shot controlling what is within.

EMOTIONAL RESILIENCE

When you break down communication skills, a large portion of it comes down to emotional resilience.

Think about it for a second.

You are about to enter a party.

And out of nowhere, you have this surge of social anxiety.

A part of you thinks that all eyes will be on you once you open the door.

Or how about, RIGHT before you are about to get up on stage to give your speech.

Feel that?

It's a surge of emotions.

Emotions and communication skills go hand in hand.

And when you don't understand those emotions, you develop a negative perception of it.

In today's article, the goal is to give CLARITY to those emotions.

Once you understand emotions, that's when you can display emotional resilience.

We often hear the word 'mental toughness' being thrown around.

And I believe mental toughness is huge for life in general.

But let's not forget the cousin, emotional resilience.

At the end of the day, the human at a core is an emotional creature.

Once you can begin controlling your inner energy, you will become unstoppable.

And every word that you say will exude a level of confidence.

Let's unlock that inner potential.

WHAT IS EMOTIONAL RESILIENCE?

'Yo Armani, are feelings & emotions the same thing?'
Nope.
'Wait, really??'
Yep.

Feelings are physical sensations in your body.
Emotions are perceptions of your feelings.

Feelings are neutral.
Emotions are subjective.

Emotional resilience is defined as one's ability to adapt to stressful situations.

That's the core of it.

You develop emotional resilience during times of darkness, not light.
Happy emotions are great, don't get me wrong.
But the resilience portion can only be exercised during times of tension.

IMPORTANCE OF EMOTIONAL RESILIENCE

Emotional resilience is important in all aspects of life.
Without it, you become overly sensitivity & will rarely take action.

Since this site is about communication skills, let's give you an example that deals within that realm.

Let's talk about giving a speech at Toastmasters.

When I first joined Toastmasters, I was a pure mess in terms of public speaking.

I'd overthink the little details & undermine the large concepts.

For my Icebreaker speech, I felt like I did a great job!

This was my first official speech as a Toastmasters member.

I'm sure I did well in the eyes of everyone.

'Well, did you?

In terms of an icebreaker speech? Yes! I did pretty well.

But not everyone felt that way.

Apparently my back was turned to one section of the audience for most of the speech.

Due to that, I was given praise.

But I was also given criticism.

Let's be real.

Criticism always sounds louder than praise.

And it was no different for me.

When I first heard the criticism, I was sad.

My emotions were hurt.

Not going to lie, a part of me wanted to throw in the towel.

But afterwards, one of the veteran Toastmasters came up to me & let me know that criticism was just a part of the game.

- *Public speaking involves humans.*
- *Humans have a lot of opinions.*
- *Opinions can boost your ego OR hurt your feelings.*

'Learn to not let good opinions get to your head or mean opinions get to your heart' he said.

Emotional resilience is crucial because it allows you to keep moving forward.

No matter which part of life you are in, we all have to deal with humans at one point or another.

We have to deal with tough emotions.

Failures.

Setbacks.

But how we bounce back is the ultimate test of character.

Think long term, not short.

HOW TO DEVELOP EMOTIONAL RESILIENCE

Developing emotional resilience comes down to knowing yourself.

Sure, you can watch motivational speeches or read a lot of books.

But at the end of the day, emotional resilience is like our thumbprint.

It's unique.

We all have different flavors of emotional resilience.

But at the core of it all, it comes down to:

Taking action DESPITE negative emotions.

Earlier on in this article, I explained the difference between feelings & emotions.

I stated feelings were neutral, while emotions were subjective.

And unless you get to know your feelings, most of the emotions will be subjective with a negative tilt.

Getting to know your TRUE self often happens in the darkness.

So explore journaling or being more introspective.

Talk to yourself about things that you try to hide.

And ponder thoughts that make you uncomfortable.

During moments of exploring the uncomfortable, you are conditioning your mind to navigate the storms.

Storms that would have thrown your past self off...

But nowadays, it's different.

When you seek to actively explore the dark parts of you, that's when you become more emotionally resilient.

- People who lack emotional resilience run away from discomfort.
- People who have emotional resilience, can sit with discomfort & take action anyways.

Which brings me to my next point.

It's okay to be nervous before you are about to be brave.

Every human has different perceptions of bravery.

But it comes down to making a move despite feeling like your world is going to end.

Reality check, more often than not, it will not end.

So when you are going up on stage to give that speech, EMBRACE the nerves you are feeling while walking on stage.

Those nerves don't define you.

You define it.

As you feel the nerves, you realize that it is quite therapeutic.

And it allows your primal brain to disengage the negative perception & engage the neutral sensations.

That's when you'll take action.

That's emotional resilience.

LEVERAGE EMOTIONAL RESILIENCE FOR OPTIMAL CONFIDENCE

Your brain & emotions are always in contact with one another.

-When your brain & heart fights, you get anxiety.

-When your brain & heart work together, you get courage.

The world of communication skills is no cakewalk.

It's the path of winners & those who want something more.

They want to use their experiences, wisdom & knowledge to influence.

The power to influence is earned, not given.

Need to put your reps in champ.

But it all comes down to learning to sit with uncomfortable emotions & take action anyways.

Adapt when you need to adapt.

As cliche as it may sound: What doesn't kill you makes you stronger.

The human brain has crazy potential.

But never forget about the human heart.

The combination of your brain & heart is what will allow you to turn that potential energy into kinetic energy.

Energy which will show the world the depths of your emotional resilience.

HOW TO THINK CLEARER

Clear thinking spills over to all aspects of your life.

'Even communication skills?'

Especially communication skills.

At the end of the day, speech is simply tangible thoughts.

So if you are a messy thinker, often, your speech will follow suit.

In this site, we are all about creating confident communicators.

So rather than focusing on the tactics, we are going to focus on the core issue.

How to think clearer?

This blog will discuss why we are messy thinkers, the process of externalization & 2 practical strategies to slow your thoughts down!

With consistency, you'll be able to tame your thoughts.

And tamed thoughts allow you to feel more relaxed.

The more relaxed you are, the more creative you become.

It's a domino effect.

So let's begin our journey on how to think clearer.

WHY IS YOUR THINKING MESSY?

'Why is my thinking messy in the first place bro?'

Your thinking is messy because you were never taught HOW to think & due to consumerism.

These aren't the only 2 reasons.

But 2 common ones that I have noticed.

To begin, we were never taught **how** to think.
But rather, **what** to think.

When you take a walk down memory lane, you realize that most of school came down to learning information which was preselected for us.
We didn't have a class on how to think effectively.
But we sure as hell were told which subjects to think about.

Next, consumerism is adding a lot of unneeded complexity to our lives.
Think about it for a second.

- How much stuff do we have in our house that we don't need?
- Are we someone who hoards?
- Do we consume a lot of media throughout the day?

Well, that level of consumerism leads to chain effects.
All the unneeded noise is making your body absorb more energy.

And the lack of production causes that energy to go unused.
Unused energy leads to more anxious thoughts.
And those anxious thoughts lead to messy thinking.

A chain of destruction.

HOW TO FIX MESSY THINKING

You fix messy thinking by taking control of your thoughts.
Now wait, don't run off yet.

I know controlling your thoughts is no easy task.

Simply trying to think your way into a calm state of mind is difficult.

Which is why people actively avoid meditation.

But it becomes MUCH easier to control your thoughts when you can see them.

In Josh Kaufman's hit book, The Personal MBA, he brings up the concept of externalization.

Externalization is the process of transforming our thoughts into some sort of external form.

When you implement the habit of externalization, you are able to think clearer.

It is easier to fix your thoughts when you have them staring back at you.

That's when you are able to see your line of thinking, rationale & cognitive abilities.

The goal is to turn the intangible into tangible.

EXTERNALIZATION THRU SPEAKING & WRITING

The beauty of externalization is that it gives you the ability to master a few things:

- You become a clearer thinker.
- Become a better speaker.
- Become a better writer.

'I become a better writer & speaker??"

Oh wait, I just told you what externalization is.

I haven't told you how to do it.

Great segway.

How does one do externalization?
Well, there are plenty of forms of expression.
But my choices are through writing and speaking.

The simple act of writing & speaking will allow you to think clearer.
Let's go through each one.

WRITING

There isn't much of a framework that I would recommend in the initial stages of writing.
I recommend you do some good ole' fashioned free writing.

'What's that?'
Write about whatever you want.

Don't get too caught up on grammar, sentence structure, word selection, etc.
Heck, it's best to think less & write more.

'Should I do the writing on Microsoft Word or pen & paper?'
I've tried both methods.
But as of late, I'm more team pen & paper.

I become much more mindful of the writing process.
That's probably because I rarely use a pen or pencil nowadays.
So the act of physically writing something out is somewhat foreign to my brain.

That's good.

This allows me to stay mindful in the act rather than doing it mindlessly.

Buy a journal and give it a try.

If you don't have a journal, then Microsoft Doc is fine as well!

SPEAKING

So this is sort of like talking to yourself.

But I highly recommend that you record the speaking process.

The problem with just talking to yourself when you first start out externalization is that you'll have the tendency to get distracted.

You'll lose focus & keep switching train of thoughts.

Remember, the goal is to become a clearer thinker.

So leverage the recording app on your phone or buy a digital recorder.

My recommended technique for this task is to take it ONE word at a time.

This allows you to focus on the micro & build up.

Speak at a comfortable pace.

In the initial stages, when you try doing a mind dump on your voice recorder, you end up getting gassed.

Just. One. Word. At. A. Time.

Step by step in the right direction leads to progress.

You'll be surprised how great ideas can be born from just one word at a time.

THINK CLEARER, COMMUNICATE BETTER

Externalization, just like any skill, has compounding effects.

You'll notice the clarity in your thoughts after a few weeks of consistent practice.

The process of turning thoughts into an external form is highly powerful.

Some of you guys may not meditate because you hate sitting alone in silence.

So in that case, try out externalization.

Write & speak.

Slow your thoughts down.

Picking up mediation in the future will feel much easier!

Overall, the chain effects take a stronger hold in your life.

The ability to see your thoughts gives you the ability to choose the narrative.

Become a clearer thinker & watch the positive effects spill over to other parts of your life as well.

Now pick your method/s & begin!

WHAT DOES WORK ETHIC MEAN?

There are a lot of people who claim to have work ethic.

They let the world know how 'hard' they work.

But a lot of these people are the same ones who set an alarm to wake up at 4 am to post a Snapchat with the hashtag #grinding.

Then they go back to sleep.

A lot of people don't have work ethic.

They simply give off the illusion that they do.

Instead of work ethic, what they have is a desire to be an attention whore.

In the real world, only a few people truly have work ethic.

And that's because it requires a lot of cognitive effort to show up day in and day out.

It's not a sexy process.

But before I go any further, you may be wondering:

What does work ethic mean??

Great question, my friend.

And today, we will be discussing this concept in more detail.

If you were to ask me what is the strongest component of someone who is mentally tough & has genius-level street smarts, then guess what I will say?

You guessed it.

Work ethic.

Let's explore this topic further.

WHAT DOES WORK ETHIC REALLY MEAN?

There are a lot of definitions out there for this phrase.
And I have my personal definition as well.
My personal definition is:
Work ethic is being consistent through uncertainty.

Don't run off yet.
This may be a brand new definition you have never heard of in your life.
So let's break down each part.

BEING CONSISTENT

All mentally tough people have one thing in common.
They are consistent as fuck.
Showing up day in and day out.

Even if it's just for a rep, session or a minute, you can count on this group to show up.
Whatever their craft is, they are consistent with it.

The exact opposite of those people are the ones who are super motivated in the beginning, stay consistent, quit for a few days & pick it up a few days later.
These people lack discipline.

THROUGH UNCERTAINTY

This is the shining difference between work & work ethic.

Those who show supreme ethic are the ones who will continue despite uncertainty.

'Does that mean they keep doing the wrong things over and over?'

No. They are very strategic.

But what working through uncertainty means is that they are patient enough to let the world bend to their reality.

They understand that good things can happen soon.

But great things take time.

So rather than putting in work & praying for instant success.

They will be patient.

And they will be consistent through uncertainty.

How is Work Ethic Valuable?

Work ethic is the most valuable trait in any field.

I always say, when mentoring or hiring someone, focus on the work ethic over their current skillset.

'Why?'

Because skills can be taught, but fire cannot.

The fire is a PURE representation of how a human deals with chaos.

Do they fold & quit like a bitch?

Or does their fire radiate more when they are pushed against the wall?

Work ethic is valuable because it is the gateway to compounding skills.

Compounding effects are mother nature's way of telling us to keep going.

Whether it's public speaking, learning to play the guitar, picking up a new language...

Work ethic is going to be the main component of whether or not someone will make it for the long term.

IS WORK ETHIC A SKILL?

Yes.

Work ethic is a skill.

That means it can be learned practiced & mastered.

From my life, I've seen people take different roads towards work ethic.

- Some were led to this road through the pain.

They were never amazing test-takers growing up..

So they grinded extra hard.

- Some were led to this road through jealousy.

They took their foot off the gas pedal & saw other people surpassing them.

This led these individuals to step up their internal game.

- And some were led to this road through their role models.

Whether it was their parents who always showed consistent work ethic.

Or a celebrity role model.

These individuals learned from their surroundings.

Anyone can implement this skill anytime in their life.

It mainly comes down to going from micro to building up.

-If you want to have work ethic, you need to be consistent.
-And if you want to be consistent, you want to be realistic.

Say your goal is to become the best public speaker in the world.
Well, as a beginner public speaker, it will be VERY difficult to give a speech every day.

So be realistic.
What CAN you do?

Well, rather than giving a speech every day, you can:

- **Write some days** – this will allow you to keep your idea muscle sharp.
- **Record youtube videos** – This will keep your body language tight.
- **Attend a weekly Toastmasters meeting** – This will keep your public speaking sharp.
- **Get a mentee** – Teaching someone twice a week will help you learn.

You broke down a big scary task into one that is very manageable.
Now staying consistent is a no brainer.

The more consistent you are, the more micro wins you stack.
With those micro wins, you build confidence.
The confidence makes work ethic second nature.

WORK ETHIC = EVERGREEN

The more you mature, the more you are able to spot what matters from what doesn't matter.

What is signal vs the noise.
You start looking out for **evergreen** skills.

I sometimes laugh at the people who get caught up in the latest fashion trends.
They buy some goofy looking clothes.
Pants with holes in them, big ass shoes, no belt etc.

Is this something you can see yourself wearing in 30 years?
Nah.
That means those clothes aren't evergreen.

The same concept holds true with skills.
There are certain skills which will be used momentarily in your life.
And there are certain other skills which will be valuable for life.

Stay consistent through uncertainty.
And trust me.
This will be a skill that will be beneficial for the rest of your life.

Begin finding creative ways to incorporate it into your life.
Your future self will thank you.

HOW TO DEAL WITH FAILURE

Times are getting tough.
And you are beginning to wonder how to deal with failure.
Not easy.

But today, I'm going to flip your mind.
'And how are you going to do that?'
By showcasing that failure is an illusion.

'Wait what?? Failures are an illusion? Nah...'
Yes.

Today, you'll learn about your perception of failures, why it's an illusion & how to deal with it.

This article can be applied to virtually any aspect of your life that has friction.

Because let's face it.

There have been plenty to times we quit too soon.

Plenty of times when 'failures' accumulated & destructed our confidence.

Not anymore.

Let's rewire our views of this phrase once & for all.

WHERE DOES FAILURE STEM FROM?

In order to learn how to deal with failure, you are going to have to go down memory lane with me.

Ask yourself when you first started discovering the concept of 'failure.'

The first memory that I remember was handing a glass of water to my uncle.

In my culture, it was seen as rude to hand over an object to an elder with your left hand.

No clue why to be honest.

But this was a well established rule.

The first time I gave my uncle the water with my left hand, he told me about this rule.

So he handed the water back and told me to try again.

I felt that this rule was stupid, so I gave him the water again... with my left hand.

This time, you could see that he was visibly upset.

He handed the water back & told me to try again.

And I repeated the process, once again.

At this point, he was pissed.

'Armani, you failed the task!'

That was my first brush of an encounter with failure that I remember.

But it wasn't my last.

By the time I went to school, I found out that teachers actually assign you this word on your deliverables.

If a homework assignment, quiz, or test didn't meet the standards, then guess what?

I would be delivered an F.

Think about the first memory you have of failure.

This will serve as a crucial component for the next section.

WHY FAILURES ARE AN ILLUSION

The reason failures are an illusion is because it is subjective.

It is intangible, not tangible.

However, our minds view it the opposite way.

Humans are placed in school for multiple years.

And multiple years being reinforced a concept will alter our thinking patterns.

The mere notion of being given an exam with an 'F' turn failures into a tangible concept for the human mind.

We start to view failures as an entity.

This sort of thinking works in school.

You need to make failure a tangible concept in order to keep students motivated to strive for more.

But this sort of thinking is awful in the real world.

Imagine I point to a Lamborghini.

Calling that Lamborghini a car is a fact. It is tangible and we can see it.

Saying that Lamborghini is cool looking is an opinion. It is intangible and subjective to the person making the claim.

When my uncle told me to give him the glass of water with my right hand, he was going by **his** principles.

In his world, I failed.

In my world, I stood up for what I believed in.

So I did not fail.

In order to deal properly with failures, you need to hit the brakes for a second.

Then you need to evaluate which stage of life you are in.

If you are in school, then yes, you should follow the school's standard as you are operating in that environment.

Also, if you are in a job where there are black & white definitions of failures, then you should comprehend the standards & move accordingly.

But in terms of personal goal chasing (like learning a profitable skill), the rules are different.

When dubbing yourself a failure, you need to ask yourself:

Whose standard of 'failure' are you operating on?

Simply answering this question will give you a lot of 'aha moments.'

HOW TO DEAL WITH FAILURE: REFRAME

I remember when I first got into digital marketing in my early 20s, I had TONS of failed campaigns.

It got to a point where I lost 1000s of dollars.

Your boy was about to mail it in.

But decided to take 5 more stabs at it before completely throwing in the towel.

4 of the campaigns were a bust.

But the final 1 was a hit.

And it was such a hit, that it allowed me to make all my money back within the next 7 months.

That campaign is still profitable to this day.

The digital marketing journey was a 13-month process.

I spent the first 6 months stinking up every campaign.

Then I spent the next 7 months making it all back.

What do you classify this experience as?

During the 6 months, I felt like a failure.
But during the 6 months & 1st day, I felt like a winner.
All those losses were required to hit that eventual win.
And that win compounded into a life of its own.

In order to reframe failure, you have to realize that a tangible form doesn't exist.
Failure is simply an absence of an act.

If I had quit on the 6th-month mark, then I did fail.
Because I quit.
Quitting leads to the absence of an act.

But until I quit, I am simply accumulating lessons for that eventual win.
Reframe 'failures' into 'data' and you'll be much more flexible in your journey.

MAKING MENTAL TOUGHNESS A MANTRA

I still have 0 clue why we are not taught about mental toughness at all in school.
But hey, that may be a good thing.
Mental toughness may be a lifestyle that is best when discovered, rather than taught.

The ultimate lesson you'll learn in respect to your life is that mental toughness is pretty much consistency.
A power to show up & show out.

It doesn't matter if you are trying to record a YouTube video.

Or start a business.
You will 'fail' along the way.
A big part on how to deal with failure is to just deal with it.

Our subconscious mind will automatically want to classify it as a failure because of the pain.
But think about it like this.

When you are in the gym, does lifting the weights hurt?
'Yes.'
Then why do you continue?
'Because the pain leads to something bigger.'
Exactly.

You don't view the pain of repping heavy weights as a failure.
Because you know that it's all leading towards the greater good.

So carry over the same mindset into the real world.
Failure is an illusion.

You figure it out when you figure it out.
That doesn't mean to not hold yourself accountable.

But that means to never quit grinding when things are getting tough.
Miracles are all about staying consistent for long enough.
So grind way & turn the darkness into light.

HOW TO HAVE CHARISMA

Have you ever wondered how to have charisma?

Such an ambiguous term.

We were never taught proper social skills growing up.

Just thrown into the lions of the communications world & expected to figure it out.

But is charisma a framework that can be learned, practiced & mastered?

I like to think so.

I grew up as a very socially awkward individual, who was shy & viewed as standoffish.

This led me to have little friends & acquaintances.

'Geez bro, that sucks.'

On the contrary, it was one of the best things to happen in my life.

'Wait, for real??'

Yes. Because I had the opportunity to reengineer my personality towards charisma.

Throughout the past 10 years, I have served as the communication chair for many clubs, worked numerously with people via leadership positions & developed my ArmaniTalks brand to help with social skills.

I was fortunate to learn about several elements of social skills.

Charisma being one of them.

Today, I'd like to talk more about this mythical concept & a SIMPLE mind hack that you can adopt to be your most charismatic self!

Let's begin.

WHAT IS CHARISMA?

Before we define charisma, I want you to picture 2 charismatic people that you know.

Could be a friend, relative or worker.

Take some time & look for the SIMILARITIES between the 2.

What do you notice?

There is a glow to them, right?

If they were to enter a room, then you wouldn't worry about it being awkward.

Rather, you KNOW that it will be lit.

Charisma is defined as a compelling attractiveness in personality that can inspire devotion in others.

A pretty powerful statement when you think about it.

This site is about communication skills & leadership.

A leader knows how to inspire their troops to take action.

They aren't like the archaic boss who just barks orders at their employees.

Therefore, if you want to improve your communication skills/leadership, charisma is no longer optional.

It is mandatory.

CAN ANYONE BE CHARISMATIC?

Our brain has neuroplasticity to develop new neural pathways to alter our life.

Most skills are not god gifted.

Rather, trained into our existence.

So can anyone become charismatic?
Yes & no.
'Huh??'
Let me explain.

Charisma is a skill that has a few fundamental frameworks.
So technically, it can be learned.
However, charisma REQUIRES a tamed ego.

An egotistical person will rarely be seen as charismatic.
They will simply spark other egos & unnecessarily burn
bridges.

'Does that mean that I have to kill my ego?'
No.
First of all, you can't kill your ego.
Second of all, you wouldn't want to do that either.
A human who tries to kill the ego becomes a 'nice guy.'
No bueno.

You want to be the person who has an ego but is not controlled
by it.
Have your ego serve as a tool.
It gives you direction, but your consciousness is the one driving
on the road.
A tamed ego is necessary because the social world is VERY
complex.
Not everything will always go your way.
And a lot of times, YOU will be the reason for a conflict.

In a situation like that, a tamed ego raises awareness.

An added awareness allows you to make intelligent social decisions.

The decisions of the charismatic soul.

HOW TO HAVE CHARISMA?

Let's cut to the chase.

How to have charisma?

Be interested rather than trying to impress.

The core of charisma comes down to that simple concept.

All too often, when we are in an interaction, we go out of our way to impress.

We want to say the 'right' words, break news, and show how cool we are.

'Do humans try to impress for malicious reasons?'

Not really. A lot of times, humans try to impress due to social anxiety.

They feel so much pressure to contribute, that they subconsciously become controlled by the ego.

Their ego takes them out of the present moment & puts them in their heads.

This leads to not paying attention, interrupting & ruining the vibe.

Here's the thing fam.

You NEED to do less, not more.

Every time you enter an interaction, your goal is to make the other person feel like the star.

You do that by having a genuine curiosity towards the other person.

Humans are very complex creatures.
So treat them as such with your undivided attention.

SOCIAL ANXIETY -> CHARISMA

Here's a life law for you champ:

When you put the spotlight on yourself, you get social anxiety.

When you put the spotlight on the other person, you get charisma.

That's why the hypeman is a universally loved figure.
A hype man knows the art of making others feel important.
And giving another human a level of importance fulfills a primal desire.
The desire to belong.

Notice, how I am not filling up this blog with 100's of practical tips on how to be charismatic.
Rather, I am just giving you ONE tip.
Be interested rather than trying to impress.

When you become interested, magic happens:

1. Your nerves will melt.
2. You will think of better questions during the conversation.
3. The other person will FEEL the attention that they are getting.
4. Both of you will feel more relaxed.

You can't fake realness homie.

Don't pretend to listen by staring at their vicinity and nodding your head.

Genuinely tune into the conversation.

And if you have a tough time controlling your focus, then I recommend you pick up mediation and/or writing.

Both these acts will make you a clearer thinker.

BE CHARISMATIC AND UNLOCK DOORS

The world opens up doors for the charismatic individual.

They shake hands with the right people & always create social opportunities out of thin air.

When you feel too many nerves in an interaction, that means you are putting the spotlight on yourself.

Become aware & gently put the spotlight back on the star of the show.

Your conversation partner.

This is an act that requires a lot of conscious effort in the beginning.

But with practice over time, you'll start to make charisma your way of life.

Charisma is not an act that you do.

But rather a byproduct of treating someone with respect.

Earlier, I told you to imagine 2 people who were very charismatic.

Guarantee you noticed how they have the ability to make their conversation partner feel like the only person in the room.

Cool, right?

That's social magic, my friend.
Forget all the gimmicks.
Be interested rather than trying to impress.
And the social superpower of charisma will be right around the
corner.

IS CURIOSITY AN EMOTION?

Have you ever had that sudden lightning struck of curiosity?

And that level of curiosity didn't just start and end in your mind.

But it started in your mind & permeated to your body.

Is curiosity an emotion?

I have always wondered that.

There are a few parts of the human that is ingrained.

2 being imagination and emotion.

No one ever taught us how to imagine, we were just born imagining.

Also, no one ever taught how to feel emotions, we were just born feeling.

So it's normal to ask if curiosity is ingrained.

And whether or not it factors as an emotion.

This site is all about communication skills.

And you'll learn that curiosity plays a major role in terms of becoming a better communicator.

Whether you are learning to be a more knowledgable person or trying your BEST to listen to your conversation partner...

Curiosity plays a role.

So let us explore this topic in more detail.

IS CURIOSITY PRIMAL?

Curiosity is a strong desire to know something.

Something is considered primal when it is considered fundamental.

Does curiosity fall into this boat?

Well, let's answer this question by studying a child.

How does a young child who is still learning, operate?

If you observe this child, you'll notice they are VERY curious.

They are always tinkering.

Asking big questions.

And trying to fit together some figurative puzzle.

No matter which part of the world you are in, you will see the same effects.

From the Western to the Eastern world, kids have the fundamental characteristic of curiosity.

So yes, there seems to be a strong likelihood that curiosity is primal.

GOOD & BAD CURIOSITY

Duality, my friend.

Whenever there is something good, understand that there is a bad version lurking around.

Curiosity is no different.

Earlier, I stated that curiosity is primal.

Therefore, it is something that will need to be used one way or another.

Question is, which direction are you aiming your curiosity?

Is it pointing towards a constructive or destructive direction?

Constructive curiosity is the type of curiosity that helps you grow.

This requires a purpose that you are leveling up towards.

You have a north star that you are chasing and your curiosities form around that north star to help you chase the right answers.

Destructive curiosity is the type of curiosity that does nothing meaningful for your life.

This typically happens when you are void of a north star.

You just wing life.

Winging life will have you getting curious about all the wrong things.

Gossip, scandals, other people's opinions etc.

This will make your life feel like a living hell.

IS CURIOSITY AND EMOTION?

Emotion is defined as:

Arousing or characterized by intense feeling.

So, is curiosity an emotion?

I do believe curiosity fits a part of that definition, but not the full picture.

Yes, curiosity often does have an intense feeling, but what sparks that feeling in the first place?

If you ask me, then we need to trace back to the core of a human, once again.

I said earlier 2 core components of a human are emotions and imagination.

Well, it seems like curiosity is a bridge between those 2 primal elements.

Think about the last time you were VERY curious.

Not just a 'yea, it'll be cool to know.'

I mean a 'I HAVE to right now because I can't focus on anything else.'

Yes, that sort of curiosity.

If you trace that curiosity back, you'll notice it stemmed from a thought.

That thought was painted with tones of imagination.

The scale of the imaginative experience will lead to the degree of curiosity as well.

'So, curiosity is the bridge between imagination and emotions?'

Yessir.

'And how does this apply to me?'

Excellent question.

HOW TO CORRECTLY BE CURIOUS

We are taught a lot of things in school.

But a big part of the real world is reconnecting with the basics.

The basics which make us who we are.

Unfortunately, we aren't how to rediscover these elements.

We are just expected to figure it out.

'Is there anything to look out for when it comes down to curiosity?'

I personally have a few points.

Let me share them & you can see which parts apply to your life.

1. DON'T TRY TO BE CURIOUS, JUST LET IT HAPPEN

What I've noticed is that I get curious about topics that help me level up, when I just flow.

Flowing is much better than treating curiosity like homework.

'How can I flow?'

One of the best ways to flow is by having fun.

'Fun?? Come on bro. Give me practical tips.'

That's the practical part, my friend.

Is curiosity an emotion? No.

But that doesn't mean that you can't follow your pleasant emotions.

When you are having fun, your mind tends to follow your natural curiosities.

It seems as though unleashing your childlike spirit is what unleashes the engine.

So find activities that you enjoy.

Just a hint.

A lot of great curiosities lie behind your hobbies.

2. DON'T RULE OFF A SILLY CURIOSITY

I'll be real.

A few years ago, I got super curious about remote control cars.

No clue why.

But I started to watch a few videos of people making these remote control cars.

Over and over again.

After a few days, I had a light bulb moment.

'You were going to make a remote control car as well??'

No.

But watching the cars being taught me a lot about electrical circuits.

This allowed me to solve a HUGE problem for my senior design project for engineering.

What started off as a silly act, served as a missing puzzle piece.

3. LEVERAGE THE INTERNET

The problem that many of us have is that we go searching for mentors too quickly.

We have a curiosity and automatically go asking for advice.

A lot of times their answers may help.

But this can rob you of the full curious experience.

Let me do you a favor.

Treat Google like your mentor.

You can virtually find any article or video on search engines nowadays.

As your curiosity regarding the topic is at the infantile stages, do some research on questions that you have.

Even if it seems silly, type it down in the search engines.

You'll notice yourself asking questions that others have been pondering about as well.

See how far those answers take you.

CURIOSITY IS THE LIFEBLOOD OF CREATIVITY

All in all, I don't view curiosity to be an emotion.

But I do think they have a lot of strong ties with one another.

In my eyes, when we see curiosity, we see the bridge between the mind & heart.

Your curiosity is something that should serve as the compass for your life.

You'll be surprised how often it leads you to the answer that you were seeking.

In today's digital age, there is information about virtually any topic out there.

You are living in the golden era of curiosity.

Follow where your internal compass takes you.

Be bold, ask yourself tough questions & allow your mind to expand.

Curiosity is the lifeblood of creativity.

Now begin to maximize it.

THIN SKIN VS THICK SKIN

The battle of the 2 skins will always be present in your life.

Thin skin vs thick skin.

Which one are you?

In the communication skills world, your response will play a big role in your success.

We all like to view ourselves to be thick-skinned.

But many of us fall into the thin-skinned boat.

In today's post, I want to get you thinking correctly about emotional states & mental toughness.

Because that's what thin skin & thick skin boil down to.

Then, I want to teach you why thick skin is so important in the social world.

How you carry yourself is always a choice.

It's easy to blame others for our problems.

But we don't do that on this side of the world.

Thin skin vs Thick Skin.

Let's see which team you are in.

WHAT IS THIN SKIN?

I like to view a thin-skinned person as someone who is **sensitive**.

They feel emotions quicker & have the tendency to personalize the effects.

In many cases, personalizing will lead to an impulsive act.

If you think about it, we are born thin-skinned.

I've never met a tough baby in my life.
We are born onto this planet crying.

But look closer...
Imagine if we yell at a 5-year-old.
What will he do?
'He will cry.'
Exactly.

He will cry because you hurt his feelings.
Your words (the stimulus) was able to get a response (output).

WHAT IS THICK SKIN?

Thick skin is when someone is **not easily offended.**
They can feel the same intense emotions.
However, they do not personalize it. Therefore, they do not make an impulsive decision.

Thick skin is exercised onto our existence.
It is something that requires patience, grit & a fuck ton of pain.
(Going to talk more about this shortly).

But thick skin people are very emotionally intelligent.
There is this misconception that they do not feel emotions.
But that's incorrect.

EVERY human feels emotions.
It's just a part of life.
But they can read their emotions like the back of their palms.

WHY IS THICK SKIN IMPORTANT IN COMMUNICATIONS?

In the communication world, you'll run into PLENTY of different personalities.

You will meet good-hearted people.
You will meet mean-hearted people.

Humans have the tendency to get stuck in the negatives though.

The negativity bias is when a human's brain places more importance on negative scenarios for survival reasons.

This often causes us to let 1 insult outweigh 10 compliments.

Thick skin is important in the world of communication skills because if you let EVERY mean opinion get to you, then you'll go insane.

Just take a look at celebrities' social media for example.

Do you ever read those comments?

Some people can be hella' mean for no reason.

And if you are someone who personalizes attacks, then you:

1. Give importance to haters.
2. Undermine your supporters.

Thick skin allows you to make more **mature** decisions.

You realize every move from others does not require a response.

And when you can internalize this, then you begin to control your behavior.

Someone else no longer controls you.

HOW TO LEVEL UP TO THICK SKIN?

We have been talking about thin skin vs thick skin.
Now, I will teach you how to level up to thick skin.
Ready?
'Yessir.'
Great.

Thick Skin Formula:
1. Conflict Chasing
2. Deal with it.

CONFLICT CHASING

You do not get in the best shape of your life by sitting on your ass watching Netflix all day, right?
'Right.'
So what do you do?
'I go to the gym & put my body through some pain.'
Bingo.

You put your body through the pain because you know that's how you will grow.
Same concept with thick skin.
You need to put your *emotional muscles* through the pain so you can grow.

Chase conflicts by always looking to grow.
If you don't know what conflicts to chase, then analyze your fears.

Scared of public speaking?
•   Then join Toastmasters.

Scared of swimming?

- Then take swimming classes.

Scared of being funny?

- Then tell more jokes.

Proving yourself right is the best way to overcome pain.

At first, when you are trying something new, you will feel hesitant.

And after failing incessantly, you will feel like quitting.

But don't...

Keep going.

Over time, you'll notice yourself toughening up.

You showed to yourself that you are able to produce thru pain.

This will have your emotional muscles stronger than ever.

DEAL WITH IT

There are certain times, doing nothing is better than doing something.

Yep, you read that right.

Everything doesn't need a response.

Imagine if someone cut you off in traffic.

It would be super easy to go on road rage mode & cut that person off as well.

However, it would require A LOT of restraint to act as though nothing happened.

Ignoring is a superpower.

Remember that.

Ignoring is such an effective way to build thick skin because you are literally doing **nothing**.

Maintaining composure when you want to snap is one of the TOUGHEST things out there.

Often, this route is tougher than conflict chasing.

So if you are able to force yourself to maintain composure in stressful times, you'll notice thick skin building.

You'll begin to feel more poised.

CREATING A SOCIAL ARMOR

The tougher that you get, the more you feel grounded in social interactions.

Don't let the fans get to your head.
Don't let the haters get to your heart.

If you are someone who considers yourself overly sensitive, then take gradual steps towards advancing.

And don't think for a second that thick skin will make you some heartless robot.

Rather, you will feel much more in tune with your emotions.

You'll know which emotions are disruptive.

And which emotions are productive.

From there, you can morph destructive into productive.
That's modern-day magic.

It doesn't matter how much of a great person you consider yourself.

Unfortunately, stupid people exist on this planet.

Keep conflict chasing & dealing with trials that you can't control.
Take your emotional muscles to the gym.

Soon, an invisible armor will form across you.
As the famous saying goes:
The thicker the skin, the less the stress.

Level up to toughness & life will never be the same.

EMOTIONAL INTELLIGENCE: SELF AWARENESS

The ArmaniTalks brand deals with communication skills.

One of the reasons I bring up emotional intelligence is because it is a major subject in the world of communication.

If you have poor emotional intelligence, then you will often have poor self-awareness.

If you have poor self-awareness, then let's just say you are burning more bridges than creating.

Humans are emotional creatures.

We love to view ourselves as logical.

But unfortunately, this isn't always the case.

We are flawed creatures, who have an ego, feel anger & have times when we feel like losing it.

Nothing wrong with that. As long as we acknowledge it.

Self-awareness is a superpower in the world of communication skills.

The more you talk to others, the more you see everything stems from self-awareness.

In today's blog post, I want to talk about the importance of self-awareness and how emotional intelligence will put you on the right path.

WHAT IS SELF AWARENESS?

There are a lot of definitions of self-awareness.

My personal definition is:

Self-awareness is the conscious mindfulness of one's subconscious mind.

Now, this may seem like a very cryptic statement, but it is not.
Look closer.

What really makes up our subconscious mind?
3 major components of the subconscious mind include:

- Emotions
- Past experiences
- Present-day habits

Those are the majority of the thoughts which make up your subconscious mind.
Often, we just carry out these tasks on autopilot.

When we feel angry, we react.
When we brush our teeth, we do it without thought.
We use past events as the groundwork for future events.

These are just a few examples of how we carry out our lives without much thought.
We just react.
Not much conscious awareness which requires thinking.

A person who just reacts without thought has low self-awareness.
A person who can view themselves from a 3rd party perspective has high self-awareness.

WHY EMOTIONAL INTELLIGENCE IS IMPORTANT FOR SELF AWARENESS

We often have a wrong understanding of what emotional intelligence means.

This causes us to undermine the subject.

In order for you to understand what emotional intelligence means, you need to understand what emotions are.

Emotions are feelings with a perception.

So what are feelings?

Feelings are physical sensations in your body.

So in summary, we feel physical sensations in our body, then we assign a perception to it.

The perception holds the narrative.

Feelings + Perception = Emotion

Positive perceptions get defined as happy, excited, ambitious etc.

Negative perceptions get defined as anxious, sad, angry etc.

The reason emotional intelligence is huge for self-awareness is because it allows you to clarify the ambiguous.

It allows you to add nuance to what many overlook.

People who are emotionally UNINTLLIGENT let their perceptions dictate their reality.

People who are emotionally INTELLIGENT know their perceptions are up for interpretation.

Those with high emotional intelligence do not allow their feelings to cause them to make a permanent decision.

Rather, they feel their feelings.

Then dissect it with their logical mind, not their emotional one.

Then, they decide what the next step is going to be via rational & sound judgment.

That's self-awareness.

When you break it down, maturation really comes down to raising your level of self-awareness.

Picture the most mature person you know.

They still feel hectic emotions like anyone else.

But they have the emotional intelligence to make their moves rationally instead of impulsively.

HOW SELF AWARENESS & EMOTIONAL INTELLIGENCE TIES INTO COMMUNICATION SKILLS

Emotional intelligence allows you to understand your internal world.

Mastering your internal world is a prerequisite to conquering your external world.

If you are someone who gets angry and just starts screaming at others, then you will not be building too many connections.

The lack of self-awareness will cause you to damage relationships.

Building self-awareness is a **painful** process.

It forces you to tame your ego.

Taming your ego is no easy task.

We are not born self-aware creatures. It is something that is exercised in our existence.

Therefore, those who tame their ego had to do it through a lot of heartaches, headaches and objectivity.

If you want to form meaningful relationships with others, then you need to be able to master your emotional states.

Learn the art of feeling a physical sensation without attaching a label to it.

One of the best times to do that is when you are feeling HEATED.

Ever had a car cut you off in traffic?

That didn't feel too good, did it?

But use that as an opportunity to sit with a lot of tough emotions.

A lot of emotions which will break people.

But just sit with them anyways.

The more you can sit with tough physical sensations, the more you develop our emotional resilience.

And the more you build the emotional resilience, the more you tame your ego.

A by-product of taming your ego is self-awareness.

Self-awareness allows you to realize that you are simply a character in this world.

Just because you are the main character of your world does not mean you're the main character of someone else's.

This core understanding allows you to make much smarter choices in the future.

BUILD SELF AWARENESS THRU EMOTIONAL INTELLIGENCE

Emotional intelligence breaks down into multiple components.

You have emotional regulation, self-awareness, motivation, empathy and much more.

This is a subject to leverage if you want to build your street smarts.

Humans are emotional creatures at the end of the day.

Those who can manage their emotions will allow themselves to conquer challenges with more poise and build long-lasting connections.

Those who can't control their emotions will allow someone else to control it for them.

Sad, but true.

Remember this, my friend.

Emotions come and go, but the consequences can come and stay.

Therefore, you always need to be mindful of your emotions.

Be self-aware even when you are the villain in the scenario.

It will not be easy.

But no one said building self-awareness was going to be an easy task.

Keep treating self-awareness like a muscle that you will continue to work on.

Soon enough, your emotional muscles will be so strong, that you will feel BULLETPROOF.

WHY CONFIDENCE IS IMPORTANT

Confidence was one of those words we used to hear a lot growing up.

And for good reason, of course.

The word represents an act that has a huge effect on our reality.

But if the word is so important, how come we weren't taught HOW to be confident growing up?

Isn't it a little strange we view confidence as the holy grail, but we were given little to no training on it?

It sure is.

As you continue to mature, you'll notice the content which actually matters in the real world, is rarely taught in school.

- Like how to concentrate.
- Social skills.
- Emotional regulation.

And so much more.

But just because you weren't' taught how to be confident in school does not mean you should not self educate yourself on the topic.

In today's blog post, I want to share why confidence is important & why you need to start mastering this skillset asap.

WHAT IS CONFIDENCE?

At the core of it all:

Confidence is a strong belief in an entity.

That is it.

You can assign what the entity is.

Example:
- When the entity is your business, then you have a strong level of confidence towards your business.
- When the entity is you, then you have a strong level of confidence towards your own competence.
  - Aka: self-confidence.

You need to have self-confidence before you can have anything else.

Without self-confidence, you got nothing OG.

I remember as an electrical engineer, I used to work on a lot of electrical circuits.

And I used to notice how complex and unique the design was once I was complete.

However, it didn't matter how great the circuit was if I had no battery.

Without the battery, the circuit simply wouldn't function.

You are the battery towards your life.

It doesn't matter how many opportunities you are given in this life if you don't have the SELF-CONFIDENCE.

Without self-confidence, you will blow most of those opportunities.

Why?

Because you feel like you aren't worthy.

However, when you are confident, things change.

It doesn't matter if you have opportunities or not.

Deep inside, you know it's coming.

You have such a STRONG belief in yourself, that you know that the belief mixed with your work ethic will CREATE opportunities.

You create a bent reality.

CAN ANYONE BECOME CONFIDENT?

Yes.

Confidence is a skillset.

It is something that can be learned, practiced and mastered.

However, there is a catch.

If you are someone who is leveling up, you have to understand that confidence is not an act, it is a lifestyle.

You are going to have to continue practicing confidence for the rest of your life.

Every new stage in your life that you go thru will require a new you.

Therefore, you need to have the BELIEF that you will eventually figure it out.

That's how you keep stretching yourself to new levels.

'Wait a minute Armani! So you're telling me that I have to be confident towards acts that I've never done?'

Correct.

The core of confidence stems from the CAPABILITY to do something, rather than having already done it.

You need to ask yourself if you are *capable* of doing the task.

I remember when I first started public speaking, I had o confidence towards the task.

It's because I hadn't successfully given speeches yet.

But that didn't mean that I just ignore the task completely.

Rather, I knew that I was CAPABLE of doing the task.

I was alive and breathing. Therefore, I knew I could speak in front of a group of people.

Confidence comes from the BELIEF where you know you are capable of doing something.

So spot something that you have been running away from.

Then ask yourself:

- *Is someone else doing it?*

If so, then ask yourself:

- *If they can do it, why not YOU?*

This will get you thinking the right way.

BEING NERVOUS IS NECESSARY

Look, you want to be real with yourself.

Imprint this quote into your mind.

It's okay to be nervous before you are about to be brave.

Even if you are capable of doing something, understand that you will still feel nervous.

Nerves are normal.

A great deal of confidence comes down to feeling nerves and taking action anyway.

That's why confidence is important.

Imagine if our history required people to feel 0 nerves before they took action.

Then, we wouldn't have any form of innovation!

It requires you to show courage to be confident.

No matter what kind of dark feelings you have, understand that they are just feelings.

Dark emotions will come and go.

Don't make permanent decisions due to dark emotions.

Rather, make permanent decisions in SPITE of dark emotions.

You'll continue to surprise yourself.

WHY IS CONFIDENCE SO IMPORTANT TO YOUR LIFE?

The reason confidence is important is because it is the lifeblood of your life.

Whatever you do, you should be doing it with intent.

Without the intent, you will half-ass the process and eventually quit.

Confidence allows you to form intent in your act.

Notice how I said FORM an intent.

You are not born with intent.

It is exercised into your existence.

So, nothing is going to be comfortable at first.

But you need to take action anyways, go through the nerves, and over time, the intent will be formed.

- *Intent creates a stronger belief in yourself.*
- *A stronger belief in yourself creates a stronger belief towards the act.*
- *A stronger belief towards the act leads to more results.*
- *And more results lead to more value.*

Confidence in yourself leads to more value for yourself and others.

That's why confidence is so important.

TREAT CONFIDENCE LIKE A SKILLSET FROM HERE ON OUT

Look...

It's okay to not feel confident at times.

A lot of the times when you don't feel confident, it's because you are about to take a new stage in life.

You arc about to level up into something grander.

So go through the process and TRUST that the nerves will go away.

Confidence is the staple of communication skills and most of the acts out there.

It's a universal skill that will be evergreen.

So invest in this skillset by doing hard shit and fighting through the emotions.

Rinse and repeat.

Over time, you will feel bulletproof mentally & emotionally.

That's when you will give yourself a pat on the back for taking the road less taken.

WHAT IS A PERSONAL BRAND?

A personal brand is a brand that is built around you.

You are the star of the show.

For the longest time, we have gotten to know plenty of mega brands throughout history.

A few of them include Amazon, Apple, Coca Cola etc.

These were not just businesses…

But rather, their brand took up a life of its own.

If you go to anyone who is a superfan of a brand, you will notice how loyal they are.

Why though?

It's because brands evoke emotion.

And emotions are the invisible glue that connects humans.

Today, I want to share what is a personal brand so you can apply brand principles to your life.

Personal brands have been growing due to the access of the internet which has allowed more people to take control of their narrative.

Let's make sure you begin with the correct understanding.

THE TYPES OF PERSONAL BRAND

I remember growing up, I had a teacher who would always say 'Armani, you are a brand. Act like it.'

At the time, I had no clue what she meant.

But as I grew up, the lesson began clicking.

She was basically trying to imply that every time I step foot outside the door, I am the person representing my life.

I am the brand ambassador for all things Armani Chowdhury.

And by the way... she made that comment to me because I'd rarely comb my hair and my clothes were always dirty.

That day, I learned that personal branding is very important in the offline world.

You may not want to hear this, but here it goes:

People judge you all the time.

Yes, it is true.

If you look and act like a slob, then you will be perceived as a slob.

If you look and act sharp, then you will be perceived as sharp.

Not rocket science.

So if personal branding is so important in the offline world, can we say the same for online?

And the answer is YES.

Online personal branding allows you to work on your brand, but on a higher level.

The beauty of online is that it is not confined to certain segments of society.

Rather, it is global.

So the 2 types of personal branding are: offline & online.

WHY ONLINE PERSONAL BRANDING IS ON THE RISE

We have been displaying offline personal branding for as long as we can remember.

Even if we did not have a word for it, we were still carrying out the acts consciously/subconsciously.

Ex: Your fear of being judged is due to the fear of your personal brand taking a hit on the offline world.

But as of late, online personal branding has been on the rise.

Why though?

It's because of the rise of the internet & social media.

The internet serves as nodes (connecting points) which information can fly thru.

The social media are the nodes.

And did I mention that YOU have control over the nodes?

For the longest time, there was a central figure which controlled the spreading of information.

A radio station, a famous newspaper company, local news provider etc.

But with the rise of the internet & social media, the spreading of information has become decentralized.

Decentralizing information has allowed more people to leverage social media rather than being leveraged by it.

IS A PERSONAL BRAND RIGHT FOR YOU?

I'm going to be very transparent with you homie.

A personal brand is not for everyone.

And if you are someone doing it for the wrong reasons, then you are building a house on a VERY weak foundation.

If you are doing it for fame, then you're NOT off to a good start.
'Why?'
Because it hurts your psyche.

In the grand scheme of things, we do not have too much data on social media and the effects it can have on our emotional states.
Therefore, as spooky as it may seem:
"We are the guinea pig generation for social media."

I say that because when you don't have too much data to fall back on, you have to level up your awareness.
Since starting my personal brand, ArmaniTalks, I have seen many other personal brands rise & fall.

The people that fell, learned that social media can be VERY addicting.
Not going to lie, I fell in that boat a few times as well.

There were times when I felt the effects of social media on my emotions, concentration levels, and confidence.
When I saw myself falling in that route, I had to REALLY learn who personal brands were right for.

The conclusion I came out with was:

Personal brands are right for the people who use it as a self-improvement tool.

Yep, a self improvement tool to get better at their craft.

Therefore, when you have a:

- Hobby that you're passionate about
- Product/service that you believe in
- Skill that you want to develop

Then, personal branding is right for you.

You are looking to develop yourself rather than just chasing fame.

The more you chase fame, the more you become addicted to social media.

The more you chase self-improvement, the more social media works for you.

WHAT IS A PERSONAL BRAND IN THE FUTURE?

The main takeaway that I have for personal branding is to just begin & develop the idea.

At first, you are going to want to overthink a lot.

But just choose your social media channel & begin producing content.

What you will learn is that your brand vision does not come out complete at first.

Rather, it comes out as an infant.

You need to give it attention like a parent. You need to **grow** the idea.

The more that you grow it, the more that it evolves.

For example, ArmaniTalks started off as strictly a public speaking brand.

But within the year, it has gone to become more of a communication skills brand that discusses public speaking and other topics such as social skills, personal branding, content creation, etc.

This is my brand evolving.

But what's been better is that the topics that I talk about have further enhanced my understanding of the skills.

I have had the opportunity to develop my speaking, writing & presentation skills.

And the fact that I share my progress publicly holds me much more accountable.

If you were to tell me a year ago that this brand would have evolved into a business, I would have laughed at you.

But nowadays, the brand has products & services which serve as my business.

These are just a few examples of enhancements to your idea which begin to take shape once you begin producing.

You will only be able to connect the dots AFTER you begin.

So what is a personal brand mean for your future?

It's hard to tell.

Only you will be able to have the say once you begin creating.

CHOOSE YOUR PATH

The beauty of starting ArmaniTalks thus far has been the whole creation process.

I still remember when it was just an idea. Nowadays, it is a global brand that helps thousands around the world.

You want to ask yourself whether you have a gift that can help this world.

If so, then record it.

No fame, gimmicks or money.

Just chase leveling up.

Everything else will follow.

Over time, you will notice your creation developing before your very eyes.

You are giving life to something via your mind.

And the more you do it for yourself, the more you will see an authentic tribe forming around you.

That's how you attract rather than chase.

With the rise of the internet and social media, it has never been easier to take control of your narrative.

Begin leveraging that power & graduate from a consumer to a consumer & producer.

FAKE FRIENDS VS REAL FRIENDS

Have you ever had that moment when a good friend turned into a snake?

I'm sure you have.

After a certain amount of life experience, we all get hit with a betrayal.

It's not a fun feeling.

Being betrayed by someone who you had a love for is tough.

And in many cases, it is a wake-up call.

Fake friends vs real friends.

How is one to spot the difference?

You know I keep it real on this blog.

In many cases, people turned on you because they were rotten to the core.

But in many cases, it was your fault.

'My fault??'

Yes.

In today's article, I'm going to shed some insight into the world of social dynamics & how you can prevent getting bitten by snakes left & right.

Each snake bite brings a lesson, yes.

But if we can spot the difference between fake friends vs real friends, then it's our duty to preserve our time.

WHAT CAUSES SOMEONE TO TURN?

I've had my fair share of betrayals in my life.

Growing up, I had no clue what happened.

But as you get older, you begin to see the patterns forming in human nature.

There are predominantly 2 reasons why people will turn on you.

1. They are rotten to the core.
2. It was your fault.

For the first group, they often leave clues.
They are always involved in a tornado of drama.
Always hating on more successful people.
Can't seem to hold any friend after a certain period of time.

These people are rotten to the core.
I have no clue why you hang out with them.
Well, scratch that, I do.
Many are charismatic & fun to get along with.
But they do a good job in hiding who they are.
Fake.

The second reason why people turn on you is because of YOU.
This is when someone feels anger & fear towards you.

Say you and this friend are chilling in a group.
They are making a point, and you disagree midway & tell them to shut up.
This person does not want to cause a scene & is a little frightened by you, so they do as you say.

But you stung their ego.
Over time, they will feel resentment.
And unless y'all solve the issue like adults, then this real friend will turn into a fake friend.

WHAT MULTIPLE BACKSTABBINGS SHOULD TELL YOU

If you are someone who gets backstabbed over & over again, then you need to take a look at the mirror.

I'm a firm believer in the <u>law of attraction.</u>

The energy you put out there is the same energy that you attract back.

If you only attract fake friends, then you may be sending out the wrong vibes.

There are 2 wrong vibes I see people send out.

1. Naive empathy.
2. Toxic behavior.

Naive empathy is when you keep forgiving left & right.

You use very little common sense & accept everyone!

Although others warn you this person is fake & you see the signs for yourself, you let your emotions overpower your logic.

You feel like you'll be the 'magical' person to change them.

Grow up.

Accept reality for what it is.

Toxic behavior is when you leave someone drained rather than empowered after interacting with them.

If you are someone who sends out bad vibes to this universe, you'll get the same thing in return.

Scarcity minds attract scarcity minds.

If it happens every now and then, don't sweat it.

If it happens multiple times, it's a pattern.

Regardless, you need to take a few steps back & work on yourself.

Develop your life & self-image.

Improve your value, so you can attract value.

I discuss practical methods of building your value in my book <u>Level Up Mentality</u>.

QUALITY OVER QUANTITY MINDSET

Once you begin improving your value, people are going to be swarming you left and right.

Everyone wants the time of the winner.

At this point, it is going to be harder than ever to spot the difference between a fake friend vs a real friend.

Therefore, from the get-go, you need to adopt a <u>quality over quantity mindset.</u>

Major key.

Our entire lives, we heard the mainstream peddle the notion that popular people have a LOT of friends.

But this simply isn't true.

In order to turn a human into a friend, you need to invest a lot of time, energy & attention into that soul.

Time, energy & attention are all finite resources.

Therefore, there's only a certain amount that you can spend.

If you try to turn 50 people into your best friends, then you will develop surface-level bonds.

These surface-level bonds will attract many snakes into your squad.

Fake friends are imminent.

On the contrary, if you invest those finite resources into 5 people, then you'll develop deep level bonds.

You'll be able to spot loyalty & filter more efficiently.

Real friends are much more likely now.

WHAT HAPPENS IF YOU STILL GET SNAKE BITES?

I wish I can give you a blueprint on how to never get snake bites.

But unfortunately, I can't.

I can give you all the precautions in the world, but at the end of the day, humans will never be fully predictable.

If you took the time to invest in yourself, attract quality people, took time to filter a strong friend circle, but still got backstabbed, then I have one suggestion:

Learn.

Yep, learn.

Sometimes, dark moments like this are not in your control.

Take some time to analyze what happened.

And ask 'what' questions vs 'why' question.

Don't be like 'why me?'

-This will make you feel more defeated.

Rather say, 'what can I learn from this?'

-This makes you feel more empowered.

Betrayal gives you wisdom that a book can never give you.

And to be honest, each snake bite made me more <u>socially intelligent</u> in the long run.

So I thank everyone who has betrayed me.

It's sort of like the trash taking itself out.

When you can view it with that mindset, then you will come out mentally tougher.

FAKE FRIENDS VS REAL FRIENDS: THE SOCIAL JOURNEY

Snakes are abundant, loyalty is scarce.

- Don't trust fast, trust slow.
- Don't cut slow, cut fast.

These are life laws that you need to learn if you want to make the most of your time.

You can't control someone else's behavior, but you can always control yours.

Therefore, take the necessary precautions & control what you are able to.

And learn from the rest.

Build a strong social circle by following the tips in this article.

Overcoming each fake friend will allow you to appreciate the real friends much more.

WHAT IS THE MIND?

I was recently scrolling thru YouTube to search for videos on 'what is the mind?'

Results?

Very disappointing.

Every video I went thru was a word salad or wasn't answering the questions that I wanted to be answered.

Most of the videos left me more confused & scratching my head.

I'm a simple guy.

I like things delivered to me in a simple way so I can process the information & execute on it.

And for years, I have been trying to learn more about mindset.

If you follow ArmaniTalks, then you know my page is mainly about helping you improve your communication skills.

So what does communication skills have to do with the mind?

It has EVERYTHING to do with it.

How others feel about you is mainly a reflection of how you feel about you.

And if you can't control your mindset, then you will inadvertently project quirky vibes to the other party.

This article is going to talk about the 3 main components of the mind.

I am not going to go super detailed because this is meant more for a high-level overview.

I am going to discuss the sense of self, conscious & subconscious mind.

Once you understand these 3 elements, you can apply the concepts effectively to your life.

Let's begin.

WHAT DOES THE MIND LOOK LIKE?

The biggest problem regarding the mindset is that we have no clue what it looks like.

When we don't have an idea on what something looks like, it has our head spinning in circles.

This is why we often ignore the intangible.

And when we ignore something, we never fully grasp what it is.

Google defines the mind as 'person's intellect.'

I believe intellect is simply a part of the mind, but not solely the mind.

My definition of the mind is:

An internal & external force which allows a human to leverage intellect, imagination, information & energy storage to navigate life.

Now, in order to bring structure to the intangible, you need a picture.

You need a personalized idea of what the mind looks like.

'Is the brain the mind?'

No.

The brain is a neural circuit board that is programmable by the mind. Once programmed, it will influence the mind.

A Neuroscience Law is:

- The mind controls the brain.
- The brain controls the mind.

Since the 2 entities are different, it gets very difficult to think of a picture.

I personally envision a picture of the mind as a universe around someone's head.

The bigger the universe, the more faculties of the mind they are leveraging for growth.

The smaller the universe, the more faculties that are being ignored.

Work actively on creating a picture of the mind as you continue to study the subject.

It will allow you to feel more engaged in studying the topic.

THE 3 ELEMENTS

Here are my high-level overviews of the mind.

- **The sense of self**– who are you & what are you working towards?
- **Conscious mind-** intellect & imagination.
- **Subconscious mind**– storage of information & energy from our lives.

Let's go thru each one.

THE SENSE OF SELF

Who are you?

What do you consider yourself?

Where do you see yourself going?

These are abstract questions that are relative to the person answering them.

A true sense of self is having the rational to understand where you are & the imagination to understand where you are going.

Which brings me to the next realm.

CONSCIOUS MIND

This part of the mind is the one you are using to read this article.

Your conscious mind holds awareness.

You can use your awareness to go from intellect, imagination or use the 2 in harmony.

- Intellect is the ability to reason.
- Imagination is the ability to see impossible.

SUBCONSCIOUS MIND

Your entire life holds data (information & energy) from your past & present.

This is known as your paradigm.

A paradigm is conditioned thoughts which you accept as your reality.

The subconscious mind is the most powerful database that you can imagine.

And this database is the one which provides thoughts to your conscious faculties.

HOW SHOULD YOU USE THE MIND?

Want to know something?

Most people have a very little idea of how to USE their mindset to their favor.

They completely neglect this topic & end up suffering in the long term for it.

The problem is the school system.

From the 3 elements of the mindset that I mentioned, the school system only focuses on intellect.

They only care about the ability to reason, pass tests & do some homework.

They completely neglect to help you identify a sense of self, how to leverage imagination & how to reprogram the paradigm within your subconscious towards your favor.

When you don't know how to use the mind, you unlock the cycle of chaos.

Here's how most people behave once they graduate from school.

1. They have no sense of self, so are not working towards anything.
2. This group uses their intellect by learning a bunch of random topics which are not moving them forward towards any growth.
3. The imagination is left unused. Results? Anxiety forms because this creative portion of the mind is untamed.
4. The subconscious spits out thoughts to the conscious. This human mistakes mind wandering as critical thinking.

Sad.

Here's how a person using the mind correctly behaves.
1. They have evaluated where they are & where they want to go.
2. They use their intellect to learn meaningful topics to help them get to their destination.
3. This group uses the imagination to visualize their future self.

4. Repeating the intellectual topics & seeing pictures of their future state helps them reprogram their subconscious mind.

5. Now the newly reprogrammed subconscious paradigm provides thoughts to the conscious to move the human forward.

Notice the difference?

How to Create a Weapon

Hopefully, you understand how the mind works now.

The NUMBER 1 thing you need to be doing is analyzing who you are & what you want out of life.

Analyzing who you are can be done by spending more time with yourself.

Finding out what you want out of life requires some pain.

But it is well worth it. Go and experiment or take a walk down memory lane and evaluate what makes you feel alive.

When you have the sense of self identified, you can then use your intellect & imagination towards your favor!

The more your repeat concepts & visualize images, the more your subconscious processes rewire.

Your paradigm shifts.

And your mindset goes from being a hurdle to a weapon!

Leverage All 3 of the Components & Rewire Your Destiny

Use your mindset to create your destiny.

Learning to be an effective communicator starts or being competent in any profession starts within.

When you are a man & woman on a mission, confidence just oozes out from your voice.

You are someone people want to listen to.

Mastering these 3 elements of the mindset will help you unlock other components of the mind not discussed in this article.

Such as curiosity, willpower, memory and so much more.

When you have something you are working towards, you unlock your **inner genius**.

Your mind is a universe living within you.

It is a muscle that can be strengthened and will grow over time.

THINK LIKE A WINNER: OPTIMISTIC PEOPLE

There's a lot of negativity going on around nowadays. Optimistic people are rare.

I remember I logged onto Facebook recently & was very surprised by what I saw.

Bitching, whining, complaining, venting & all the above.

'What were they so negative about?'

Wrong question.

The right question is: 'What were they not so negative about?'

Sad.

Our society nowadays glorifies negativity & scoffs at positivity.

I remember a while back, I went to a restaurant with a bunch of old friends.

Soon as we got in, they began complaining, talking about why the place sucks & the food is bound to be bad.

Well, guess what??

Their food was bad.

While mine was delicious.

Want to know why?

'Why?'

It was based on their thinking.

You see, they thought their food was going to suck & their perception led them to view their taste buds in a negative light.

Those people were running a race with an anchor tied to them.

It's time for a change.

My page focuses on optimism & thinking like a winner.

But what does that really mean?

And if you think like a loser, can you still change the game around?

Yes.

Your damn skippy you can!

And in this article, I am going to help you break out of your negative Facebook whining ways & carve out the path of a winner.

Today, I am going to give you an insight into the minds of optimistic people.

WHY ARE PEOPLE SO NEGATIVE?

People are so negative nowadays because negativity sells.

If you tune into the news media, you are not seeing stories of positivity, abundance & wins.

You are seeing political scandals, murders & crimes.

I'm not saying making the public aware of the negatives in our world is bad.

But nowadays, mainstream entertainment & media focuses predominantly on that to capture & keep attention.

This is dangerous because it is influencing your thought patterns.

You ever heard of: **you become what you eat.**

'Ya.'

Well, in the real world there is another one. It is: **you become what you consume.**

Consuming negative trash will have you thinking negative thoughts.

Repetition and visuals are the languages of your subconscious mind.

And when you repeatedly watch graphics with negativity, your subconscious mind will become polluted.

The polluted subconscious mind will relay negative thoughts to the conscious mind.

And the polluted conscious thoughts will reaffirm the paradigms to the subconscious mind.

Aka: The circle of death.

This extends past consumption of content though.

This also deals with the squad you hang out with.

Who do you hang out with homie?

Negative clowns?

Because your immediate squad will play a massive role in your thinking, make no mistake about that.

PESSIMISM VS OPTIMISM.

You've heard the old analogy of the glass filled with water to the middle.

The pessimist sees the glass as half empty.
The optimist sees the glass as half full.

Although this may seem like a small detail to you, the concept is HUGE.

This is what truly separate the losers from the winners.

A pessimist looks for 100 reasons as to why it will not work out.

The optimist looks for 1 reason as to why it will.

It's sad because the pessimist actually gets happy when it doesn't work out.

Their strange mind thinks 'told ya so.'

Now I'm not saying having some pessimism automatically makes you a loser.

I think strategic pessimism is great.

It builds awareness and allows you to see something that you were not initially considering.

But pessimism becomes a problem when it is a character trait.

You start talking yourself out of opportunities before you even begin!

And to make matters worse, you may be subconsciously doing the same for your friends as well.

Optimistic people, on the other hand, have empowering thoughts & then fact check with pessimism.

And optimistic people every now and then run some ideas by pessimists.

But a winner is not a pessimist.

Not now, not ever.

HOW OPTIMISTIC PEOPLE ARE BORN

'So Armani, if pessimism is so bad, then why are so many people choosing that lifestyle?'

Because they are either unaware they are pessimistic or lazy.

I remember one of my cousins was a HUGE pessimist. And one day after discouraging me left & right, I gave him a piece of my mind.

He was shocked when he found out I viewed him as a pessimist.

He had no clue!

Emphasis on **he had no clue.**

Now there is another group who has a clue.

But they think nothing is wrong with the lifestyle.

Pretty sad considering their low energy affects not only their life but their surroundings.

But it's deeper than that.

Often these people don't have what it takes to put in the WORK to become optimistic.

Optimism requires work.

And often, optimism is born from pain.

A human is born happy & carefree.

Then this human is taken thru the school system & released onto the real world.

In the real world, they deal with MULTIPLE failures in a repeated fashion which causes them to become pessimistic.

They become negative & jaded.

Well, one day something traumatic happens.

The trauma depends on the person.

Sometimes the trauma can be something as small seeing other people move up while they remain a bum.

Anyways, during the moment of darkness, this fellow learns that they need to fix their life.

They need to shift their thinking or they will remain in darkness.

That's when they become AWARE of being optimistic.

THE BRIDGE BETWEEN PESSIMISTIC PEOPLE & OPTIMISTIC PEOPLE

Once this fellow becomes aware of optimism, they do 1 major life exercise which will change their life.

'Which is?'

Gratitude.

Gratitude is the bridge between pessimism & optimism.

It is the bridge that can change your thought patterns.

When you are being grateful, you are conditioning your brain to think with the 'glass is half full mentality' vs empty.

Huge key.

Your brain is either predominantly pessimistic or predominantly optimistic.

But it can't be both.

Making gratitude a habit is what will allow you to shift your paradigm & become a winner.

- Count your small wins.
- Write it out or say it out loud
- Do it in the morning & night.
- Soon, you'll be counting your big wins on autopilot.

That's the key to thinking like a winner.

BE GRATEFUL & THINK LIKE A WINNER

If the whiners on Facebook would practice gratitude every now and then, then whining on any social media would not even be a consideration.

Really is that simple.

Gratitude rewires your brain & installs new neural pathways in there.

A huge key to change your world.

Think like a winner.
Feel like a winner.
Act like a winner.

ACTIVE LISTENING: A HOW TO GUIDE

A major key to improving your communication skills is thru active listening. Therefore, knowing how to do it is **crucial**.

I often say that it is the listener who determines likability & the flow of the conversation.

If you are someone who is overly eager to speak, then this guide is for you.

I've met plenty of people in my life & I can tell you one compelling insight.

'What is that?'

The best listeners are the best speakers.

Why you ask?

It's because they are very precise with their wording & have no wasted movements.

If you want to unlock your charisma, then learning how to leverage your active listening is the key.

In this article, I am going to break down a successful interaction, types of listening & how to execute!

Social skills are a weapon, so let's add active listening to your toolbox.

HOW A SUCCESSFUL SOCIAL INTERACTION WORKS

Humans love talking about themselves.

When humans talk about themselves, they often feel the same pleasure as sex.

No lie.

But this presents a boatload of problems.

'Like what?'

Well, when everyone loves talking about themselves so much, that's when social disruptions begin!

No one wants to learn how to level up their active listening because they're too busy wanting to yap away.

But this is good for you.

'Good how?'

Well, abundant is rarely valuable. But scarce is when the demand RISES.

With all the people wanting to talk all the time, listeners are a prized possession!

There is a huge supply of talkers, but listeners are the ones in demand.

An ideal social interaction consists of a balance between talking and listening.

- If you talk too much, then you spark the other person's ego.
- If you listen too much, then you get treated like a wallflower.

We are going for the middle zone.

THE 2 TYPES OF LISTENING: SPONGE VS TRAMPOLINE

There are 2 kinds of listening styles out there.

One is the **sponge technique** & the other is the **trampoline technique.**

Sponge is when you absorb the other person's points.

They talk & you listen.

This type of listening typically has a lot of head nods & 'mhms.'

Sponge listening is perfect for being a shoulder to cry on.

When someone is going thru a tough time, aim to adopt sponge listening.

Trampoline listening is when you get the other person's points & amplify them.

You amplify their points by:

- Asking them to expand their points.
- Contribute.
- Ask relevant questions.

Trampoline listening = Active listening.

This sort of listening is what I recommend for most social interactions.

When you are networking, talking to a friend or family member, aim for trampoline rather than sponge.

You will be more memorable & build a stronger connection.

HOW TO LEVEL UP ACTIVE LISTENING

Active listening comes down to heart & mind, then ears.

Counterintuitive, I know. I'm sure you thought I was going to say lead with the ears, but nah.

- The heart is first.

This is very difficult for people to do because they enter an interaction with the ego.

Big mistake.

When you enter an interaction with the ego, then you have the tendency to yap away & ramble.

When you enter the interaction with the heart, you make the interaction about the other person.

Remember earlier how I said humans LOVE talking about themselves?

Well, give them that!

If you give them the spotlight, then they will try to give something of value back to you.

They will try to listen.

- The second element of active listening is mind.

A big part of a social interaction is staying present.

If you lose track of reality & begin going off to la-la land, then that's fine.

Just make yourself **aware** & come back to the present moment.

A present mind has you enjoying the social experience rather than drifting away from it.

- The final element is the ears.

If you got your mind & heart in unison, then listening becomes a byproduct.

When you level up your active listening, you realize:

Listening is not something you do, it's something that you embody.

When you lead with compassion & remain present, you have no choice but to listen.

You end up asking someone to expand on a point you need clarification on.

You'll contribute when you find the time is right.

And finally, you'll ask questions that are relevant to the conversation.

This allows you to not make the interaction about yourself & start being a diamond in the rough.

ACTIVE LISTENING = CONSCIOUS TO SUBCONSCIOUS TRANSFORMATION

So here's the deal.

If you're like most of the population, then you have been raised as a predominant talker.

You have neural pathways set for talking a lot.

Well, in this case, you are going to have to take an active approach to begin active listening.

At first, it is going to feel like work.

But focus!

You will feel like there are a lot of moving variables.

'Armani, are you telling me I have to be compassionate, remain present, ask questions, contribute, listen and all that???'

Yep!

At first, it seems like mission impossible.

When you are talking, you just focus on 1 variable.

But active listening is a whole different ball game.

Picture it as upgrading from riding a bike to driving a car.

When you were first driving a car, pretty sure you felt like you were having to do a lot at once, right?

'Yea.'

Well, same with active listening.

But continue on anyways.

Eventually, the variables will come in unison.

At first, driving in the park felt difficult as fuck, but nowadays, you can drive on the highway without even thinking!

When the unison of variables happens with active listening, you will begin to flow MUCH better in social interactions.

That's when you will do the act on autopilot.

HOW TO BECOME AN ACTIVE LISTENING SUPERSTAR!

This is a lifestyle champ.

You aren't just trying to be an active listener interaction by interaction...

Rather, make it a life philosophy.

It helps you a ton in the grand scheme of things.

'You mean active listening extends PAST social interactions?'

Yes!

You end up raising your awareness as a whole.

Life is a game of leveling up your awareness.

And when you are able to recondition your mind to active listen, you learn like a beast & develop more perspective.

An excellent way to hack your maturity.

Now you know how to level up your active listening skills, so be sure to execute!

Charisma & a memorable personality awaits.

HOW TO BUILD RAPPORT

Everyone wants to know the answer to the golden social question: *How do you build rapport?*

Rapport is the language of social interactions.

Without it, you cap out at being liked.

With it, you can be lazy & still be loved.

Why is this?

It's because humans love humans who they share certain traits with.

A few years ago, I had no clue.

I was an awkward engineer who struggled with communication skills.

Thought of conversations in a very logical fashion.

Therefore, I entered each interaction giving a whole lot of 'what' statements & expecting others to be swayed.

'Were they?'

Absolutely not.

Exact opposite.

When I tried to influence with logic, they just dug their heels deeper into the ground.

Very frustrating point to be in considering I needed to get my message across to move up in my company.

Therefore, I decided to reverse engineer the entire rapport-building process.

After years & years of trial & error, I was able to finally understand how to build rapport!

In today's article, I am going to give you a couple of insights on how to develop this skill.

'Skill?'

Yup! Learning the art of building rapport is a SKILL.

So you can learn it by getting the fundamentals down & practicing.

Ready?

'Yessir.'

Perfect, let us begin.

WHY RAPPORT BUILDING IS CRUCIAL

There are a lot of weirdos in the world.

Every day, you hear news about murders, kidnappings, burglaries & so much more.

Sad.

Therefore, humans have built a subconscious filtration system.

They put up an invisible guard to avoid falling in the trap of wasting their time or having anything malicious happening to them.

Think about it for a second.

Analyze your personal life.

Who are some of the people you click the MOST with?

I'm sure it's the people who make you feel understood.

Noticed what I said?

UNDERSTOOD.

Most people think rapport is only about finding similarities.

But that is not true.

Rapport is about making someone's ideas & emotions feel understood.

Often, that happens when 2 people have similarities, sure.

But is it always the case? Nah.

But you NEED to make the other person feel understood if you want to know how to build rapport.

Really is that simple.

Once you make them feel understood, you will penetrate into their world.

Their guard is down.

And now you can build a social bond & strengthen it.

THE GOLDEN RULE ON HOW TO BUILD RAPPORT

The golden rule to understand is that building rapport with individuals is different.

You can have a set framework, but be able to adjust depending on the person that you are speaking with.

By understanding that every human is different, you are going to be much more dynamic with your movements.

You are going to make everyone feel like the main character in their world.

This is a mega key because those who build rapport are able to adjust at the whim.

Look closer...

If you want to know how to build rapport, then you need to know how to analyze.

Analyze social cues, so you make the right moves.

Here are a few moves that you can pull out from your bag of tricks to spike rapport:

QUESTIONS

Questions = Collecting data.

This is huge because it helps you tame your ego.

We often like to talk about topics which interest us.

Therefore, we try to pound this topic into another person's world to have them think it's interesting as well.

But that is the wrong strategy!

Remember:

We are not trying to pull them into our world, but rather, we are trying to enter theirs.

Use questions to extract information from them.

What exactly is it that makes this person tick?

You'll always be very surprised.

I remember a few years ago I was talking to the CEO of my company.

After asking him a few strategic questions, I found out his passion was racing.

Huh??

Dude was a polished 60-year-old man.

Never would have thought of him as a racer.

But strategic questions led me to that insight.

SEE IF YOU CAN FIND SIMILARITIES

During your questioning, see if you can gather some similarities.

You'll be surprised by how similar humans are when you look deep inside.

And it may be something that you may have never expected!

I shared a similarity with my English professor from high school in regards to which sport we played as youngsters.

But once you find a similarity, there's a subconscious hook point.

They FEEL like they can relate to you.

Go back & forth regarding this similarity.

Share stories on it, ask questions, follow up etc.

Really hammer it home.

You're strengthening the rapport bridge.

WHAT IF THERE ARE NO SIMILARITIES?

If there are no similarities, then don't panic!

Remember earlier how I said rapport is about allowing the person to know they were heard?

Well, then do just that!

The CEO who I was referring to earlier loved racing.

It was a passion of his.

Therefore, I let him talk about it.

I asked strategic questions. Questions which were **relevant** to the conversation.

His eyes glowed as he saw my interest in the topic.

Afterwards? He left energized by the conversation.

He called me into his office the next week so we could schedule lunch.

Don't panic if you can't find any similarities, rather find their passion.

TALK ABOUT DARKNESS

One way you can learn how to build rapport is by talking about darkness.

Pains, trials & tribulations.

This is a more advanced move, so no need to do it yet if you feel uncomfortable.

But I recommend adding this to your toolbox.

What do I mean?

Well, when the CEO and I had lunch, we talked about how his mom passed away from cancer.

I listened with compassion.

And I steered the convo onto how he handled the situation.

He went onto talk about how the death of his mom lit a fire in him.

Every move he was going to do from here on out will be in memory of his mom.

As he transitioned from the death of his mom to his rise, he felt a level of honor.

Talking about the darkness allowed him to see how far he had come.

Seeing how far he had come gave him positive FEELINGS.

And those were positive feelings he associated with me.

We all have our trials & tribulations. When someone asks about it, it touches our human side.

Being vulnerable is a key to building rapport quicker.

So don't only ask about someone's tough times, but offer stories of your own.

BODY MIRRORING

I used to think body mirroring was bullshit.

But it isn't.

It a subconscious hack which allows you to enter rapport quicker.

There is an art to it though.

Don't be the person being obvious with mimicking the other person's body language.

The name of the game is being SUBTLE.

Transition smoothly into the other person's body language.

See which moves they like to do a lot, and do it every now and then.

See the tonality & pacing they use behind their voice.

And do it.

Are they crossing their arms?

Cool. Do it then!

No need to do every single movement.

Just body mirror every now and then.

Treat it like a seasoning in a dish. Overdoing it will give off creepy vibes.

HOW TO BUILD RAPPORT LIKE A CHARISMATIC BEAST!

These are moves you can apply whenever you are building rapport.

But understand that it will change based on the person you are speaking with.

Which is why it is crucial to know WHO you are speaking with so you can adjust accordingly.

Building rapport beforehand allows you to deepen a social bond much quicker.

A deepened social bond allows you to **influence**.

You'll rarely (if ever) be able to influence someone who doesn't even trust you.

But when they trust you? It becomes 10x easier to lead them.

Use rapport building for good.

There's nothing worse than entering someone's world, then souring the interaction due to a poor character.

Be a high integrity individual & leave everyone better after interacting with you than before!

Not only will you know how to build rapport, but you will know how to be a human of value!

Now go out there and kill it.

7 SOCIAL SKILLS ACTIVITIES TO BUILD YOUR CHARISMA

If you are currently out of the social game, you may be wondering, what are some good social skills activities to build your charisma?

This is a good question considering that the social world is not stagnant, rather dynamic.

What does that mean?

It means that adaptability is king.

If you are someone who is just coming out of monk mode (strategic exclusion for self-improvement purposes), then you may be wondering how to become social?

But first, let me ask you something.

Why is it that you want to be social again?

Try to identify it before proceeding with the rest of the article.

When you have a purpose for the desire behind your social activities, you'll notice which activities to pick up & which ones aren't for you.

The major goal is to always be social, yes.

But have an understanding of where you want to go with your enhanced social muscle.

Are you someone who just moved to a new city & wants to make some friends?

Do you want to build a powerful network?

Do you want to start finding a life partner?

Do you want a squad to party with?

Etc.

Once you identify, then proceed on with the rest of the article.

Being social is a superpower in today's world.

Having the ability to put yourself out there requires courage & will help you in the long run.

So let's begin.

AVOIDING THE #1 SOCIAL SIN

I want to tell you something.

There is no one more unlikable than someone who is needy.

It is the biggest social sin out there.

Neediness stems from lack of self-worth.

Why is the person's self-worth low?

It's because this fellow hasn't taken the time to invest in themselves.

When you refuse to invest in yourself, you approach each social interaction as the lower social valued creature.

Is that what you want?? Well??

'No no, that's not what I want!"

Great.

You want to be charismatic.

You want to be someone who provides more value than they take, right?

'Yessir.'

Well, in that case, you need to become **valuable**.

When you take the time to invest in yourself, you fix your mindset.

This allows you to approach interactions from a place of value rather than needy.

People will automatically be able to sense your level of self-assuredness.

Go on a journey to level up & you will thank yourself later.

HAVING A ROUGH OUTLINE FOR YOUR SOCIAL SKILLS ACTIVITES

Having a rough game plan can never hurt anybody, right?
Well, that's the same with social skills activities!

Your game plan should lead with your predominant desire.
Let's use an example:

Say you want to build a stronger network for your career.
Well, that is your predominant intent.
You are still going to be social in other aspects of your life, of course.
But you are going to lead with building a stronger career.

When you assign your brain an intent, you move with more purpose.
If you are someone who is just moving aimlessly, then you are someone who will have deflated movements in your social interactions.

Have you ever had that moment when you were at a networking event, but had no clue WHY you were there?
What happened?
'I was very low energy & unsure of my moves.'
Exactly!

So have a very rough gameplan for what is your main goal.

Then you will begin to move with intent.

The intent is a staple of confidence.

7 SOCIAL SKILLS ACTIVITIES

In this section, I want to give you a few ideas to help you get started. You don't have to use all 7.

But choose the ones which fit into your game plan.

And remember, your social skills activities will grow, not stagnate as you stack up more experiences.

When that happens, you just adjust & adapt!

The list is in no particular order.

1. MEETUP GROUPS

Meetup groups are great if you are someone who is new to a location or simply want to find other like-minds.

Download the Meetup app on your smartphone.

From there, you can choose groups that interest you & attend.

Most are free, some are paid.

Keep going & you will be able to do fun activities to keep your social skills sharp.

2. TOASTMASTERS

I'm a big fan of Toastmasters & have been a member for 5 plus years.

Toastmasters has gotten the reputation as the #1 public speaking club on the planet.

But personally, I think it's better for your social skills.

Surprising, I know.

The clubs have very supportive members who help you become a better communicator.

Many of the clubs have an 'After Hour' where the members go to an event afterward to network.

Find a Toastmasters club near you.

3. SPORTS

Sports is one of the best ways to be social.

I remember when I moved to Virginia a few years back, I didn't know anyone.

I would always kill time by going to shoot at the basketball court.

During my time at the basketball court, I'd always have someone who'd come and ask if they could shoot with me.

Then more people came....

And before you know it we are all having an intense basketball game, engaging in teamwork & building a sense of camaraderie.

Many of those people went onto becoming great friends.

4. SOCIAL MEDIA GROUPS

I am a firm believer in digital charisma.

Let's face it, the world is changing.

Digital presence is something that can expand your message from your local city to the entire planet.

Find a social media platform of your choice to build on.

And once you get on the platform, find other people with similar interests as you & engage with their content.

Soon, you are becoming friends with people from different cities, states or countries.

Combine all the members & start a group to talk about similar topics.

Also, you can always just request to join a group. I know facebook is popular for their groups.

5. THROWING A PARTY

One of the best social skills activities to keep your ax sharp is by throwing a party.

I remember a few years ago, I used to be the external vice president of my fraternity.

My job was to work with other organizations to throw events.

Often, I was in charge.

I kid you not, those were some of the most stressful times of my life.

I had no clue who was going to show up, if something was going to go wrong, whether people were going to have fun etc.

But after each event, I left with wisdom that helped me with the next party.

And managing all those egos made my social skills sharpen to new heights.

Try throwing a small party & work your way up from there.

6. NETWORKING EVENTS

If your goal is to build a network, then go to networking events.

You will find plenty by going on Google, Eventbrite or Facebook in your local city.

Use networking events as an opportunity to sharpen your social muscle.

'What if I have no one to go with?'

Then go by yourself.

Going by yourself is huge because you may be nervous as fuck, but you continue anyway.

Going to a new event where you don't know anyone isn't easy, so it works out your social muscle 10x stronger.

You'll come out feeling more alive.

7. GOING OUT

Going clubbing & bar hopping gets a bad rep.

But I don't think it's bad as long as you carry yourself with class.

Don't be the clown getting fucked up & getting into a fight with the bouncers.

But rather be the person who is enthusiastic & using it to connect with others on a personal level.

People tend to open up much more when they are out in a nightlife setting.

So if this suits you, give it a try!

One of your friends may be the one who hits you up. But if not, then make an event happen on your own!

8. TRAVELING

One of the best ways to create strong memories is by traveling with people.

I remember a while back, the mere idea of camping disinterested me.

Why the fuck would I go in a hot, stank area without electricity for?

But it was my friends birthday, so I agreed.

We drove 7 hours to the location & had a blast.

I don't know what was more fun, the drive there or the actual camping part.

Point being, travel with your squad.

You'll solidify your bonds further.

INVEST IN YOUR SOCIAL SKILLS ACTIVITIES

Being social is a great investment in your long term happiness.

When you are leveling up, it's hard to find the time to always connect with people.

But aim to keep this muscle strong.

Your social skills will continue to sharpen over time & you will become better at it.

The stronger the social muscle gets, the easier you can adapt to social situations.

You will become much more charismatic.

Life becomes much easier when you have a network of people who not only like you, but respect you as well.

HOW TO REFRAME
SOCIAL ANXIETY

I want you to take a second to analyze your anxiety.

Which thoughts lead you to feel emotional sensations in your body?

Take some time to find 2-3 experiences.

Got it?

Cool.

Now I want you to take some time to analyze those thoughts.

How many of them deal with people?

'Uh… most of them.'

Aha! A major insight has been spotted.

Isn't it a tad bit funny?

So many of us have our lives inhibited by anxiety, but we often simply react, rather than respond.

How often do we take some time to analyze the root cause?

If you delve deep into your anxiety, then you will see that a majority of it deals with people.

Which is why I say that:

Social anxiety makes up a majority of your anxiety.

You aren't afraid of failing.

You are afraid of being JUDGED for failing.

Not judged by yourself, but by others.

This is a massive clue into engineering a comeback, because you now have spotted the root cause.

Reframe your perception of social anxiety & a lot of your anxiety will melt in the process.

But the question is, *how*?

And that is a great question!

Reframing social anxiety will be the core of this article.

Learn the power of perception & how to engineer it to your favor.

THE POWER OF FRAMING

Imagine if you are sitting in an audience.

The host gets on stage and is about to introduce the new speaker.

'Allow me to bring on stage, Paul Johnson! Mr. Johnson was voted the best public speaker for 5 years in a row. He is an 8 times Toastmasters champion. Has helped millions of people overcome speech anxiety and is an all-around winner. Put your hands together for Paul 'The Rockstar' Johnson!!'

Automatically, your perception has been set.

In your mind, Paul is some magnificent speaker.

Want to know what's funny?

Even if Paul gives a rather sloppy speech, you'll be more forgiving because the frame has been set in your mind.

Now, let's flip the scenario.

Imagine if the host simply introduced Paul Johnson by his name, and that was it.

In this case, if Paul gave a sloppy speech, then you'll be less forgiving & wonder why he didn't prepare.

'So what does this all mean?'

This means that the power of framing is CRUCIAL.

And you need to frame to your advantage, not disadvantage.

ANALYZING ANXIETY VS. EXCITEMENT

Have you ever looked into the physical feelings of anxiety & excitement?

Picture yourself on the top of a roller coaster. How do you feel?

'I feel very excited!'

Now picture yourself getting ready to give a speech in front of 500 people. How do you feel?

'I feel very anxious!'

But look closer into your imagination.

FEEL THE SENSATIONS.

The 2 feelings are practically identical.

However, one gives you a positive emotion & the other gives you a negative emotion.

'Any idea why?'

Yes. It's because you have stacked the perceptions against you.

REFRAME SOCIAL ANXIETY AS SOCIAL EXCITEMENT

If you think about it, our ancient ancestors didn't have words. They only had body language to operate on.

Eventually, society designed words.

And words play a MAJOR role in our present-day psyches.

You can set up your frame by simply choosing your words more carefully.

Using '**social anxiety**' is stacking the cards AGAINST your favor.

The word automatically implies a *negative* connotation.

Once you inhibit your mind, your behaviors will follow.

You will be much more restrictive, paranoid & feel like everyone is watching you.

But change the game!

Use '**social excitement**.'

Excite implies a *positive* connotation.

This automatically plays to your favor. You've energized the mind.

You are like the host who gave Paul Johnson that magnificent intro.

And your behavior will match your empowered mindset.

Same feelings, but different behaviors.

This concept is LIFECHANGING.

You just need to be consistent.

Anytime you are entering a new social event & begin feeling flustered, stop.

And hammer in the new paradigm shift.

Instead of saying you feel 'social anxiety,' say that you feel 'SOCIAL EXCITEMENT.'

You'll immediately feel the benefits in your psychology & physiology.

Charisma will follow.

THE TRUTH ABOUT SOCIAL INTERACTIONS

Here is the plain reality.

Human interactions often require a level of tension.

We are creatures of energy, you know.

But what happens is when you go to a social event & you feel a surge of energy, you feel a little taken aback.

'What is all of this energy I am feeling out of nowhere?' your brain wonders.

And it automatically assigns it a negative label due to the unfamiliarity. This is social anxiety in a nutshell.

You try to suppress the energy because you think it is something bad.

And by doing this, you simply make your anxiety worse.

But that simply shouldn't be the case!

You should welcome the energy with open arms.

All human interactions have energy.

But since you are entering a new social situation or bigger social situation, you simply feel more energy.

That's your body energizing you!

When you welcome the energy, something magical happens.

You become expressive.

Expressing energy = Charisma.

You just need to learn the art of reframing.

A mindset concept that I discuss more in Level Up Mentality.

OVERCOMING SOCIAL ANXIETY

Overcoming social anxiety is a beautiful feeling.

You begin noticing a lot of other thoughts which made you anxious, goes away.

Why?

Because you learn the power of reframing.

Simply by consciously calling anxiety, excitement, you begin to take a massive control back of your life.

You have displayed emotional intelligence.

And your renewed paradigm shift makes you feel more powerful in social situations.

This allows you to take up new challenges which you were previously running away from.

Keep the momentum going champ.

Your mind is more powerful than you can ever imagine.

WHY EQ IS MORE IMPORTANT THAN IQ

Yup, you read that correctly.

Your EQ is more important than your IQ.

'Huh?? What the fuck are you talking about? What is EQ?'

Good question.

And this is a good question because you were never taught about the subject growing up.

Pretty sure if you are like most people, you were only taught IQ.

There's a certain time in people lives when they take their IQ exam.

Maybe it was when they were a little kid who was just entering school.

Maybe it was when they entered a certain job.

Or heck, maybe it was when they got curious and tried out an online exam.

But once they get the score, they are told it is a set score.

You can't raise your IQ, they say.

It is a fixed score for life.

Is this the measure of intelligence?

For decades, that is what we have been taught.

But is the human brain that fixated of an entity?

Is intelligence so black & white that you can measure it with a test score?

Ha! That's laughable.

However, I want to be clear about something.
This article is not me shitting on the IQ exam.
I understand the importance of the IQ test in today's society.

However, I want to take it a level further.
I want to introduce a new measurement that you have been deprived of in the school system.

It is none other than emotional intelligence.
Your emotional quotient.
Your EQ.

WHY IS THE IQ EXAM THE MEASUREMENT OF INTELLIGENCE?

Humans love clarity.
Clarity gives us understanding and makes it feel like we solved a problem.

So why should intelligence be any different?

There are billions and billions of humans on this planet.
There must be a way to quantify the processing powers of the human brain, right?
Right!
So the IQ exam was developed.

A structured exam that measures a human's pattern recognition abilities, critical thinking and reasoning skills.

'Was the exam successful in accomplishing what it attempted to do?

Yes!

The IQ exam is a brilliant test to measure your critical thinking abilities.

In many ways, it knocked it out of the park.

'So why is it flawed?'

Because critical thinking is only **one** element of the Umbrella of Intelligence.

WHAT IS INTELLIGENCE?

The dictionary definition of intelligence is:

The ability to acquire & apply knowledge & skills.

This simple definition leads massive insight into the world of intelligence.

Critical thinking is simply one building block for intelligence.

The Umbrella of Intelligence:

1. Critical thinking skills
2. Creativity
3. Emotional intelligence
4. Social Skills
5. Mental toughness

Picture one skill that you are VERY good at.

Were you able to acquire AND apply it thru critical thinking skills alone?

Fuck no.

·   You needed to be able to show the ability to connect dots (creativity).
·   You had to regulate past emotions that made you want to quit (emotional intelligence).
·   You connected with others to find missing answers (social skills).
·   You persevered through the good and the bad (mental toughness).

Does critical thinking play a MASSIVE role in **acquiring** knowledge? Absolutely.

But in terms of applying?

It requires creativity, emotional intelligence, social skills & mental toughness.

Simply having knowledge without **applying** is like sticking a key in a lock & never turning it to see what's behind the door.

Your intelligence can't be measured by a damn exam.

Your IQ score can, sure.

But from the umbrella of intelligence, bullet points 2-5 are all internal.

And internal leads to ambiguity which is not measurable by an exam.

What's funny is that some of the most 'woke' people are completely unaware of this.

They shit on the school system left and right.

But will take the IQ exam as the only measure of intelligence to their grave.

Cognitive dissonance much?

The IQ exam was implemented by society & reinforced by the school system to clarify the ambiguous nature of human beings.

But when you do that, you simply lead to more questions.

THE TRUE NATURE OF HUMANS

Not sure if you are aware of this, but humans are emotional creatures, not logical ones.

The emotional states are influenced by a human's subconscious mind.

And the subconscious mind dictates 95 percent of human behavior.

Therefore, thinking logically is a great gift to possess, but it will only measure a fraction of your ability to thrive in the real world.

That's where EQ comes in.

'But Armani, I thought you said the internal world cannot be measured by society?'

That is true.

But the internal world can be measured by the person themselves.

Knowledge can be measured externally.

Awareness must be measured internally.

There is no test to measure your awareness.

But awareness is the CORE principle of EQ.

HOW TO MEASURE YOUR EQ

Here is my definition of EQ:

EQ is measured by the self awareness of an individual to gauge their ability to showcase emotional literacy, ability to regulate emotions & understand the emotional states of others.

In order to self assess your own EQ, you are bringing awareness (which is stored in the conscious mind) to your internal emotions (which is stored by your subconscious mind).

You are bridging together your 2 minds.

As a beginner, I want you to be aware, honest & analyze.

For the following three steps, measure where you stand from a score of 1-10.

1 being awful & need massive improvement to 10 being great & have a strong grasp.

I. THE ABILITY TO REGULATE YOUR EMOTIONS.

Are you able to turn destructive emotions into positive fuel?

Life is going to be a game of coexisting with your emotions.

It doesn't matter if you are the smartest test taker in the world.

If you are someone who is always clouded with anxiety, you will not get far.

It's like trying to drive a shiny car with a busted engine.

Doesn't work.

Your ability to control your emotions with your mind (emotional intelligence) will dictate your success.

Can you change states at will?

Score yourself 1-10.

2. THE ABILITY TO UNDERSTAND OTHERS EMOTIONS.

How well can you read the emotional states of other humans?

You've heard the phrase, your net worth will be determined by your net work.

Understand that HUMANS ARE NOT LOGICAL CREATURES.

As Dale Carnegie said in his blockbuster book How to Win Friends & Influence People:

When dealing with humans, we are dealing with creatures of emotion, creatures bristling with prejudices and motivated by *pride* and vanity.

Your logical IQ thinking goes straight out the window when dealing with humans.

IQ thinking: If I do A, I will get B,C,D.

EQ feeling: If I do A, I may get Q, R, V, D.

Rate your ability to understand emotional states from 1-10.

3. EMOTIONAL LITERACY

How well can you put precise words to ambiguous emotions?

When you just feel an emotion & react, you are operating with the amygdala.

-The center of the brain responsible for perception of emotions like anger, irritation & fear.

When you feel an emotion & are able to logically verbalize it, you involve your prefrontal cortex.

-The part of the brain that deals with regulation of emotions.

The more nuance you can add to your emotions, the more emotional intelligence you possess.

Are you just angry?

Or are you irritated with a tad bit of disappointment due to lack of sleep which is making you angry?

Big difference.

Measure your emotional literacy from 1-10.

Tally up your final score and measure out of 50.

This exercise will get your awareness onto your strengths & areas of improvement.

WHY EQ IS MORE IMPORTANT THAN IQ

As I stated earlier, IQ is important for acquiring knowledge.

But EQ is important for applying knowledge.

In the school system, you are measured by your ability to score well on tests.

But in the real world, you are measured by your ability to work with people.

Look at everyone at the top.

They have the ability to WORK with people.

That's how the human race progresses.

'What about a very techie role like coding?'

Same thing.

Your IQ will help you learn the frameworks, structures & process for coding.

Step 1 is a very logical process.

But then ask yourself.

Who are you designing the code for?

You are designing it for a consumer.

Therefore, you need to be able to assess their needs & empathize with their pain points.

Emotional intelligence.

Anything that you learn in life, you will notice that it is first learned with your logical brain.

But after practicing for a while, it becomes intuition & controlled by your emotional brain.

Life is a game of working with people.

I don't make the rules, I simply share it.

So amplify your knowledge.

But make sure you have the emotional intelligence to be able to apply it.

LEVERAGING YOUR EQ & IQ

Having a high IQ with shitty EQ is like having a great product with shitty marketing.

It really is that simple.

Don't use your IQ as a crutch to display how 'smart' you are.

You are only smart when your ideas are producing results for other people.

It doesn't matter how great your brain is if your heart is in disarray.

So apply the 3 step formula, analyze your self assessed EQ score & see where you stand.

By clarifying your internal world, you will feel 10x better.

And fixing your energy allows you to fix the energy that you send to the world.

It's not what you know, it's who you know.

It's not what you say, it's how you say it.

It's not how many people you know, it's how many people know you.

Humans never made sense.

But that's what makes learning the subject so damn compelling.

HOW TO TAME YOUR EGO

The ego gets a bad reputation in the real world.
And to be honest, you can't blame people.

Look left.
Now, look right.
Do you see that?

I see a bunch of people who have their ego's controlling them.
They have untamed egos and they are not even AWARE of it.

'Whoa whoa Armani, back up a little. What exactly is an ego?'
Ah, good question my friend.

Let us go through the basics of the ego & teach you how to wield it to give you an advantage.
If you apply the tips in this article, you will realize that an ego is a TOOL.
And you were the master all along.

Let us begin.

WHAT IS THE EGO?

In plain terms:
The ego is your identity or sense of self.

Every experience that you have had growing up, people that you have encountered & traumas that you overcame shaped your ego.

The ego rests between the conscious and subconscious mind.
It serves as a bridge.

All the events that you have been through have been stored in the database of your subconscious mind.
And your conscious mind gets data from that database, forms it with perception & that creates your self-image.

The ego gives every human their sense of uniqueness.
And an ego is something that can either aid you in your level up journey or make it a living hell.

WHAT IS AN UNTAMED EGO?

You ever met that person who only saw life through their eyes?
A brutal narcissist with little or no empathy.
A person who magically made every conversation about themself?
Yes, that person has an untamed ego.

But you can even take it a level further.
People with untamed egos are not always loud and brash.
Many of them can actually be timid!

Believe it or not, social anxiety is a form of having an untamed ego.
'Huh???'
Yes!

Think about it.
Why is someone socially anxious?
It's because they are self-conscious in social situations.
Why are they self-conscious?

It's because they feel like all their moves are being watched.
'Why do they think all their moves are being watched?'
Because they feel **special**.

When you get to the root cause of the issue, it seems rather silly that everyone will be watching one person.
Can you fly?
'No.'
Then other people are not watching your every move.

But guess what?
Your ego paints an **illusion** that people are. Also known as the Spotlight Effect.

The ego is your self-image & an untamed ego is magnifying that self-image.
You feel like your sense of importance is manifesting into other people's lives.

Therefore, an untamed ego can produce a very brash personality or a very meek one.

SHOULD YOU KILL THE EGO?

I often hear people say 'I am meditating so I can kill my ego!'

What a foolish statement.

You can't kill the ego.
It is your sense of self!

If you try killing it & have no sense of self, then you are simply replacing it with a renewed ego.

Your perception of yourself will be a nobody.
Which is why there can never be a void.
There is always something that fills that void of self-image.

But killing the ego is a poor strategy as well.
An ego gives your life a sense of purpose.
You know what happens when you minimize it?
'What?'
You get a nice guy.
A nice guy is a people pleaser who does not value themself.

Result? They become a doormat in the process.

You don't want that!
'So what is the solution?'
You tame your ego.

How to Tame Your Ego

A tamed ego is a beautiful thing.
It makes your life so much easier & more fulfilling.
You stop personalizing negatives, stop forcing your beliefs onto others & maintain a clear vision along the way.

A tamed ego helps you in your level up the journey.
It allows you to have a poised persona that is not easily rattled.
You mature along the way.

'Whoa man! This seems too good to be true!'
It sort of is.
'Why?'

Because a tamed ego often comes thru pain.

Look at people who are very mature for their age or just mature in general.

They didn't just get like that.

They were crafted into that from hardships & overcoming those hardships.

Therefore, taming your ego is not a finite state.

It is a lifelong journey.

You will continue to tame it more and more with each chapter of life that you tackle.

Each conflict that you overcome with poise will allow you to gain perspective.

Each perspective gained allows you to maintain your sense of self AND comprehend your place in the universe.

You have to understand, that everyone is fighting a battle.

Everyone is the main character in their own life.

When you digest this, you can work on your mission & respect other people for where they are in their lives.

I want to give you some tips on taming your ego quicker than the average bubba.

Because understand this:

You don't mature with the age.

You mature with the pain, introspection & re calibration.

1. MEDITATE

Meditation has proven scientific health benefits. It allows you to maintain a more responsive behavior versus reactive.

Reactive is when you are being impulsive to the whims of your emotions.

Responsive is when you are understanding those emotions to make a rational decision.

Meditation will help you understand your sense of self & tame your ego in the process.

Every day, find a quiet spot & count your natural breaths.

When you find your mind losing focus, gently make yourself aware & focus back on your breath.

Start off with 1 minute & work your way up.

That's it.

2 . BUILD A GRAND LIFE PURPOSE

Your life purpose should not be to get a bonus on your paycheck.

Think BIGGER.

Designing a grand life purpose is something that is very counter-intuitive.

You're designing it in a way where it cannot be obtained, but it gives you direction.

'Huh??"

Say your life purpose is to become the most confident person on the planet.

By becoming your most confident self, you are going to help other people become their most confident selves.

Well, that is very grand!

How do you go about achieving something like that?

You do it by overcoming hardships, providing value & being consistent in your chosen craft.

These 3 tasks are not something that you just achieve one day so you can mail it in.

Rather, these 3 tasks are stuff that you can do for the rest of your life!

You are building your value from within.

You are providing value to the external world.

A combination of mastering your internal & external world melts the untamed ego & tames it in the process.

And more importantly, you continue to grow in the journey.

3. WELCOME HARDSHIPS

If you were able to follow step 2 correctly, then you will notice a lot of hardships being thrown your way.

If you don't have any hardships being thrown your way, then you didn't paint a big enough vision!

But a grand vision will continue to level you up.

It will continue to present new problems.

You will feel self-doubt, will be backstabbed & feel emotional pain etc.

But that's good!

Remember, pain teaches you how to tame your ego.

Pain gives you perspective.

Pain gives you courage!

And most importantly, pain lights your **FIRE**.

You need to welcome hardships.

While most people are sitting on their ass watching Netflix all day, you are stretching past the comfort zone.

As you stretch past the comfort zone, your ego will recalibrate.

It will maintain its sense of self, but will tame so it is aiding you in your journey vs. taking you off the path.

That's how the game was meant to be played.

USE YOUR EGO AS A WEAPON

A tamed ego hacks your maturity.

You stop personalizing attacks, stop behaving impulsively, and are much more calculative with your moves.

It allows you to clarify your life.

You now provide with the tamed ego rather than take all the time with the untamed ego.

Your nerves will melt in the process & you will feel **much** more powerful along the way.

Learning how to tame your ego is by no means an easy journey.

Which is why only a rare few are able to do it.

But when you do enter the club, you feel as though you have an advantage that money can't by.

You have clarity.

And that clarity helps you carve your path as you work towards your grand vision.

HOW TO DISCIPLINE YOURSELF

One word that you can expect to hear when you begin your level up journey is the word 'discipline.'

Self-improvement would not be the same if you were just winging it the whole time.

But let's ask a serious question, does discipline live up to the hype?

The word is so common in self-improvement spheres that there HAS to be some kind of catch, right?

Well, that depends.

'On what?'

On **you**.

Discipline can be your best friend or something that doesn't really impact you.

It all depends on the mindset that you approach discipline with.

Just like anything else in life, if you give a half-ass effort, you will get a half-ass result.

Not rocket science.

But that doesn't have to be you.

As long as you can get a few core concepts about discipline down, then you will be someone who stays for the long run, not someone who is discipline when they feel like it.

There is a huge difference between an act & a lifestyle.

We are going for the latter: Lifestyle.

But before you learn how to be disciplined, you need to learn *why* you are incorporating it into your lifestyle in the first place.

THE CHAOTIC CREATURE

Picture this.

Your 5-year-old self or another 5-year-old kid.

What do you notice about them?

'They cry, act out, show a lot of emotions.'

Sounds accurate.

We are born onto this planet crying & being emotional.

At the core state, humans are chaotic, irrational, emotional creatures.

If you don't take any PROACTIVE measures to counteract that, then you will remain a chaotic, irrational, emotional creature.

How many 'adults' do you know that act like they are still 5?

They throw hissy fits, whine & are whimsical etc.

Those are the adults who never grew up.

Their disruptive emotions overpower their mind.

When disruptive emotions overpower the mind, you get immaturity.

DISCIPLINE EXERCISES STABILITY

When your mind overpowers disruptive emotions, you get discipline.

Pretty fascinating, huh?

A small mental switch that can turn your **entire** life around.

Discipline is powerful because you are exercising the POWER of your mind.

You are fighting against the CORE chaotic self to bring on a structure.

And when you do that, you gain back a massive control over your world.

But look a little closer!

Having your mind being strong enough to overpower disruptive emotions is not only discipline, it is also **maturity**.

Mature people feel a roller coaster of emotions just like you.

They just know how to control themselves when faced with it, rather than being impulsive.

Therefore discipline allows you to:

Strengthen your mind

Gain back control over your world

Facilitate maturity

Pretty good deal if you ask me!

HOW TO DISCIPLINE YOURSELF

Now that you know the predominant purpose of discipline & how it will enhance your life for the best, you are ready to begin.

In order to start this journey, you need to get a few frameworks right.

You need to get the following 3 in harmony:

1. *Mind*

2. *Why*

3. *Routine*

When one of the elements are off, you risk becoming a half-asser.

A half-asser is someone who incorporates discipline some days, forgets it on the other days, then picks up where they left off.

This sort of behavior prevents you from ever building up momentum & seeing any results from your discipline.

Don't be a half-asser.

If you are going to be disciplined, then commit to the process.

If you can make all 3 align, then you are are going places.

Let's go thru each one.

I. MIND

Get your mind right by preparing correctly.

Many people who begin their discipline journey think it's supposed to be all rainbows & butterflies.

Ha! Nope.

There will be days where you do not want to be disciplined.

You just want to be a lazy sack of shit & watch Stranger Things all day.

And that's fine.

Expect those days so you are not rattled when you come across those days.

Just by expecting hiccups, you prep your mind to play for the long run.

Also, understand this major concept:

Discipline is not an act, it s a lifestyle.

Get this core concept registered in your mind!

If you treat it like an act, then you WILL quit.

But if you treat it like a lifestyle, then you will do it on autopilot.

Getting your mind right is the major factor of discipline.
So make sure you:
- Plan early for roadblocks.
- Treat it like a lifestyle.

2. WHY

In order to treat it like a lifestyle, you need a Why.
Without the why, you become someone just doing a bunch of random productive tasks.
Doing a bunch of random tasks will have you working **aimlessly**.
Identifying the why allows you to work **purposefully**.

Is it to maintain a stronger control over your emotions?
To strengthen your mind power?
Reach some sort of end goal?

Don't matter!
Identify a Why so you become more invested in the task.
Plus, your why will refine over time, so don't spend too much time on this section.
Just have a rough idea so you can begin.

3. ROUTINE

Without a routine, you will fail at discipline.
It really is that simple.
The whole point of being disciplined is executing a routine!

Without it, you got nothing.

Question is, how do you get a routine?
Great question.
The most simple answer is ***Experimentation***.

I wish I could give you a more detailed answer, but nope.
Experimentation it is.

Everyone has different routines.
If you do a carbon copy of someone else's routine, you may not feel as invested.
'Is it fine to use other people's routine for inspiration?'
Sure!
You can use it as a baseline in the initial stages to get started.
But aim to add your own unique twist as well.

Once you get some creativity involved, **you** will feel much more involved.
That's because you used your mind power to design a lifestyle framework, which will have you feeling more invested.

MIND HACK: Refer to your routines as rituals. No clue why, but it makes you feel more invested.

HOW TO DISCIPLINE YOURSELF FOR THE LONG RUN

Want to know something?
At first, discipline feels like work.
But after a while, it will feel like your safe haven.

You eventually come to realize that the world is a very chaotic place.

When you learn this, you realize that a little structure could never hurt anyone.

People get the misconception that discipline makes you boring.

Wrong.

Discipline makes it easier to enjoy yourself when you are out.

That's because you are not worrying if you still have work left lying around.

PS: *Make sure you don't only use discipline to be productive, make sure you also schedule in social time.*

If you do that, you will realize the beauty of discipline & how powerful it was all along.

You'll be stunned by how you had spent so long just letting life happen to you.

Why?

Because you had the power to architect it all along.

STEPS ON HOW TO MEDITATE

In the world of communication skills, one of the best habits to pick up is meditation.

The art of training your mind to become still can work wonders.

But let's be real...

There is so much information out there on HOW to meditate.

Analysis paralysis is bound to ensue.

Some people talk about having meditation apps.

Others talk about having meditation music.

And let's not forget the group who talks about having candles!

All those things are **not** necessary for the beginning stages.

If you want to add them in later on, you can.

But when you are first starting off, the goal is to keep it simple.

I've spent years looking for practical strategies on how to meditate.

And after a lot of experimentation, I found my core principles.

In this blog, I will be sharing why meditation is important & the steps to pick it up.

Without further ado, let us begin.

WHY IS MEDITATION IMPORTANT?

A distracted mind is a useless mind.

One of the biggest causes of unhappiness is a wandering mind.

I'm sure you can relate.

When you are hopping from thought to thought, you put yourself in a state of panic.

Not fun.

Meditation is important because you learn the art of CO-EXISTING with your thoughts.

Not eliminating your thoughts, but coexisting with them.

When you learn the art of coexisting, you are able to detach your identity from thoughts.

No longer do temporary events define you.

Seeing the situation for what it is allows you to recognize that thoughts are simply waves.

They come and go.

But the core of your identity is the ocean. It will remain.

SIDE BENEFITS OF MEDITATION

Learning to coexist with your mind is just one of the many benefits.

When you invest in meditating, you begin to unlock another flurry of benefits as well.

Those benefits include:

–**Concentration**– You do not succumb to distractions as easily.

–**Less impulsive**– Temporary thoughts make you do silly things. Detaching from them allows you to mature.

–**Compassion** – You begin accepting ALL of you, which makes it easier to accept others.

–**Confidence**– The confidence levels rise when your mind has been tamed.

–Ability to Handle High-Pressure Situations– The weak are controlled by their breath. The strong control their breath.

Science is backing up mediation as well.

You learn the art of calming the Default Mode Network portion of the brain, which is responsible for mind-wandering

Gray matter increases.

And you are able to process more data from the prefrontal cortex (responsive) rather than the (amygdala).

Lesson?

Meditation is a great skill to leverage in ALL facets of your life.

STEPS ON HOW TO MEDITATE

So I'm going to keep it simple.

Going to give you a 3 part strategy for steps on how to meditate:

1. Start off SMALL.
2. Pick a target to focus on.
3. Bring awareness to distractions.

Most people who begin meditation don't stick to it long term.
Tsk tsk...
Don't be a statistic.

1. START OFF SMALL

It will be very tempting to do 30-minute meditation sessions from the get-go.
You feel sooo motivated.

But that will simply overwhelm your brain.

Gotta EASE yourself into it.

Your brain has been programmed with wandering thoughts for years.

Rewiring that will be no easy task.

My personal strategy is to make the beginning portion so easy that you'll feel guilty for quitting.

For me, that was 1 minute a day.

If I couldn't commit to 1 minute a day, then I wasn't going to commit long term, period.

In his blockbuster book, Atomic Habits, James Clear brings up the importance of working your way up.

Spend 1-week doing 1-minute meditations.

The next week, do 2-minute meditations.

And you'll start a chain from there.

2. PICK A TARGET TO FOCUS ON.

Meditation is all about making the mind 1 pointed.

Choose 1 thing and stick by it.

A few options are:
- Breath.
- Sensations in your body.
- An affirmation.
- Visualization image.
- A physical picture.

Etc.

I recommend choosing 1 target and sticking with it for a few weeks.

Rather than doing breath one day, then a picture the next day, and an affirmation the day after.

Just focus on 1 target for now.

This allows you to build an intimate relationship with the target.

Your mind is wild at the moment.

So don't confuse it too much in the taming stages.

3. BRING AWARENESS TO DISTRACTIONS & REFOCUS.

Once you have picked your time limit & your target, now it gets fun.

Your 2 goals are:

1. Focus on your target.
2. Make yourself aware when you have gotten distracted and gently bring yourself back to the target.

How you focus on the target is up to you.

For breathing meditations, I recommend counting your breath.

For targeting your mind towards a picture, you just need to look at the picture with all of your attention.

Here's the issue though.

Most people are too harsh on themselves.

When they lose focus, they start feeling defeated & being negative.

But that's not the point of meditation.

Like I said earlier, meditation is not about eliminating thoughts.

It's about learning to coexist with them.

Your goal is to build your AWARENESS.

Every time you get distracted, make yourself aware. And gently bring yourself back to the target.

Be proud that you made yourself aware rather than remaining distracted.

Each time you do that, each time you gain power over your thoughts.

After a lot of practice & consistency, you'll be able to notice quickly when you get distracted.

It's all a process.

TAMING THE MONKEY MIND

A distracted mind is an unhappy mind.

A still mind is a confident mind.

In the world of communication skills, the last thing you want to do is be all over the place.

Communicating comes down to making your mind tangible.

And if your mind is sloppy, then your speaking skills will be sloppy.

Meditation is one of the best skills to pick up.

You now have the steps on how to meditate.

With the endless list of benefits, it's a skill that you don't want to postpone any longer.

And if you did the act before & quit, no worries.

Pick up where you left of.

Tame the monkey mind & you'll future self will give you 2 pats on the back.

How to Focus Better by Leveraging Emotions

There are different paths to build focus.
It's highly dependent on the personality type.

What works great for one person may fall flat for someone else.
And vice versa is true.

Yet, we have been approaching focus with a one size fits all attitude.
That may explain why focus levels are so shit nowadays.

In this article, we are going to hit the topic of focus from a nuanced approach.
Our personality type is going to be the leading factor for the actions we take.
It's our internal world that will determine our internal states.

What Is the King of Focus?

We act as though focus is only a game of the mind.
And oftentimes, we may even delve deeper and say it's only a game of the intellect.

BIG MISTAKE.

'If it's not a game of the intellect, then what is it a game of?'
It's a game of emotions.

It doesn't matter how smart you are...

If you can't control your emotions, then focus will be impossible.

Even the best swimmer in the world knows they can't swim against a tsunami.

Likewise, the smartest person should know that swimming against emotions is not strategic.

Rather than swimming against the emotions, work with them.

HOW TO DIRECT EMOTIONS

Emotions are like little children.

You need to coax your emotions to let them know that you're on their side.

A lot of people get interested in focus & try meditation for 1 hour on their first session.

This overwhelms emotions.

Rather than doing that, adopt the:

-Curiosity approach.

-Micro approach.

Let's go thru both.

CURIOSITY APPROACH

Imagine someone tells you that they heard gossip about you...

But they weren't going to tell you what they heard.

This got your curiosity.

You want to know what is being said about you.
There is a STRONG desire.

Yet, this individual is stubbron.
They aren't saying a word.

Well, as 2 months pass on by, they FINALLY decide to tell you.
They have a 30-minute story to share.
Once they share the story, you'll be all ears.
You'll be all focus.

This shows that when curiosity is activated, focus is a byproduct.
What does this mean for you?
Study subjects that you are naturally curious about.

PROVE to yourself that you are already capable of focusing.
This wins the emotions over.

MICRO APPROACH

It's better to meditate 1 minute every day rather than 1 hour out of the blue moon.
Micro is a big friend to the emotions.

Why?

Because micro doesn't overwhelm the emotions.
Micro eases good habits into the world of energy.

So in order to pick up a micro approach to focus, identify what micro means to you.

Different situations will require different definitions of micro.

Whenever micro is involved, GET A TIMER.

Let's say your room is messy as shit.

Give yourself 1 burst of 20 minutes of uninterrupted focus to clean the room.

Take a rest.

Now another 20 minutes.

Repeat until the room is polished.

During moments of the micro sessions, focus SOLELY on the task.

These micro sessions should feel like a game.

It should not make your head hurt.

FOCUS IS A SKILL

Curiosity & a micro-based approach (plus a timer) to productivity will get you ahead of the curve.

2 variables...

Not too difficult right?

We aren't making it any more complicated than that.

While many humans immediately try working with the head...
Be better.
Work with the heart, the head will follow, guaranteed.

Humans are creatures of emotions first & they justify with logic later.

Flow with the tsunami, so the swimmer's job becomes tensionless.

During the burst of leveraging curiosity & doing the micro approach, *be highly present.*

Be aware of what's going on.

How does it feel to focus?

Understanding the physical sensations of our body gets us associating a positive emotion with focus.

It doesn't feel like work.

Your emotions LOVE it when it hears something isn't work.

Just like anything in life, focus works in exponential returns.

It's a process of iteration.

The prior rep builds on the latter rep.

And the skillset of focus gradually increases over time.

EMBODYING FOCUS

Not only does focus compound over time..

Eventually, it becomes a mode of living.

There are 2 predominant states of the brain:

Default Mode Network: mind-wandering state.

Task Positive Network: focused state.

Most humans spend their time in default mode.

That's because they practice that state the most.

Going from thought to thought.

By taking a mindful approach to building focus, we gradually start shifting to a *task-positive network.*

Our nervous system rewires when we constantly make ourselves aware of something.

Where attention flows, energy goes.

This is the beauty.

So keep practicing focus until you become focus.

That's a beautiful state to be in.

A state of utmost presence.

Great spiritual teachers have said that there is no past or future.

The only time that has ever existed is the NOW.

Keep using bursts of focus thru curiosity & micro reps…

Until it becomes the main mode of living.

That's working with your emotions to the tee.

CONCENTRATION IS MORE THAN A MERE ACT

We often confuse focus as being something that only works with productivity.

While in reality, that's not remotely the case.

Focus is an aid for social skills, courage, emotional management…and productivity also happens to be on the list.

And still...I'm only scratching the surface.

So see how curiosity & micro reps can be leveraged in context to your life.

Curiosity is innate in us.

That's the gut instinct for the mind.

Find out what you're curious about & learn about it.

This shows you that you are already great at focusing.

As for the micro reps, break things down & use the timer.

The timer keeps ya on track & gets you thinking in micro -> macro reps.

The nervous system gradually becomes rewired to match our intentions.

Focus is a gift that all humans can get once we change our way of thinking.

Unlock it thru the art of repetition.

Matured focus is a new state of being.

That's living in the present moment.

3 GRATITUDE EXERCISES TO GO FROM A ZERO TO A HERO

Gratitude is a powerful way to exercise the mind.

Not only do you exercise the mind...

You also change the way that you communicate.

Imagine a guy who is constantly entertaining negative deflating thoughts.

Then put him against a guy who is entertaining powerful thoughts.

Who will communicate better?

The answer is obvious.

By the way... Let me be clear.

I'm not an advocate of only positive thinking.

I'm an advocate of acceptance thinking.

My hierarchy goes like this:

- Positive thinking beats negative thinking.
- Acceptance thinking beats positive thinking.

Acceptance thinking is conditioning the mind to thrive under whatever is thrown our way.

We use a wide range of experiences as data to extract lessons and continue to power up.

The 3 gratitude exercises in this blog are meant to unlock **acceptance mode** thinking.

Thrive & speak with power.

It starts with changing the thought waves.

1. COUNT TINY WINS

It's easy to go to our biggest wins when doing gratitude exercises.

'Are you saying that is wrong?'

Not quite. But it is suboptimal.

Acknowledging only the big wins will build blindness to the small wins.

Heck, it may build a resentment towards small wins!

You're conditioning the mind to be like, 'who needs small wins anyways?'

Another danger in only counting big wins is that it makes you a parrot.

Let me guess... every morning, you are reciting the same 5-8 things you're grateful for. Am I right?

'How did you know??'

You ain't that special homie.

Focus on the micro.

This automatically forces you to *think* & engage your memory banks.

The smaller that you get, the more you FEEL changes in your body over time.

Acknowledging the small wins easily allows you to acknowledge the big wins.

Being grateful for making 1 dollar online will make you ecstatic when you make 100 dollars.

2. TREE METHOD: ACKNOWLEDGING THE ROOTS

What do you see when you see a tree?

'I see the tree.'

What don't you see?

'The roots.'

What is holding the tree up?

'The roots.'

Would it be comical to say that the roots are **just** as powerful as the tree?

'No, that makes all the sense in the world....'

The roots of your life are the losses you took to get to the win.

Without the losses, you will not have a tree.

Be grateful for losses as well.

This is what acceptance thinking is all about.

Losses of the past make more sense in the present.

If I gave you 10 minutes to think of a moment that you hated going through in the past, but are now grateful for.

You'll be like, 'keep your 10 minutes. I already got 3 things that came to mind.'

Make your mind acknowledge the losses that led to the win.

Connect the 2.

Don't just acknowledge the loss and leave it at that.

CONNECT the loss to the win.

Talk about how the roots and the tree are connected.

Talk about how it required you to get fired from your dream job to start the business which led you to become financially free.

Get it?

'Got it.'

3. FIND THE PRACTICAL ASPECTS OF GRATITUDE

I'm not going to lie, but I used to think gratitude was bs.

Thought it was another trick to get me thinking in a certain way to ignore the truths of life.

However, I came to realize that I was doing it incorrectly.

The reason I was doing it incorrectly was that I was not doing gratitude with a purpose.

It's like reading.

Reading for the sake of reading is better than not reading at all.

However, when you read to complement a life vision, then it's a different ball game.

Now, each book serves as a **puzzle piece** pulling you forward in your path.

Same with gratitude.

My perspective regarding gratitude changed when I saw a noticeable difference in my communication.

Because speaking is the byproduct of thinking.

This line above is EXTREMELY important.

This means that thinking is the orange.

While speaking is the orange juice.

You can't have orange juice without the orange.

When trying to improve speaking skills, the naive mind goes straight to speaking.
While the wise mind addresses the root of the issue:
Thinking.

Gratitude gets the mind to think empowering thoughts.
It alters the narrative.

If you did exercise 2, you'll see how present-day losses can lead to a future tree.
Making connections like that alters the speaking game entirely.
Leading to a powerful voice, clear thoughts, and passion for the topic.

To do gratitude with intent, work on creating a list of 50 PRACTICAL benefits that gratitude will have for your life.
No need to create the list at once (unless you are able to).
You can also build it over time as more ideas come to you.

The more practical benefits you see for gratitude exercises in relation to your life, the more likely you are to stick with the practice long-term.

BONUS TIP: WRITE DOWN GRATEFUL THOUGHTS

As a beginner, write your gratitude down.
'Can I speak it?'
Sure.
But something about writing makes it more real & frozen in reality.

The reason I consider this an exercise is because it **physically** feels a certain way.

'What can be so hard about typing?'

Who said I told you to type?

HANDWRITE.

You may be the person who hasn't written by hand in a *long time*.

So, when you start writing by hand, there will be tension in your forearms and fingers.

GOOD.

Get gel point pens to **ease** the feeling.

Now the mind & body are being worked **together**.

This creates a stronger mind-body connection which leads to clear and concise communication skills in the future.

MAKE GRATITUDE EXERCISES A LIFESTYLE

I'll give you another mini bonus tip since you made it this far.

Exercise gratitude like an athlete rather than an artist.

An artist is great.

But in this field, we want to be an athlete.

Grit, determination, and consistency.

You'll need all of that.

If you decide to do my micro gratitude method, then you'll have days where you can't think of anything.

A part of you may want to quit.

Don't.

Be an athlete.
Push that extra rep.
Then another.
And another...

Over time, you will be done with your 10 reps for the day.
These 10 reps continue to add up & begin to change the way that you think.
It will eventually have you thinking grand thoughts on autopilot.
That's the acceptance mode being unlocked.

How to Deal With a Boring Texter

Have you ever met someone who was boring on text?

- They gave 1-word responses.
- Only answered questions but never asked them.
- And took forever to respond back.

However, there was a *twist*.

'What?'

They were pretty cool in real life.

If they were so cool in real life, why couldn't they behave the same way via text??

To make matters worse, it felt like their text personality drowned out their real-world personality.

Because real world interactions come and go.

But texts are fixed in time.

Which one do you think is easier to replay?

The purpose of this blog is to share how to not be a boring texter and how to deal with boring texters.

Boring texting is an epidemic in the age of seamless communication, so let's make sure we don't fall into that boat.

Why Texting With Personality Is Important

You may have read the intro and thought:

'Oh snap, I'm a boring texter!'

There are multiple reasons for boring texting. A few reasons are:

1. The texter doesn't care about the person they are speaking to.
2. They are nervous.
3. The texter normally talks pretty dry with everyone.
4. They do not place much importance on digital communication in general.

For the 1st one, they are speaking to someone who is annoying and keeps asking them for stuff.

This causes them to be short via text on purpose.

The 2nd reason for being a boring texter is due to nerves.

In real-world conversations, it's easy to share the first thing that comes to mind.

But with text, there's a higher likelihood of overthinking and overanalyzing.

The 3rd reason for being a boring texter is because of a naturally dry personality.

For this group of people, it's not personal.

They just talk like that with everyone.

And for the 4th reason, it's because they don't place too much importance on digital communication.

For them, they subconsciously think:

'When I meet them in person, they'll see what I'm about.'

All reasons for boring texting.

HOW TO BE MORE ENTERTAINING ON TEXT

The first step into being more entertaining on text is to actually care.

Articulate the importance of digital communication.

Rather than viewing it as a chore, see it as an opportunity.

'How can I view it as an opportunity?'

Well, for 1...you can craft your perception at will.

Attractive writing is a skill set.

This is when the personality seeps into the words.

Rather than focusing on the act of texting, focus more on the person you are speaking with.

Remember, the phone and the telecommunications are just the medium.

The texter's goal is to focus less on the medium and focus more on the recipient, so the message takes care of itself.

To make this easier, smile while texting.

Smiling makes a person feel better.

When they feel better, they write better.

'Cool! So, articulate the value of texting, remember that I'm talking to a person, and smile. Anything else?'

Yes. Practice!

Practice is fundamental to developing communication skills.

Even the most well-intentioned people need to shake off the rust every now and then.

Therefore, practice with all types of personalities.

'All types?'

Yes, this brings me to my next point.

HOW TO DEAL WITH BORING TEXTERS

When dealing with a boring texter, the first reaction may be:

'They want to be short with me?? Do they even know who I am??'

However, this is the perfect time to reframe the scenario.

If we only get better at attractive writing through practice...

Do we want a good texter to practice with or a bad texter?

In my opinion, trying to breathe life into a dead conversation is a better workout.

It forces the texter who is trying to improve their attractive writing to:

- Ask more open-ended questions.
- Make more jokes.
- And make comments that illicit some response.

To do any of the above, it's best to assume that the bad texter is nervous.

'Why view them as nervous? Because I think they are snobby.'

When we view someone as snobby, it's difficult to put in the effort to help them.

However, when we view them as nervous, it's easier for us to make the effort to loosen them up.

By viewing them as nervous, it's easier to view ourselves as the higher social valued creature.

All comedians, speakers, and leaders realize they are the higher value.

Which allows them to have a gentle cadence and not rush.

Therefore, to deal with a bad texter:

1. Assume they are nervous.
2. View them as practice opportunities to strengthen the attractive writing skillset.

CREATING OPPORTUNITIES THROUGH TEXT

Offline communication is great.
Something about face-to-face will never get old.

However, don't view the importance of offline communication as the unimportance of online communication.
The average person hangs onto their phone.
Impressions are made and solidified through the phone.

Often, what happens with the phone is that it will either:

- Create opportunities.

or

- Take opportunities away.

If you are a boring texter, that's not good at all.
Enthusiasm means *unlocking the God within.*

If you can't be somewhat enthusiastic about writing a text, it's difficult to assess the opportunities which are silently being taken away.
'Does that mean I have to be enthusiastic forever?'
Eventually, the enthusiasm can wane once the rapport has deepened.
That's when short texts aren't mistaken for a lack of interest.

Instead, short texts are seen as normal to keep the dialogue
ping-ponging.

In the beginning stages, effort is required.
Practice doesn't make perfect.
Practice makes progress.

5 TIPS TO CONTROL YOUR ANGER

Your anger can be your best friend or your worst enemy.
It all depends on the perception that you set for it.

Do you use your anger as an excuse to throw a temper tantrum or to produce?
Your answer to that question will show whether anger is your best friend or worst enemy.

In this post, I want to explain what anger really is & how you can control it.
But I want to take it a level further & show you how to PRODUCE with it.

In my eyes, anger is one of the most unique emotions out there & needs to be leveraged.
With that being said, let us enter the wonderful world of emotional intelligence.

WHAT IS ANGER?

Anger is an emotion that indicates a sense of displeasure.
But let's delve deeper.

To understand anger in a more nuanced light, you need to be able to distinguish between emotions and feelings.
'I thought emotions and feelings were the same thing?'
Nope.

Feelings are the physical sensations your body produces & emotions are your perception of those feelings.

When we think anger, we automatically go to the perception.

We think, 'anger is bad because it indicates a sense of displeasure.'

But in order to leverage anger, you need to focus on the FEELINGS before the emotions.

Once you can do that, then your perception of anger will go from negative to neutral.

And when your perception switches to neutral, you can use anger to produce a lot of masterpieces.

But how do you focus more on the feeling rather than the emotion?

By getting out of your head & into the present moment.

-When something makes you angry & you keep focusing on getting revenge, you stay in your head & recondition a negative perception towards the emotion.

-But when something makes you angry & you let it slide so you can focus on the present, you focus on the feelings.

In order to make the mental transition, apply the following 5 practical tips.

TIP # 1 – SLOW & SILENT BREATHS

In order to control your anger, being present is a **must**.

Your breath will prevent you from making impulsive decisions & allow you to engage logic.

Engaging your logic is huge because rather than making a short-sighted reaction, you think bigger picture.

The breaths slow down your movements & allow you to make a rational decision that you can feel proud of later.

The breath is the remote controller for your emotions, so dial it at your will.

TIP # 2- FOCUS ON THE PHYSICAL SENSATIONS NOT WHAT CAUSED THE ANGER

When you focus on what caused you to be angry, you begin plotting your revenge.

When you focus on the physical sensations from your anger, you remain present.

Remaining present WHILE angry allows you to understand yourself on a much deeper level.

You are able to understand that anger is not the boogeyman.

Leverage awareness.

-What exactly happens to your body when you are angry?
-Which body parts are warm?
-Which muscles are tightening up?

Be as aware & curious as possible so you can understand that anger literally is:

Physical sensations + Perception, not reality.

Your mind gets to control your moves, not your emotions.

TIP # 3 – HAVE A HEALTHY CREATIVE OUTLET

A few years ago, if you were to tell me that anger makes you more creative, I would have laughed at you.

But a few years later, I would be lying if I didn't notice the effects of anger on creativity.

Creativity is when the brain thinks on higher thought frequencies.

When you are calm & relaxed, you are thinking on a regular thought frequency.

But when you are angry, you spark a hidden side of your imagination.

Most people are not aware of this because they use that imagination to plan out a retort, throw a temper tantrum, go into road rage, etc.

But if you can hold that anger & channel it on a creative channel, you'll notice yourself producing on a surreal level.

Whether it's writing, painting, building a speech, you will notice anger can often make the quality of your content skyrocket.

Your content becomes a lot more unpredictable & you captivate in the process.

This is a productive way to control anger.

TIP: 4 – BE HEALTHY WITH YOUR ANGER

The best way to be healthy is by getting your ass to the gym or playing a sport.

A few weeks ago, this dude cut me off in traffic & flicked me off.

I was extra heated because I was following the speed limit, was already having a bad day & was minding my own business.

I was so close to tailgating him & cutting him back off but decided it wasn't worth it.

A few controlled breaths later, I was now at the gym. Don't remember exactly what I was working out because everything felt like a blur.

Your boy was lifting heavier & ultra-focused.

I had reached a state of flow that felt like therapy.

The feeling of anger didn't go away, it was simply used to lift weights.

Use your anger to lift & power-up.

You'll realize that anger is your body's pre-workout, coffee, Red Bull & so much more.

Note: For tips 3 & 4, I gave you a vehicle to channel your anger on.

You never want to bottle your anger for too long.

When you bottle your anger, you recondition a negative perception towards it.

And the negative perception grows over time.

An emotion that you try to bury goes to the gym & comes back 10x stronger.

Have a channel to release the energy on.

TIP 5- FORCE A SMILE

A smile changes your mindset & emotions.

The next time you want to really blow up on someone, try smiling.

You'll notice that you feel a sense of ease.

Also, you will maintain frame.

Understand this major life concept:

The person being angry or trying to make someone angry loses social value.

The person who remains unaffected maintains and/or skyrockets social value.

You understand this life principle the more you mature.

And the smile low key rattles the other person who is trying to make you mad.

So:

1.   Maintain frame.
2.   Exercise a positive perception towards anger.
3.   Enhance social value.

The smile is a no brainer.

LEVERAGE THE TIPS TO CONTROL ANGER

One major thing that you'll learn in the emotional intelligence world is that anger will never go away.

However, your perception of it will change if you bring **awareness** to it.

Use the 5 tips in this post to change your perception towards this emotion.

Rather than letting it take you on a downward spiral & make some silly decisions, aim to **build** with it.

You will find that a lot of your most unique creations will come from anger.

And each time you produce when you feel this strong emotion, you take a little bit more control over your reality.

Those small fragments of control, allow you to build momentum.
And the momentum will snowball into significant life changes.

Leverage anger.
And level up your emotional intelligence along the way.

The End

Check out the other books in the series